Still Life

For
Megan Vaughan

— Still Life —

Hopes, Desires
and Satisfactions

—Henrietta L. Moore—

polity

First published in 2011 by Polity Press

Polity Press
65 Bridge Street
Cambridge CB2 1UR, UK

Polity Press
350 Main Street
Malden, MA 02148, USA

ISBN-13: 978-0-7456-3645-0
ISBN-13: 978-0-7456-3646-7(pb)

A catalogue record for this book is available from the British Library.

Typeset in 11 on 13 pt Sabon
by Toppan Best-set Premedia Limited
Printed and bound in Great Britain by MPG Books Group Limited, Bodmin, Cornwall

The publisher has used its best endeavours to ensure that the URLs for external websites referred to in this book are correct and active at the time of going to press. However, the publisher has no responsibility for the websites and can make no guarantee that a site will remain live or that the content is or will remain appropriate.

Every effort has been made to trace all copyright holders, but if any have been inadvertently overlooked the publisher will be pleased to include any necessary credits in any subsequent reprint or edition.

For further information on Polity, visit our website: www.politybooks.com

Contents

Acknowledgements   viii

1   Thinking Again   1

2   Still Life   30

3   Slips of the Tongue   55

4   Other Modes of Transport   77

5   Second Nature   106

6   Arts of the Possible   136

7   New Passions for Difference   170

Notes   206

References   215

Index   235

Acknowledgements

This book was written during a period of leave made pos-sible by the award of a Major Research Fellowship (F/07 004/AL) from the Leverhulme Trust. I am deeply grateful to the Trust for their generous and much needed support.
    I always find that every book draws inspiration from particular scholars whose ideas and insights flow through the text, shaping it in ways that exceed the possibilities of citation. In this case, the work of Henry Jenkins, Lauren Berlant and Rosi Braidotti has had a profound impact on my thinking.

– 1 –

Thinking Again

This book is an attempt to think again about how to analyse the worlds we share with others. One part of this challenge is how we might understand what being historical means; how do we create the personal and political horizons that define our understandings of the present, as well as the forms of belonging and interconnection that characterize it? The present, of course, is never still, never fully present. We may be haunted by our pasts, but human social life is equally lived in a relentless forward gear. It's not just that we are open to the future, to potentialities and possibilities, but also that our perceptions and evaluations of change are formative both for ourselves and for the times we live in. It may be that 'the times they are a-changing', as the old Bob Dylan song goes, but perceptions of time and change are connected to historically specific modes of being, particular understandings of ourselves as subjects and agents in history. The Enlightenment, for example, is often said to be both a period of history and a way of being in the world, characterized by certain sorts of individuals with particular ways of thinking about the world; so too modernity. How we are placed in time and space links to modes of being – specific ways of thinking, feeling and acting, of relating to things, to others and to ourselves. Political and economic changes alter these ways of being, and new ways of seeing and understanding drive forward further possibilities for change. In the chapters that follow, I puzzle over the challenge that analysing social change presents, and the dilemmas posed by trying to think about the connections between the kinds of people we are and wish to become, and the times we live in, with all their promise of technological, political and social transformation.

In the contemporary moment, as many chapters in this book demonstrate, there is a huge interest in self-making, and self-stylization. This is not just about self-cultivation as a form of individualization or the embrace of possessive individualism, but more properly as Foucault described it, a desperate attempt to imagine the present, 'to imagine it otherwise than it is, and to transform it not by destroying it, but by grasping in it what it is' (1998: 311). Stylization in music, in dress, in politics and in all aspects of personal and intimate life is part of a drive to give form not only to the self, but to the world, and to relations with others. It is an obstinate search for a style of existence, a way of being. It accounts, in part, for the massive drive towards authenticity, truth and reality that is observable in so many different domains of life around the globe. A palpable commitment to the value of the present. This drive towards, and demand for, the 'real' is evident not only in contemporary forms of religious stylization, but also, and perhaps more surprisingly, in the engagement with virtual worlds and financial markets, as well as in the collapsing of distinctions between art, entertainment and politics (see Chapters 5 and 6).

After Globalization

What tools do we have at our disposal for analysing these forms of self-making and their relation to lived understandings of the demands of the present and the processes of transformation that seem to undergird contemporary life? Periodizations are always contentious; there is no settled agreement as to the nature of the Enlightenment, modernity or globalization, for example. My interest is not in trying to define a specific era, but rather in understanding the present as a set of lived possibilities and relations, what it might mean to say that we share our worlds. It is often said that we are living in times of great change, of speeded up connections and distortions of space and time. We are more connected than ever before, and the problems of this enhanced and, as some would have it, unwelcome proximity are manifest in the clashes of culture, faith and ideology with which we are all so familiar. For many, the root of these problems is a rapacious form of whirligig capitalism that self-devours by spinning on its own axis, moving inexorably across the globe. Before the financial crash of 2008, it seemed impossible to get off this alarming funfair, and yet now its violent arrest threatens to hurl us all into space, a frightening no-man's-land of dispossession.

Global capitalism, and globalization more generally, are the forces that allegedly bind us together, and speed up our interactions. However, globalization as metaphor and process has been the subject of extensive critique and debate (e.g. Bisley, 2007; Held and McGrew, 2007), and more recent approaches emphasize its uneven, nonlinear character. The plural, unpredictable nature of processes of change and transformation means that analytical frameworks can no longer depend on the earlier binaries: local/global, inside/outside, micro/macro (Moore, 2004). It is one of the paradoxes of globalization that it is not global. It exists as a partial condition that has no teleology of completion and cannot do so. Likewise, global capitalism is not a single, coherent entity or set of forces, but rather a dynamic set of processes establishing and disestablishing uneasy, shifting, often provisional connections that continually seek out new sources of profit (e.g. Harvey, 1990; Bayart, 2001; Tsing, 2005). The result is that change may be all around us, but its directions, pulses, propensities and outcomes are maddeningly difficult to analyse and predict. This does not stop anyone from trying; from politicians, corporate leaders, entrepreneurs, academics and NGO activists to ordinary farmers. What it does ensure is a great deal of theorizing, reflection and debate. As Weber suggested, people's ideas, and the 'world-images' they create in consequence, determine 'the tracks' along which action is pushed (1948: 280). Particular ways of conceptualizing the world bring about material consequences, and drive change. Ideas matter, and so talk of globalization, occurring as it does everywhere from the academy to international organizations, policy forums and the boardroom, matters.

And yet, ideas are not enough, so what value and significance should we assign them? Social critique is a form of political action, but its limitations are frequently all too apparent. In Chapter 6, I discuss the disabling effects of the melancholia that has overtaken the Left since the 1980s as a consequence of our inability to imagine viable alternatives to global capitalism. My interest is in the theories that social theorists put forward, and the kind of relationships they have with the theories of ordinary people. Social theorists are part of the worlds they investigate, and their passions and fears are often very similar to those of the people they study and write about. Successful social theory must stay close to the theories, concerns and experiences of the people being studied, but it has to be something more than mere description. When critique collapses into description, I suggest, melancholia is the inevitable outcome. The proliferation, commodification and politicization of differences under contemporary capitalism have been extensively documented by social theorists, but we have not been able to develop theories of difference that provide certain terrain either for political change or for moral and ethical critique (Judt, 2010).

In Chapters 3, 4 and 6, I explore this problem by examining how our concepts and languages of analysis and understanding are caught up in formulations of difference that impede analysis. In a series of discussions about values, faith, gender, sexuality and politics, I try to develop forms of critique that are not indebted to the pre-theoretical assumptions underlying current discourses on globalization. In attempting this task, I do not suggest that the processes of interconnectedness and integration we usually refer to by the term globalization do not exist, or are not significant. Rather, I mine many instances of such processes to demonstrate what current theoretical preoccupations leave insufficiently theorized. My aim is to mark a definitive break with some of the presuppositions that adhere to the idea of globalization and which continue to haunt it even when they have been disavowed and extensively critiqued. Chief amongst these are notions of pessimism and loss. Discourses of capitalism – most particularly those on the Left – always invoke the ghostly spectre of change understood as the erosion of ways of life. Insofar as theories of globalization are the inheritors of specific theories about capitalism and modernity, they continue to carry with them traces of the antinomies between tradition and loss that have always animated such debates. This is true, in my view, even of those critics who have highlighted the unexpected and unstable outcomes of globalization, and its simultaneously heterogenizing and homogenizing propensities. There are many writers who have suggested that we need to move beyond the confines of the relation between the modern and the non-modern, beyond hybridity, beyond also the collapse of culture, the McDonaldization thesis, the waning of affect, and the endless play of différance.[1] However, the pre-theoretical assumptions underlying the conceptual framework of globalization constantly return us to worn out formulations of similitude and difference that invoke modernity versus tradition, authenticity versus loss.

Part of the difficulty here is the way that information technologies and the media stand in for the modern and the new. The internet and information transfer have not only become dominant metaphors shaping our conceptions of globalization (Castells, 1996; Cooper, 2005: 96), but they function as the conceptual and performative framing for the pre-theoretical assumptions that characterize the nature of the global. We all know that we live in the age of information technology, global capitalism and globalization. What this invokes much of the time is a nostalgic, pessimistic and unproductive oscillation between the celebration of identity and authenticity on the one hand, and fears about the loss of culture and cultural selves on the other. The language of analysis is instructive here: hybridity, mimicry, resistance, reappropriation. These strangely etiolated terms are deployed to typify encounters between different world-views, systems of power and distributions of resource, and as a way of characterizing differences in reception and responses to what are assumed to be 'external' influences. In Chapter 3, I argue that such terms reflect a set of western preoccupations and concerns, and are too leached of meaning to provide us with sufficient analytical purchase in the contemporary moment.

Why might this be so? We need first to begin with a point of clarification. All cultural meanings and forms of cultural production require mimesis, repetition and reappropriation. Interpretation at its most fundamental involves the repositioning and repurposing of meaning. This process is not always one that works through direct reference; as well as cognitive and evaluative components, it also frequently proceeds through emotion, affect and somatic engagement. For example, Brent Luvaas discusses young Indonesian fashion designers who rework such things as corporate logos, the album covers of foreign rock bands and a variety of international images, and then incorporate them into their designs. Their selection process is eclectic and 'borrows from anywhere and everywhere, other places and other times, from the disco 1970s of New York to the demure Victorian era of England, without any consistent allegiances or affiliations' (Luvaas, 2010: 7). Their innovative compilations are based on a form of fashion remix, but this is not one that is concerned with imitation, nor even with hybridity or reappropriation as these terms are usually understood and deployed in social theory. The whole point of their designs is to signal that the material comes from elsewhere, that what is being offered is a form of visual citation and commentary on otherness, one that both incites pleasure and creates innovative cultural forms. Luvaas, following Turkle (1995) and others, dusts down Lévi-Strauss's notion of bricolage and repurposes it for a computer-mediated age, suggesting that we see these young designers as bricoleurs. Lévi-Strauss's original notion of bricolage was about meaning-making, about putting existing things to new purposes. The Indonesian designers, like the African youth I discuss in Chapter 3, are doing rather more than that. They are seeking ways of contributing to cultural production, leaving their mark on the world – to use Luvaas's phrase – projecting themselves into history – to use mine. The world of transnational capitalism, transnational faith and interconnected geopolitics is now the world these young people inhabit. Their aim is not to resist modernity or western culture, or even to appropriate it or subvert it, but rather to take up their place as producers of culture within a new set of cultural possibilities.

Luvaas suggests that beginning the analysis by asking whether the designs are examples of resistance and subversion or whether they are typical of the forms of individualized subjectivity under neoliberalism rather misses the point. 'These designers are not trying to throw off the conceptual shackles of cultural imperialism; they are trying to assert some degree of direct control over the new commercial world they live in. [They] . . . are less concerned with subverting international commercial culture than working with it, or perhaps more accurately, inserting themselves into it' (2010: 13). Luvaas argues that they are attempting to reproduce themselves as global citizens, but what is clear is that we cannot gain much insight into the complex cultural forms these young designers are producing, and the forms of self-stylization with which they are engaged if we reductively conceptualize them as hybrids, a mixture of pre-existing western and Indonesian cultures, or as involved in resisting or appropriating modernity or western capitalism.

The processes Luvaas describes are enormously facilitated and speeded up by access to digital resources and new technologies, but the crucial point, I would argue, is that they involve novel forms of belonging, novel performances of self, new ways of imagining our relations to others, to objects and to the wider social and cultural worlds we inhabit. New technologies enhance these capacities, but they do not create them. What is significant about information technologies is not just their distributed, interconnected nature, but the fact that they allow users – individuals and groups – to create and develop spaces and opportunities for emergent forms of sociality, in ways that enhance familiar cultural capacities and competences. I argue this case in more detail in Chapters 5 and 6, but I want to signal here the distance between the argument I am making and those who argue that these remediated forms of cultural production are somehow inauthentic, leached of value and meaning, mere simulacra because they are fully co-opted by capital, intrinsic to neoliberalism and technologically mediated. To take such a view seems strange – and certainly very melancholic – and we might start once again by asking whose vision is it, and how well does it capture the situations we observe?

Globalization as metaphor and as a conceptual framework for understanding processes and interconnections across the realms of economics, technology, culture, politics and media took shape in the 1990s. It seems reasonable to suggest that 20 years later, we might step back and ask what the processes and interconnections we normally label globalization would look like if we were to place a different analytical frame on them. It is a paradox of theories of globalization – given that they are about interconnections – that they overemphasize difference, starting with the differences from market, modernity and the West which undergird the whole edifice. I would suggest that the example of the Indonesian fashion designers demonstrates the value of abandoning a view of globalization that is too dependent on the binaries of impact/response, capitalism/culture, western/non-western. The point surely is that these young Indonesians are Indonesian, and their cultural productions are part of contemporary Indonesian culture in all its complexity. They certainly see themselves as interconnected global citizens, but their perspective is not one that is fractured along the lines of western/non-western, global/Indonesian. Their vision is one premised on exploring affective and cognitive dispositions, as well as the possibilities engendered by engaging with the potentialities and possibilities their connected world offers. Their interest is not in hybridity, resistance or even reappropriation, but rather in creating new connections, new meanings, novel forms of relation.

Of course, inequalities of power, resource and opportunity continue to play a key role. Processes of inclusion and exclusion are constantly in play, creating new possibilities of connection and disconnection, identification and disavowal. But, the substantive point is that communities like the young Indonesian fashion designers are not just consumers; they are also creators and producers, and what they create are not just products, but new forms of the imagination and of knowledge, new ways of connecting to each other and their object worlds, new forms of desire and satisfaction. In the chapters that follow, I examine ways in which we might analyse these desires and satisfactions by focusing on specific connections and forms of relation as they are lived, imagined, maintained and transformed. I want to explore the theoretical and political possibilities of a conceptualization of others and otherness that is not overdetermined by figures of difference.

Culture, Subjectivity and Ethics

My interest in this book is in the aspirational character of our relations to others, to knowledge and the world. The way that hopes, desires and satisfactions are part of the making of selves, social relations and social imaginaries. Issues such as these – what we might term relationality – inevitably involve an engagement with problems of meaning and problems of value. Here we are unavoidably returned to a discussion of culture. I do not intend to engage here with the many debates in social theory about the definitions and validity of the term culture. It is worth noting, however, as many others have done, that social theorists became disenchanted with the notion of culture at almost exactly the same moment as many outside the academy were enthusiastically embracing it. This dissonance – or misapprehension – is one of several reasons why I am turning my thoughts once again to the question of the relationship between critique and politics (Moore, 1988; 1994). Contemporary forms of cultural objectification and reification are historical constructs, a particular way of configuring otherness and identity. Some have suggested that even in an increasingly interconnected world, forms of incommensurable difference continue to proliferate (Povinelli, 2001: 320). Recent formulations of culture as resource, asset and/or property tie the notion of culture to identity in very specific ways. Key to such formulations are ideas about heritage and authenticity, and, like older notions of culture as tradition, these tend to concentrate attention on history, autochthony and the past. What is evident is that those who claim incommensurable alterity are involved in specific deployments of power and power relations (Harrison, 2003). We are familiar with the historically specific way in which identities are linked to belonging and emplacement, and although these linkages have been extensively criticized in the social sciences, they nonetheless continue to exercise considerable dominion over people's imaginations and aspirations (Geschiere, 2009), as the many examples of war and conflict around the globe attest.

Contemporary social theory may take it as axiomatic that cultures are not fixed and bounded entities, that they are internally diverse and that individuals may have allegiances to more than one simultaneously, but this view is not one that is necessarily shared by many of the individuals and communities who make claims about culture around the globe. In this book, instead of focusing on forms of strategic otherness, on culture as difference, I want to return to the notion of culture as an 'art of living', as a means of engagement with the world, and develop new vocabularies for the analysis of change and social transformation, as well as new registers for addressing issues of belonging, meaning and value. In so doing, I am concerned to emphasize the constructive tension between the views of cultural change held by individuals and groups around the world, and various theoretical or analytical formulations developed in social and cultural theory. My overall contention is that social scientists and critical theorists have been so preoccupied with the deconstruction of 'culture' as entity/analytic category, and/or its complicities with the strategic deployment of power, that they have paid insufficient attention to the specific reconfigurations of cultural productions, capacities and relations characteristic of the contemporary moment. What is more, in examining theories of cultural change and social transformation, it seems that, despite protestations to the contrary, pre-theoretical assumptions about difference, carrying as they do the traces or residues of authenticity, tradition and belonging, continue to haunt many of our efforts.

The reasons for this have much to do, I suggest, with the way theoretical frameworks link critique to the recognition of difference. Since the 1980s, social constructionist and poststructuralist theories have emphasized the centrality of difference, and, across a wide range of scholarship and political activism, the recognition of diversity and difference has been consistently linked to the determination of political rights and political agency. The demand to be heard, to be recognized, has served as the basis for authentic claims, not just about rights and resources, but about identities. Identity has become a legitimate and defining feature both of self-expression and of group membership. It is curious that this development has occurred at the same time as performative theories have emphasized that identity is not something you are, but something you do. In theoretical terms, identities may be conceived of as non-essentialist and constructed in and through difference, but in practice the various deployments of performative theory – often contra the intentions and philosophies of their original architects – have ended up privileging the performance and expression of identity, if only through the performative transgression of identity itself.[2] Identity as an analytic notion has expanded to fill the screen, and there is talk, both inside and outside the academy, of gender identities, sexual identities, class identities, nationalist identities and much more. In Chapters 2, 3 and 4, I discuss how individuals in Africa, Southeast Asia and elsewhere imagine, create and deploy links between culture and identity, and I explore the limitations of existing frameworks of analysis and suggest new ways forward, alternative pathways to approach old questions.

One possible pathway – in an analogous fashion to the arguments I make about globalization – is to explore notions of culture that are not overdetermined by theoretical formulations of difference. In suggesting this, I am not advocating the dismissal or disavowal of differences, and their evident political, economic and cultural consequences. Rather, I am interested in the ways that the recognition of diversity and difference produce particular kinds of self–other relations through engagements with specific forms of hope, desire and satisfaction. One aspect of this is already captured by existing approaches that take as their starting point the assumption that all individuals and groups wish to be recognized in and for themselves. I do not deny this – indeed, recognition and identification are crucial for the making of self–other relations on which selves, social relations and social imaginaries rest – but I ask the question what happens if we begin from elsewhere, what then does the terrain we usually refer to by the term culture look like? In this book, I attempt to rethink belonging, emplacement, identity and culture. I do so by emphasizing that the recognition of diversity and difference is not a simple matter of self-presence, of the differences that exist between pre-existing individuals, entities or units, because the making of selves, social relations and social imaginaries always involves both being yourself and being other to yourself in ways that create new possibilities for imagining self–other relations. I discuss these ideas in more detail in Chapters 3 and 5, but critical to this approach is that, instead of reading culture backwards, looking at it in the past tense, I examine how it is deployed as a means for dealing with the alterity of the future, with the not-yet. More properly speaking, I suggest that we should think about culture as the radical potential for creating meanings, relations and values and that we should do so by reading culture forwards rather than backwards, exploring the relation between the present and the future through the conditional and future perfect tenses (see Chapters 6 and 7). Many contemporary processes of cultural creativity, expression and relation are not concerned with the authenticity or origins of the forms they employ, but with processes of subjectification and self-stylization that depend on cultural diversity and cultural change, on borrowing, mimesis, identification and projection, as I argue in Chapter 5. The key analytic issue here is how we deal with the potentialities created by new forms of sociality and new forms of knowledge.

In discussing these issues, one persistent difficulty is how we envisage and theorize what links human agency and human subjectivity to forms of the possible, to ways of living that open up new ways of being. In Chapters 6 and 7, I look at recent theories of change and social transformation that draw on biological and vitalist models to develop alternative views of social transformation and the human subject. A critical reworking of these innovative and provocative theories demonstrates very clearly why theories of social transformation are so closely linked to specific theories of agency and the subject. What is important here is the way these theories focus on affect, and on the capacity of embodied experiences and affective states to refuse and/or exceed social subjection and social constraint. The 'affective turn', as it is sometimes termed, is not just about new theories of change, but about new ontologies, new ways of conceiving of the human subject and their relation to the world. Affects encompass the human and the non-human, life and matter. They function through non-lineal connections, potentialities that circulate and are qualified in context, and while they are the stuff of everyday life, they are not held to reside in or be possessed by any single body or subject. Affect theory thus displaces the centrality of the human subject, but reconnects it to the vitality of the world, where the potential for change resides in radical forms of relationality and indeterminacy. These theories have been extremely influential in social theory and philosophy, and I focus on them as a way of returning to the kinds of relationships that social theories have with the theories of ordinary people, and as a means for re-examining how social theorizing is necessarily influenced by the social, economic and political contexts in which it is carried out. Affect and other vitalist theories are often explicitly described as an antidote both to the melancholia of the Left and to the limitations of the poststructuralist subject, constituted in language and founded on an ontological lack, precisely because they offer a way of reconnecting human subjects to the material world, and to its potential for change and transformation (Braidotti, 2002: 57). In Chapters 5, 6 and 7, I explore how well these theories serve us in an attempt to understand the world we share with others, and its interconnected and technologically mediated nature. One of the questions I raise is how such theories might take account of people's own projects of self-making, including their desire to transform the conditions that make them. Once again, my explicit interest is in asking what significance and value we should give to people's own theories of the self and social transformation, given that we know such theories play an important role in driving social change.

The Ethical Imagination

Theories of self always entail theories of self–other relations, and any discussion of the self in relation to others must necessarily engage with questions of the ethical (Foucault, 1998: 287). Ethics, however, is not a simply a matter of rule-following, a question of moral imperatives (Laidlaw, 2002; Zigon, 2007). As Foucault, drawing on Aristotle, so cogently reminds us, the ethical must always be distinguished from mere obedience or transgression, and it is this distinction, I suggest, that allows us to expand our ways of thinking about social change and how it occurs. In this book, I am not concerned with ethics per se, but with what – following various precedents – I want to term the ethical imagination:[3] the way in which technologies of the self, forms of subjectification and imagined relations with others lead to novel ways of approaching social transformation. As already discussed, existing theories of globalization and culture invoke a series of oscillations between determination and subversion, mimicry and resistance, tradition and freedom. Such antinomies continue to animate many of our analyses, and one consequence of their spectral presence is that we find it difficult to recognize what Foucault called the stuff of ethics, 'the strategies that individuals in their freedom can use in dealing with each other' (1998: 300). I take the question of how we deal with each other to be part of the larger problematic of understanding the world we share with others, and comprehending the forms of complex relationality that pure piffle

characterize it. The forms and means, if you will, through which individuals imagine relationships to themselves and to others, and this is what I intend by the phrase 'the ethical imagination'. Foucault's invocation of freedom in regard to self–other relations envisages it as a practice, a human possibility, rather than as a given state of affairs or actual set of capacities (see Faubion, 2001: 88–90). He recognizes that ethical practices are not invented by individuals, but are rather 'proposed, suggested, imposed upon him by his culture, his society, and his social group' (1998: 291). But equally, in *The Use of Pleasure*, Foucault (1985) makes it clear that neither culture, nor society, nor rules provide absolute limits to the ethical imagination or to ethical practice (Faubion, 2001: 89–90). They are not, and cannot be, absolutely determining. In a similar manner, forms of subjectification and the technologies of self, while engaged with the normative and with distributions of power, cannot completely bind people to identities, particular forms of the self or external powers. What remains open, unforeclosed, unfinished is present in its active possibility.

Consequently, the ethical imagination is, I suggest, one of the primary sites of cultural invention (Foucault, 1998), precisely because it deals with the self in its relations with others, both proximate and distant, and as such provides for historical possibilities. In contexts of social change and transformation, it is brought into play by the advent of new information and new ideas, new ways of being and acting, new forms of representation and their mediation. However, it does not always involve conscious thought and is not always based on a privileging of language. While we must always have regard for the kind of interpretive talk the ethical imagination makes possible, we need to attend equally to the importance of affect, performance and the placement and use of the body. More than this even, we have to acknowledge that identification and fantasy often proceed through forms of unknowing and types of incomprehensibility. I have in mind here such things as speaking in tongues, the imitation of dance styles, ritual secrets and the impact of texts and media productions that are written and produced in languages other than one's own. I elaborate on these points in Chapter 3. It is a paradox that forms of unknowing can engage the ethical imagination every bit as much as explicit ideologies and well-worked-out theories. The forms of identification involved may vary, but hopes, desires and satisfaction work most often through the relays and connections they establish between pleasure and identification, where pleasure is a consequence of thought and unthought forms of reflection, experimentation and reformulation. Here fantasy plays a key part in creating and maintaining forms of identification and belonging through establishing new possibilities for connection, as I argue in Chapter 4. These connections do not need to be based on explicit meanings. Meaning, as it is used in English, is an amorphous term, encompassing everything from the dictionary definition of words to the broadest understanding of what gives value to our lives (Weinberger, 2007: 169). Explicit meaning – ostensible reference – is only one facet of meaning. What is of more significance, I suggest, is the general underdetermination of cultural meaning, its ambiguity and indeterminacy, its debt to forms of affect and unknowing which provide the core conditions not only for subjectification, fantasy and identification, but for self–other relations, the making of connections, cultural sharing and, ultimately, social transformation. If cultural meanings were fixed, not open to interpretation, without ambiguity, then subjectification would not be possible. Human beings would be too overdetermined to become human subjects. It is a feature of human subjectivity that we are born into and make ourselves under conditions that we may then choose to transform. In this sense, culture provides for historical possibilities; it is the radical potentiality within subjectivity, as I argue in Chapters 3 and 5. The logical corollary of this is that the indeterminacy of cultural meaning, said by some to be characteristic of global capitalism, might be better viewed as the enhancement of a general condition rather than the inauguration of a new one.

Cultural meaning involves itself in myriad ways with the formative conditions of subjectivity and subjectification because debates over cultural meanings and values have a substantial role in the diverse and conflicted formations of subjectivities in the modern era. But, we cannot hope to understand these processes if we reduce them to cognitive and evaluative processes or see them as overdetermined by particular distributions of power and resource. When we consider everything that underlies behaviour, we have to recognize that thought alone is not enough to bring about change. We need to take account of the way in which thought is bound up with fantasy, affect, emotion, symbols and the distortions of space and time. Our reifications and objectifications are only partially the product of conscious thought. More than this, our forms of reflection, experimentation and stylization are also bound up with symbolic systems and intimate relations that are not of our own making, and with which we have a fantasized relation, one that is set up in representation (Moore, 2007). The ethical imagination links human agency to the forms of the possible, and I suggest in this book that it does so primarily through a refiguring of self–other relations, and that key to this process of reconfiguration is fantasy. This provides for a series of complex links between objectifications, stylization and agency. I suggest in the chapters that follow that exploring these specific linkages gives us an alternative way of understanding emerging forms of relationality. And this in its turn provides us with an alternative framework for understanding many of the connections and interconnections we usually refer to by the term globalization. Through this process, the ethical imagination becomes a means to explore the historical refiguring of technologies of self and of self–other relations, with their constitutive engagements with thought, fantasy and affect.

In order to explain how a focus on the ethical imagination might lead to novel means for approaching social transformation, we need to return to the connections between ethics and knowledge. Foucault argues that ethics involves a relation with self, not merely self-awareness, but a regard for self-formation, an attention to the ways in which it is possible and desirable to constitute oneself as an 'ethical subject' (Foucault, 1985: 28–30). Self-formation necessarily takes place in historically given contexts, where specific ethical problems arise and provide the conditions for the 'problematization' of self. Much of Foucault's work, for example, is about locating the areas of experience, as well as the forms in and through which sexual behaviour is problematized. His general thesis is that at any given moment there may be several areas of problematization – thematic complexes – within the general terrain of sexual behaviour: for example, the nature of the body, marriage, sex with men, the truth of sexed being (Foucault, 1985: 23–4). Such problems or difficulties pose challenges both for politics and for self-formation and self-understanding: am I a paedophile? will my desires expose me to the terror of being labelled a paedophile? Consequently, the experiences we have of ourselves at specific historical conjunctures always involve certain forms of problematization that 'define objects, rules of action, modes of relation to oneself' (Foucault, 1998: 318), and which bear on the question of how we are constituted as subjects of our own knowledge, the kinds of selves we are for ourselves and for others.

Foucault's overall interest is in how particular forms of knowledge or problematization involve necessary intersections between the development of a specific politics, a form of government of the self and the elaboration of an ethics in regard to oneself. This provides the basis for his analytic triumvirate: knowledge, power and ethics. What makes his notion of problematization provocative is that it emphasizes what happens when something stands out from the general terrain of human life and experience, when something emerges as an object of thought, and we start questioning 'its meaning, its condition and its goals', reflecting on it as a problem (Foucault, 1998: 117). There is something here that is akin to Weber's 'world-images' that determine 'the tracks' along which action moves because, as Foucault says, for something to be problematized, 'it is necessary for a certain number of factors to have made it lose its familiarity, or to have provoked a certain number of difficulties around it' (Foucault, 1998: 117). The factors that make a particular problem or object of thought stand out or coalesce are the result of specific social, economic and political processes, but while they may initiate the process of problematization, they do not and cannot completely determine its form and character. This is because problematizations are never simply the direct consequence or expression of socioeconomic and political change, but a series of historically specific responses that take a variety of forms, and which may be contradictory and conflicting. What makes all these responses possible, as Foucault says, is the general terrain or character of what is problematized and the way in which it nourishes them in their diversity and in spite of their contradictions. 'It is problematization that responds to these difficulties, but by doing something quite other than expressing them or manifesting them: in connection with them, it develops the conditions in which possible responses can be given; it defines the elements that will constitute what the different solutions attempt to respond to' (Foucault, 1998: 118).

In this book, I suggest that it is our relations with others, the vexed question of what we share, of how we set our personal and political horizons, the character of contemporary forms of belonging and the complex relations they entail that have become problematized.[4] Within this general terrain, a set of thematic complexes – culture, religion, values, environmental sustainability, the nature of anthropos, life itself – offer a series of problematizations to which diverse solutions are being proposed. We can see this diversity at work, for example, within the ethical domain of culture, where some seek solutions in culture as proprietary asset and primordial identity and others in bricolage and the exigent demands of cosmopolitanism. The preeminent challenge posed to politics is our shared world and how we can and should share the many worlds that comprise it, from our most intimate relationships to questions of citizenship, international governance and planetary concerns. This challenge has certainly been instigated by social, economic and political changes, but cannot be reduced to them or seen as a direct expression of them. One of the reasons for this is that people's own theories of change, of self-formation and self–other relations, their ethical imaginations, play a major role in developing the very conditions in which their possible responses to the challenges and difficulties they perceive can develop and find form. Where my thinking parts company with Foucault's formulation is in my insistence that problematization is always more than a work of thought or reflection. It also involves affect, emotion, the placement of the body, fantasy, and relations with objects, technologies and the material world. The ethical imagination, I suggest, is the primary site for cultural invention because it engages with and refigures self-stylization and self–other relations in the context of all these factors. To grasp it in all its fullness, we have to recognize that it is not just about conformity to the normative or to power, but is about the strategies that individuals 'in their freedom' can use in dealing with each other.

Hopes, Desires and Satisfactions

Problematizations necessarily engage with hopes, desires and satisfactions because they are about the ways in which selves and lives are given value and meaning in relation to themselves and to others. One of the terrains in which hopes, desires and satisfactions are played out is that of *oh god!*

anticipation or what we might more broadly term the alterity of the future. By this I mean more than simply the unknowable character of temporal processes. Rather, I want to emphasize the radical potentialities of human agency and human subjectivity, their essential openness to meaning-making and therefore to new ways of being. Hopes, desires and satisfactions can never be fully captured by forms of regulation. This means that they emerge as possibilities, forms of improvisation, within cultural and social contexts. In this book, I take them up as questions, as methods for exploring both the relationship between critical thought and politics, and the dynamics of intimacy and meaning in cultural and social life. My aim in thinking about the 'ethical imagination' in this context is to use it as an analytic lever to engage with the broad terrain of self–other relations as they are experienced, felt, imagined, cognized and performed, as well as the forms and potentialities of the relationalities they engage and make possible. My interest is in the way hopes, desires and satisfactions attach us to the world, to ourselves and to others through imagination and fantasy. In several places in the book, I explore how new technologies powerfully enhance these capacities, and thus augment our potential for connection and sharing. Knowledge of ourselves and others is open to the future, driven as it is by the affective, embodied, cognitive and evaluative consequences of engagement and connection. New forms of knowledge create new forms of sociality which have the potential to create new ways of seeing, doing, feeling and being. Life-making is profoundly attached to forms and terms of value – culture here acts as the enabling matrix, as well as a set of coordinates – but the ethical imagination has scalar dimensions, as I explain in Chapters 3 and 4, that link us both to those with whom we are most proximate and intimate, as well as those who are very distant. Within the domain of the ethical, the fantasmatic nature of intersubjectivity plays a key role in maintaining forms of identity and belonging through establishing new possibilities for connection that are animated and propelled by hopes, desires and satisfactions.

In talking about hopes, desires and satisfactions, we have to have regard for the way that they too are operative at different experiential and analytic scales. Here the interconnections between the abstractions of social and cultural theorists and the experiences of ordinary individuals need to be carefully explored. We may all have our personal hopes, desires and satisfactions, but these remain at some distance from general theories. In Chapter 6, for example, I draw on the work of Hirokazu Miyazaki to explore hope as an analytic category and its interface with the specific hopes of individuals. Hope – like desire and satisfaction – is an affective disposition as well as a cognitive evaluation, and this inserts the action or agency of hoping into historical analysis on different temporal, as well as analytic scales. For example, Miyazaki analyses it as something that redirects critical thought within individual life plans, but the forward thrust of hope can also refer to longings, yearnings and impossible dreams, as well as to states of being or situations such as the second coming of the Lord. Hope for change stretches from the personal to the messianic, from the private to the realm of citizenship and onwards to modernity and the future of the planet.

It is for this reason that I do not attempt definitions of hope, desire and satisfaction in the book. Rather, I explore them as a series of different affective and evaluative dispositions and/or orientations that animate the ethical imagination, as well as resulting forms of agency, both conscious and unconscious. What this draws attention to is the way that the boundaries between hope, desire and satisfaction cannot be rigidly established, for they overlap as shifting constellations in human life, forming a dynamic matrix. What they share is the forward direction of our appetite for attachment to the world, to ourselves, to objects, to others, and to the relationships we establish between all these things and the meanings and values we create and attribute to them. Recent theories in social and cultural theory (actor network and affect theory) have turned our attention towards the agency of objects and non-human actors, towards the role of non-conscious actors in networks of hybrids, and the movement of affects that are not centred on the human subject. These theories are extremely powerful and valuable, and I suggest in Chapter 7 that we need to build on them. But if we are charged with understanding that we are part of a world made up of the human, the non-human and the inhuman, and that this is a constitutive feature of our vital being, we also need, I suggest, to retain a regard for what is distinctively human about being and doing in the world. For our theories of being and doing have a direct impact on the formation of that world, which, of course, is not the same thing as saying that they fully control or determine it.

It is often argued that modern digital and information technologies are making humans ever more hybrid, cyborgs immersed in virtual worlds. In Chapters 5 and 7, I take up this theme and critique it. Arguing that humans have always been virtual, that subject–object distinctions can never be rigidly imposed, and that this must necessarily be so because of the way we become subjects through engagements with and attachments to the world and its objects, I go on to suggest that while new technologies enrich our capacities for being virtual and extend our cyborg character, they do not create such capacities or qualities. However, through their deployment of sensation and affect, they do productively enhance the animating effects of hopes, desires and satisfactions. Starting from very different premises, some critiques of capitalism make a parallel point, arguing that we are lured into complicity with capitalism through consumption and our desire for goods. The formation of our tastes, and thus of our desires and satisfactions, is necessarily bound up with the proliferating differences of capitalism and their seductions. Consequently, we are all part of a desiring machine within an industry of erotics that animates subjects, but leaches subjectivity and lives of meaning. There is much to recommend this influential and authoritative body of work, and there is certainly no purpose in suggesting – indeed it would be egregious foolhardiness – that such processes are not at work. However, as before my interest is in asking what such perspectives leave under-theorized; what would the terrain of enquiry look like if we began from elsewhere, if we were to focus instead on the enabling and animating aspects of hopes, desires and satisfactions?

Satisfaction is a familiar term from economics, where utility is a measure of the happiness or satisfaction gained from a good or service. While the idea that humans are rational actors who seek to maximize their utility has come under sustained critique, the utilitarian notion that the maximization of utility should act as a moral compass for the organization of society has persisted. In its most recent form, it has emerged as a concern for well-being, part of a larger desire to find 'happy versions of capitalism' (e.g. Layard, 2006). Several western governments have recently followed Bhutan, in expressing a desire to measure the happiness of their populations, and arguing for a revision of the assessment of well-being by replacing GDP (gross domestic product) as a measure with GPI (genuine progress indicator), thereby shifting the grounds for the measurement of the performance of the economy from one based on the production of goods and services to one based on satisfaction.[5] Recent discussions focus on how much social inequality, unemployment and ill-health erode the quality of people's lives even in so-called rich countries, and on the necessity of understanding sustainability (e.g. levels of indebtedness) and environmental costs (e.g. carbon emissions) as part of broader conceptualizations of economic performance (Stiglitz et al., 2009; Oswald, 2010). This is clearly a positive trend, but what is interesting is the way that in the process happiness is becoming an object of knowledge, a performance indicator and a form of governance (see Ahmed, 2007; 2010). There may be something both optimistic and slightly sinister about governments seeking to ensure, and possibly engineer, the happiness of their citizens. However, this 'happy turn' does draw attention to the recursive relationships between social and cultural theories and those of ordinary people. As research on happiness escapes the confines of the academy to become part of government policy, popular understandings of the good life and how to live it – everything from self-help manuals to concerns about social justice and the planet – influence the way researchers conceptualize and problematize happiness.

One important aspect here is the way happiness is conceived of as a form of labour that involves effort and perseverance, a goal towards which one should address one's efforts. A whole industry has grown up, as Lisa Blackman notes, to advise on and manage the practices and techniques of the self required to achieve happiness, involving life coaches, self-help guides and the like (2007: 15). A related development is what some have described as a rapprochement between psychology and economics, evident in recent research which takes not just well-being but mental health and 'emotional prosperity' as objects of enquiry (e.g. Oswald, 2010). Prominent in this research is the idea of happiness as affect, as something that works through body mimesis, sympathetic identification, suggestion or contagion. Discussing this, Blackman points out the renewed interest in viral models in social and cultural theory as a means to explain a diverse range of phenomena relating to self-cultivation and contemporary technologies of the self. She also very cleverly points out that in the nineteenth century, ideas about 'bodily affectivity' – how affect, feelings and belief were thought to move from one individual to another – were linked to the emergence of media technologies such as radio and the telegraph which were often envisaged as forms of agency at a distance (2007: 17–19). As I discuss in Chapters 6 and 7, contemporary theories of affect are clearly linked to contemporary technologies – including web 2.0, the mobile phone, transbiology and nanotechnology – and the way we envisage them as open systems of ramifying connection and information transfer based on pulses, bytes and cellular replication.

Recent work on politics and information technologies takes up older themes in social theory about how ideas and sentiments animate groups and populations (e.g. Connolly, 2002). Blackman reminds us that late nineteenth- and early twentieth-century thinkers like William James and Gabriel Tarde saw suggestibility as key to understanding sociality (Blackman, 2007: 19). These ideas re-emerge in reconfigured form in the writings of contemporary feminist philosophers and cultural theorists, as I discuss in Chapters 6 and 7 (Blackman, 2007: 24). My general proposition is that recent analyses of culture and politics are frequently trapped in a strange and unproductive liminality between theories that figure them as wholly or substantially captured by capitalism and vitalist theories that posit the movement of affect as the primary motor for change. In both cases, there is a turn away from the hopes, desires and satisfactions of individuals. In Chapters 5, 6 and 7, I try to think about the historical circumstances in which these different theories have emerged and about the analytic purchase they offer for understanding how social groups and social imaginaries based on hopes, desires and satisfactions come into being. Such forms of belonging, imagination and identification can be very temporary, but they are evidently based on the satisfactions of sharing, connecting and creating.

The collaborative nature of cultural production is intrinsic to the way that values and meanings are bound up with and constitutive of relationships. It is a feature of the human capacity for the virtual that relationships with others – including objects, the non-human and the in-human – can extend across space and time. As I have already suggested, modern information technologies enormously enhance these capacities. They therefore augment and supplement the ethical imagination, in ways that are in evidence from online games to political activism, file-sharing and the collaborative construction of second worlds, as I argue in Chapters 5 and 6. One of the things that digital technologies allow is the objectification – and consequent sharing – of forms of self-stylization. These may actively supplement pre-existing forms of self-styliza-tion, as in the use of digital technologies by religious groups to link their adherents and share their experiences of faith. Alternatively, they may provide new opportunities and new means for self-stylization. Good examples include iTunes playlists and the tagging of photos on Flickr. Taking photographs and listening to music are hardly new, but what is novel is the way that information technologies allow individuals to assemble data – images, sounds, any-thing – in ways that are meaningful to them and then share these arrangements as metadata. These piles of informa-tion are not based on expert or pre-existing classification systems, but on people's interests, on the way they interact with their lived worlds. Objects of all kinds are becoming available to us freed – at least partially – from older systems of classification, hierarchies of value and distribu-tions of power, and enabled by new forms of the ethical imagination, new fantasies of self–other relations (Wein-berger, 2007).

It is evident that the assemblages or 'profiles' that emerge from these activities can be manipulated, as individuals clearly do on social networking and dating sites, and it is a fact of life that such information is of enormous interest to marketing companies and corporations. In 2010, for example, there were several complaints against the social networking site Facebook for releasing user data to those who had an in interest in mining it for commercial pur-poses. But, the entanglements of autonomy, choice and self-stylization with the market and capitalism should not be a reason for turning away from the hopes, desires and pleasures that arise from such meaning-making, with its links to the ethical imagination, and fantasized relations with others – including objects, the non-human and the inhuman.

However, in focusing on the aspirations and pleasures of our relations with others, with objects and the world, we should not lose sight of the fact that our satisfactions are frequently ambivalent, as are our hopes and desires. Emphasizing the fact that human behaviour is not just a matter of rational calculation leads us to focus not only on the role of affect, suggestion and contagion, but on fantasy and identification. Our unconscious desires exert a powerful influence on our subjectivities and our behaviour. They also structure the form and expression of our manifest desires. There are many competing theories of desire – Freudian, Lacanian, Foucauldian, Deleuzean – but no absolute definition of desire is possible. Any satisfactory theory of desire must, however, link its powerful physical and psychic effects for individuals to broader circulations and configurations of desire within societies, communities, bureaucracies and polities, to the way we displace desire onto other things, and invest objects, situations, fantasies and people with affect. Desire is both personal and relational, and as such it is always bound up with self-stylization and self–other relations: who am I for myself and for others? Desires, like satisfactions, are very often ambivalent or opaque. We don't always need what we want, and we don't always want what we get. When we desire something, we are hopeful. As Lauren Berlant suggests, 'all attachments are optimistic' in the sense that they provide a means and a reason to 'keep on living on and to look forward to being in the world' (2007: 33). However, we can also be attached to hopes, desires and satisfactions that keep us from thriving, that are simultaneously enabling and disabling (2007: 35). Hopes, desires and satisfactions are not necessarily liberatory, but they are human possibilities, conditions within which we find our possibilities, part of the strategies that 'individuals in their freedom can use in dealing with each other'.

waffle again

– 2 –
Still Life

In this chapter, I discuss how ideas about culture have become involved in contests of knowledge and value in a community in northern Kenya. My interest is in demonstrating how and why debates about culture engage with particular ways of thinking about selves and self–other relations, and with specific forms of what I have termed the ethical imagination. Discussions about culture and cultural practices have emerged in response to particular socioeconomic and political changes. As a consequence of expanding personal and political horizons, culture appears both as an object of knowledge, and as a specific kind of challenge or problem. I sketch two different theoretical propositions that might shed some light on the mechanisms of 'problematization' before going on to discuss the theories and ideas offered by community members in an effort to comprehend and confront the challenges they face. As with the other chapters in this book, I draw on several theorists and theoretical traditions, but my intention is prismatic rather than synthetic. I am not trying to provide a single model for culture or cultural change – such a task, in my view, is neither desirable nor possible – rather, my aim is to try and maintain a creative tension between different starting points, conclusions and aspirations, exploring what happens to theoretical frameworks when we begin from elsewhere.

In the contemporary world, debates about culture are very often debates about politics. Culture has become a particular form of the political. There is also considerable irony in the fact that culture has become the idiom through which opposing sides of the debate – capitalists and anti-globalization supporters, nation-states and the communities that seek self-determination within them, corporations and the guardians of traditional life-ways – all make their claims to uniqueness and authenticity. It seems as if notions of culture are being reconfigured within a progressively narrow definition of property over which groups seek to assert monopoly rights. As David Harvey (2002) points out, monopoly rights confer monopoly rents which, in their turn, depend on seeking out criteria of speciality, uniqueness, originality and authenticity. This may explain why nations, corporations, communities and individuals are concerned not just with culture in the broadest sense, but with what one might term the elements of culture: melodies, motifs, designs, images and the like. Every bit of culture can be made to have a value, and most particularly in recombinant forms because changes in form potentially make for new value claims, as well as new regimes of commodification. However, the problem is not just one about commodification – a voluminous literature exists on cultural property, and on the interrelated questions of who owns culture, whether it should be traded, and whether or not it can be copyrighted (e.g. Brown, 2003) – but a larger one about the recentring of meaning in personal and collective life (Moore, 2008). Cultural struggles over meaning and value are reverberating across the world, and through every domain of life, from changes in processes of subjectification and intimate life, to the rise of choice, individualism, religion, ethnicity and the defence of cultural property and heritage (e.g. Anheier and Isar, 2011).

Part of the problem is what the recognition of difference should entail. Starting at different times in different places, a particular form of politics of representation gradually emerged and became integrated into government policies in a number of countries around the world, most notably from the 1970s onwards. This politics placed emphasis on the recognition and government of difference. It was and is institutionalized by states – often through policies of multiculturalism – structured through legal instruments, championed by new social and indigenous movements and NGOs, promoted by the media, and celebrated through a wide range of consumer products and practices. It also underpins much academic theorizing in the humanities and social sciences, as I discussed in Chapter 1. What is compelling about this particular politics of representation, as George Yúdice notes, is that no one group or set of institutions controls its proliferating forms (2003: 129), and consequently it inaugurates long-running and irresolvable conflicts over value. This is one of the reasons why the prime ministers of Spain, France, Germany and the United Kingdom have all recently pronounced the death of multiculturalism, arguing that it has not successfully integrated immigrants. Other countries, such as India, Malaysia and Indonesia, prefer the term diversity, but the recognition and management of linguistic, ethnic, cultural and religious differences is still a challenge.

Notions of cultural diversity – often treated as if it were analogous to biodiversity – and cultural identity have been heavily promoted since the 1980s by international bodies such as UNESCO, ILO and WIPO, and more recently by national and international NGOs (Yúdice, 2003: 78–9; Moore, 2008; 2011).[1] A number of scholars have tracked the emergence of the idioms of heritage and inheritance in determining the character and ownership of cultural property, and the term is revealing in itself (see Brown, 2003; Anheier and Isar, 2011). For example, the 1948 Universal Declaration of Human Rights guarantees fundamental rights relating to, inter alia, labour, culture, privacy and property, including the right to own collective property and not to be deprived of it. It also provides for the safeguarding of moral and material interests in scientific, literary and artistic productions. The ILO's Convention 169 concerning indigenous and tribal peoples in independent countries requires states to adopt special measures to safeguard the institutions, property, culture and environment of indigenous peoples, and to respect 'the special importance of the cultures and spiritual values of the peoples concerned of their relationship with their lands or territories . . . which they occupy or otherwise use, and in particular the collective aspects of this relationship'.[2] UNESCO has also developed a series of conventions on intangible cultural heritage and cultural diversity, taking the task of 'defending the cultural heritage of humankind' as a priority (Moore, 2008), and there are many other examples (see Coombe, 1998; Brown, 2005).

The result is an uneven, but evident, trend towards forms of citizenship based on the logics of cultural identities, and group needs, desires and imaginaries. These cultural elements become the basis for making claims on state resources, such as education, welfare and health. Cultural claims become political resources, and contests of value occur not only around actual resources, but also with regard to the forms of representation of identities, needs and desires, and how they will be translated into legal, administrative and political realities (Yúdice, 2003: 165; Povinelli, 2006; Ewing, 2008). Yúdice argues that in such contexts politics takes the form of cultural antagonisms structured by inequalities between dominant and subdominant groups. Entitlement shifts to struggles over the interpretation of representations, democracy advances through spectacle and style, and the result is an aestheticization of mainstream politics in which the media and the market play key roles (Yúdice, 2003: 165–8). Other writers have suggested that the 'culturalization' of economic and political life has changed the character of culture itself and our relationship to it (e.g. Jameson, 1991), and that as culture becomes the basis for the management of populations and value differences – a form of governmentality – it is effectively instrumentalized and emptied of content (e.g. Young, 2000; Phillips, 2007).

Walter Benjamin famously warned that 'All efforts to render politics aesthetic culminate in one thing: war' (1992: 234). He developed this theme by distinguishing between what he termed 'the cult value' and the 'exhibition value' of a work of art. He argued that in the context of traditional rituals, paintings, statues and other cultural objects were important for what they did, and access to them was often restricted to those of special place or purpose within the ritual. However, once such objects become emancipated from their ritual context, increasing opportunities for their exhibition and display arise, and consequently the manner of their consumption and use alters. Benjamin suggested that this is because the value of art objects is necessarily calibrated differently when it is based on their exhibition and display rather than on their value and use in context. The contests and character of public presentability become the domains in which value is created and assigned to cultural products, while their original use and its values fade away (Benjamin, 1992: 218). Benjamin made this observation against the background of what he termed the 'age of mechanical reproduction' – that is, the changing nature of the technical means of artistic production, and the advent of forms such as photography and film. His point was that these new technical means of reproduction actually change the character of art itself, transforming it and its relationship to values.

I want to take up these themes of the culturalization of politics and the politicization of aesthetics, and tie them to the idea that our relationship to culture is partly a feature of its 'reproduction' or mechanisms of objectification, but to make a break with the view that this necessarily implies instrumentalization and the emptying of content. I want to investigate how public debates about culture and cultural practices allow for new forms of problematization that, through an engagement with technologies of self, forms of subjectification and imagined relations with others, lead to novel ways of approaching social transformation. I want to explore the ways in which the relationship between culture and identity is creating new forms of pleasure, desire and satisfaction, as well as being entangled in processes of governmentality and supra local forms of belonging. Joel Robbins has argued in relation to Christianity that anthropologists have a tendency to emphasize 'localization' and 'indigenization', and that they prefer to stress the importance of adaptation and cultural continuity (Robbins, 2003: 221). This is connected, as Robbins and others have argued, to the comparative project inherent in the anthropological notion of culture. In the material that follows, we see how subjectification is more than a local process, and how a focus on the ethical imagination allows us to refigure standard assumptions about the links between belonging, emplacement, identity and culture.

Culture As Object

I want to turn to my own field research (see also Moore, 2009a; 2009b) to explore what has happened and what is happening to certain key aspects of culture in Marakwet District in northern Kenya. There are a number of interrelated issues I wish to discuss, and to do this I will need to give some sense of what has occurred in relation to changes in female initiation and female circumcision in the Kerio Valley over the past two to three decades. The majority of the significant changes in ritual practice have actually taken place over a much shorter period of time, beginning in 1999, and have been as a result of intensive activity on the part of local NGOs, teachers, advocates and, to a lesser extent, the government. When I was working in the valley in 2005–8, these changes are encapsulated for many by the incomplete, but nonetheless substantial, abandonment of the female circumcision ritual and its replacement by a new ritual, designed by NGOs, called an ARP, or alternative rite of passage. In this process of transfiguration, female circumcision had become disembedded from its original context of use and value, and placed on public exhibition as something to be analysed, condemned and eradicated.

One significant factor here is the way that the very notion of Marakwet culture has become reified in the contemporary moment in a way that would have seemed inconceivable in 1980 when I first began research. The speed of this transformation in the nature of culture, its reification and objectification, is rather dramatic, and has taken place in large part since the end of the 1990s. The reification of certain cultural practices and their disinterment or distinction from a broader understanding of life world is intentional on the part of those who see themselves as 'agents of social change in Marakwet', and in fact owes much to the discourse and discipline of anthropology as it is mediated through social consultants employed by NGOs, as well as through local Marakwet pastors, many of whom have received training in 'African traditional religions' in their theological colleges as part of a broader education about the proper relationship of Christianity to local cultures. The term 'rite of passage' – relating to ritual stages connected to life transition events – was originally coined by Arnold van Gennep (1961), and is a staple of all undergraduate teaching programmes in anthropology and other social sciences, from whence it has migrated to NGOs and development workers, many of whom have training in the social sciences. The reification and objectification of cultural practices through academic discourse creates its own counterparts in development and NGO practices: the anthropologization of everyday life.

My contention is that the reification of female circumcision as a distinctive aspect of something called culture is a necessary step in any programme of eradication. I make this argument because in order for female circumcision to become an object of action, it has first to undergo a transformation that constructs it as a new kind of object of knowledge, one that would be potentially susceptible to new forms of agency and governance. In the past, circumcision was the fulcrum of a rite of social transformation that prepared girls to be mothers and wives, and provided them with the maturity and the knowledge to produce children who were themselves the embodied link between the ancestors and the future well-being of the community. Intense secrecy surrounded the activities and teachings of *kapkore*, the girls' initiation house. These secrets were, however, a prelude to other secrets, other songs, dances and teachings that would be progressively revealed to married couples at different stages of the ceremonies associated with marriage, the last of which would not be performed until a couple had two or three children. These forms of knowledge were based on a model of revelation through progress, and initiation both for girls and for boys marked the assumption of social adulthood because it began that process of revelation. Talking to individuals today and in 1980 has often elicited the response that the knowledge once revealed could be disappointing, insufficiently momentous, and yet even now no adult will reveal the details of their acquired knowledge unless they know that they are talking to someone who already knows it, someone who has already passed through the requisite stage.

Knowledge of this kind not only provides powerful bonds of social cohesion, but reinforces intergenerational hierarchies and underpins forms of governance in this society without traditional chiefs, because it is linked to the formation of the age-grades that result from cycles of initiations. I have interviewed men and women extensively and asked whether they talk over aspects of this corpus of knowledge when they meet privately amongst themselves, but all my informants have always been adamant that these matters are never spoken of except when their performance is required (Moore, 2009a). Knowledge (as well as its interpretation) is a type of practical understanding, taught primarily by example and highly sensitive to particular circumstances and sets of social relations. It is not to be imagined as an extant body of information that is stored and transmitted as a corpus nor as a body of knowledge that can be drawn on and elaborated on in the manner that text-based religions can be, for example. These are forms of knowledge that are bound together not by rules or by systematic relations between the system's components, but rather cohere through habitus, through situated practice that is often discontinuous in space and time, and yet always potentially applicable. It makes of adulthood a sort of mastery, but a mastery without explicit and stable content (Barth, 1975; 1989; Beidelman, 1997; Moore, 2009b). Marakwet rituals – of all kinds – as observed across space and time often exhibit marked degrees of variation and innovation, as well as redundancy. 'We are following the ways of our fathers' is a phrase commonly heard, to be followed quite often by a great deal of debate as to whether this or that action or practice should or should not be allowed at this time or in this context.

I am certainly making the obvious point here that Marakwet culture is about living tradition, but I am going beyond that to suggest that the situated and enacted nature of traditional knowledge depended for its success on a lack of explicit reification – therein lay its power and its purpose (see Barth, 1989). The lived habitus of a world so constructed is both flexible and resistant to change. In order to bring about the upheaval required to displace female circumcision and girls' initiation from their fulcrum position in terms of social and societal continuity and well-being, something had to happen which made these practices cultural objects around which contests of value could legitimately take place. These contests of value were not like the old ones concerned with the appropriateness or not of specific situated practices, but were rather about the nature of knowledge itself and its effectiveness in modern contexts. In this process, something happened to what we might term the technical means of cultural reproduction, and as a consequence the very idea of culture, as opposed to that of a lived world, was created. Culture in this form proved more amenable to change because it could be acted on in a new way (Moore, 2009b).

Different categories of actor in Marakwet hold different views about exactly what Marakwet culture is, both in terms of its content and in terms of what kind of object it is. These differing views provide individuals with different capacities or potentialities for action. The notion of Marakwet culture that has recently emerged is a specific kind of object of knowledge, one which, as I have said, is potentially subject to new forms of agency and governance, but also one that is linked for many individuals to specific forms of self-fashioning and self-stylization with their accompanying forms of self-objectification. The drivers of change here are Protestant Christianity and education – the history of their development in the valley is in any event intertwined – but together they have produced new sets of ideas about individuals who are specific sorts of moral selves and who also have responsibilities for fashioning themselves and for changing their communities.

A Short History of the Campaign Against Female Circumcision in Marakwet

In April 2002, the remote district of Marakwet in the Rift Valley Province of northern Kenya and, in particular, its adherence to the practice of female circumcision suddenly broke onto the world stage with dramatic consequences.[3] A local NGO called the Centre for Human Rights and Democracy (CHRD), sponsored by Ashoka[4] and funded by donations from the USA, brought court cases against the parents of 16 Marakwet girls to prevent them from circumcising their daughters. The parents were angry, confused and frightened, and feared that they might go to jail. The use of legal proceedings to prevent female circumcision in this way was made possible after Kenya became a party to the International Children's Act;[5] but female circumcision, despite condemnation by the government over the past 30 years, is still not actually illegal there.

In 1982, President Moi issued an official statement against FGM (female genital mutilation) after the deaths of 14 girls from complications of excision, and he instructed the police to pursue murder charges against people who carried out the procedure with fatal results. The Director of Medical Services also ordered that no health official should carry out the procedure without the office's specific permission. In December 1989, President Moi called upon Kenyan communities where FGM was still being carried out to stop the practice immediately, and in 1990 the Assistant Minister for Cultural and Social Services announced that the government had officially banned FGM. But, despite this commitment of the executive to introduce outright prohibition of FGM, the legislature has not yet passed any laws banning the practice. Indeed, in November 1995, a proposal to outlaw the practice was defeated in the Kenyan Parliament. In 2006, forced female circumcision was originally scheduled to be included in a new Sexual Offences Act, but was subsequently withdrawn. However, a new bill outlawing the practice is scheduled to be introduced into the Kenyan Parliament in 2011.

In his submission to the court in April 2002, the director of CHRD argued his case on three grounds: first, that FGM contravenes the Universal Declaration of Human Rights because it subjects a person to torture and/or cruel and inhuman treatment; second, that under section 5.14 of the Children's Act no one shall subject a child to FGM, early marriage or other cultural rites, customs and practices that are likely negatively to affect the child's life, health, social welfare, dignity or physical and psychological development; and third, that under the Kenyan penal code FGM amounts to grievous assault. The court granted temporary injunctions in all 16 cases, and although mention was made in the record of the fixing of a date for a further hearing, no additional legal action was pursued. The girls and their parents were stunned by the media furore that followed, much of which was orchestrated by CHRD as a means to dissuade other parents from similar actions – no one wanted to be labelled as 'the person who was sued by the daughter' – and as a strategy for gaining further funds from abroad for their work. The acclaimed director and documentary filmmaker Kim Longinotto made a film on the court cases with a British anthropologist, combined with other material on female circumcision, called *The Day I will Never Forget* (2002). None of the girls involved has ever seen the film and those I have interviewed have claimed that they do not wish to do so because of the social stigma and embarrassment surrounding the events and their subsequent fall-out. They feel that they were foolish to be taken advantage of by many different social actors, all of whom had their own reasons for wanting to be involved in anti-FGM activity, but who, it subsequently transpired, at least from the girls' perspective, did not have their interests at heart.

In many ways, the cases themselves are less interesting than the series of actions that had preceded them and made them possible. CHRD had been involved in December 2000 in bringing a court case against the father of two sisters, Edna and Beatrice Kandie from the neighbouring Keiyo District, to stop him from circumcising the girls. This case had also received wide publicity and was taken up by the New York-based NGO Equality Now. Equality Now had established an FGM fund in 2001 to direct financial aid to local grassroots organizations and to support local initiatives designed to raise awareness about the health and human rights implications of FGM, with the aim of working for legal change against the practice. Using the FGM fund, Equality Now organized, through CHRD, a speaking tour for the Kandie sisters in the Rift Valley Province, including Marakwet District, where they went to schools and spoke to other girls about the dangers of FGM and the success of their legal victory in securing their safety. This speaking tour was only one such event in a raft of schemes employed by local NGOs from 1999 onwards as part of the eradication campaign against female circumcision. At the heart of all their efforts was a well-thought-out and steadfastly executed series of workshops, consciousness-raising groups, seminars, public meetings and training sessions. These campaigns escalated further after the success of the Marakwet court cases in 2002, when CHRD was able, with enhanced funding, to place a network of 12 local FGM monitors in various villages to drive the campaign forward and to help girls in need of legal support, but the overall strategy of training, education and consciousness-raising had actually begun slightly earlier in the late 1990s.

The main instigator of change in the Kerio Valley part of Marakwet District where I have been working has been the Christian development and advocacy NGO, World Vision. They first moved into the valley in 1984 and based themselves in a small settlement called Tot, adjacent to Sibou, the village where I did my fieldwork in 1980 and am doing so again now. Their initial efforts were focused on food aid and then on child sponsorship and family development programmes, the latter being particularly unpopular with the villagers. A reassessment of strategy in 1995 based on a baseline survey saw the NGO begin to examine local needs more closely and it started to work on the development of schools and educational quality and attainment. Around 1997, their sponsors, World Vision Germany, encouraged them to investigate more thoroughly the reasons for the poor attendance and performance of girls in school, and out of that work their involvement in female circumcision grew. In line with World Vision's interest in and commitment to children and their development and needs, all their initial anti-FGM work from 1999 onwards was concentrated on children. These children were targeted through the close relationships World Vision had already established with schools in the area, as well as through their connections to churches, primarily the African Inland Church and its network of pastors.

The membership of these networks substantially over-lapped with local elite networks comprising school teachers, councillors, administrative chiefs and influential community members. This was intentional, and from the very beginning of its work in the valley, World Vision employed and promoted members of the local community drawn primarily from the same elite networks. It also reached out into the community predominantly again through the Africa Inland Church, and identified teachers, pastors, Sunday school and nursery teachers and others to be trained as advocates for the anti-FGM campaign. The result was substantial penetration into, and consolidation of, local networks based on the small, but significant educated, Christian elite within the community. My own research has shown that many of the Marakwet women who spearheaded the first stages of the anti-FGM campaign were known to each other from childhood and from school – links that in many cases originated with the mission hospital and its work in Kapsowar in the highlands of Marakwet from the 1930s onwards. This strategy of penetration and consolidation was both successful and fatally flawed. It was successful in that it meant that World Vision primarily employed the educated Christian elite of Marakwet to change their own cultural practices. This was not an example of an exogenous NGO working at one remove from the community. However, it was fatally flawed initially – although this was later corrected – because it focused on young girl children in a community where hierarchies of age and gender are the foundation for social cohesion, and it marginalized ordinary women and men as parents and social actors. A close examination of the histories of the 16 girls who brought court cases against their parents shows that they were all influenced by two local men – one a pastor and one a primary school teacher – and that they all came from a cluster of villages within a single location and attended the same primary schools and churches. All these girls had to be spirited away from their homes with the help of local chiefs and

assistant chiefs, some of them being subsequently dis-
patched to school under police guard or even removed to
places of safety outside the District, before being sent to
the World Vision ARP ceremony held in Tot in December
2001.

The idea of the ARP as a substitution for the teachings
in the girls' initiation house (*kapkore*), and for the coming-
out ceremony (*kibuno*) which marks the reintegration of
the initiands into the community at the end of the seclusion
period, was mooted in the very first proposal made by
World Vision Kenya to World Vision Germany in 1998.
The explicit aim of the ARP was to draw on positive cultural values and meanings, but without 'the cut', and its
role in the teaching and training of girls, teachers and local
community leaders was crucial in the period 2000–8.[6]
More concretely, its stated aim was to integrate traditional
values with modern family life and education. However,
the original idea of an ARP is credited to the Maendeleo
ya Wanawake (a women's NGO) which conducted the first
such ceremony in Kenya in 1996 in Meru District
(Mohamud et al., 2006).[7] In the broader context of Kenya,
World Vision, along with other NGOs like PATH and Save
the Children and government donor agencies such as GTZ
and NFPK,[8] have played a crucial role in documenting,
consolidating and implementing ARPs, which have now
emerged as a set of identifiable processes and practices, not
unlike rapid rural assessment or any other development
tool.

The ARPs in Marakwet District involved a week's training (usually 5–6 days in practice), were most often located
within primary or secondary schools, and were led by local
teachers, pastors and community leaders. The topics
covered during the week included spiritual growth, the
harmful effects of FGM, respect and discipline, the rights
of the child, HIV/AIDS, personal hygiene and courtship.
The age of the children varied and some children attended
more than once. They might also have attended other anti-
FGM workshops or church youth camps which covered

the same or very similar topics. ARPs are often referred to in other parts of Kenya as 'circumcision with words'.

Just as with the traditional *kibuno*, so graduation day at the ARP was about social recognition. Considerable emphasis was placed on the importance of being and looking smart, and on the special costumes that the children wear. There was an explicit attempt at establishing a link between the ARP graduation and *kibuno*, as a means of co-opting aspects of the 'traditional ceremony' through the imitation and copying of dress codes and their symbolism. In discussion with the many different kinds of social actors involved in these ceremonies, it became clear that the ARP graduation had been designed to make explicit reference to what were locally viewed as key cultural and community values, the first of which is the public and community recognition and affirmation of the girls' achievement. In the traditional *kibuno* ceremony, this was the core feature of the rite, with its public acknowledgement of adulthood and the future roles of the new adults in the community. At an ARP in 2006, the Children's Rights Officer for the District was asked to cut the ribbon which began the graduation, and he had this to say:

> I would like to talk of this thread because I was told to cut it; because if I cut I will know that these children have graduated to be grown-ups; when they are crossing over here, they are starting a new life and after here no one will go again for circumcision, for you cannot be circumcised twice. . . . If there is anyone who wishes to go back to *kapkore* [traditional seclusion] stand up before I cut this thread, because this is like swearing and if you swear and go back to be circumcised it is up to you. . . . You stand firm with that principle for you to save Marakwet, to save the Rift valley. You are the ones to save our communities.

This was a very strong statement of recognition and affirmation, and makes explicit reference to the transition to adulthood and the responsibilities consequent upon that transition, but it also ties the girls' refusal of circumcision to the future of the Marakwet community and to the larger entity of the Province; in this way it is both continuous and discontinuous with traditional ideas of the community and its values. At the traditional *kibuno* ceremony, the girls would have received recognition from village and clan elders, from their parents and kin, and in some cases from their prospective marriage partners. ARP graduation was also a day when important people and parents were invited, and a small number of boy supporters were also there to publicly affirm their commitment. But, the 'important people' at the ARPs were in fact very different, and their job was to affirm and connect to a very different understanding of community. They comprised administrative chiefs, government officers, NGO heads, councillors, members of community-based organizations and so on. The parents of some children did attend, but at the six ARPs I attended parental attendance and participation were very poor. Part of the reason for this is the way that parents were so often represented as being attached to culture and thus as a potential threat to the new versions of community and of the future that ARP graduation represented. At an ARP in 2006, one location chief had this to say:

> Long time ago the elders had their rules, the women and also the children. So even now you have your own principles. For example, child's rights. I would like to congratulate the government because . . . everybody now has his own rights. A child has his/her rights and a father has a right of education and of providing you with clothes and shelter. . . . I want to assure you that if there is a parent who is disturbing you to be circumcised, please run to where we (the leaders) are. We shall help you where necessary. . . . If there is someone who is forcing you to be circumcised or a parent who is forcing, we shall deal with him. . . . A child has his/her rights. . . . When your father disturbs you, you have your own right. When he continues

disturbing you come to where we are. . . . We shall arrest
the father or mother.

The majority of children listening to this speech were
between the ages of 12 and 15 years, and for them it represented a rather explicit message about where power lies,
and about the community to which they should refer and
owe allegiance. Increasingly, power has shifted from
parents, kin networks and clans to teachers, pastors, NGO
representatives and the like, and in that process the very
definition of community has changed. It is no longer the
community of the village or the clan or even of the Marakwet, but of the larger entity of the Kalenjin,[9] the Province,
Kenya and even the world. It is these new communities
that have decided that female circumcision is morally
repugnant, of no further or future worth. For many individuals I interviewed, the repudiation of FGM was strongly
associated with a rejection of traditional culture understood as what is local, and with a desire to be seen as part
of a larger world. As one leader put it in his speech at the
ARP: 'You know we Kalenjins, we take time to accept
changes and we have ever been backward, but I thank God
we are changing slowly by slowly and are going where all
the people are.'

Education as a Form of Knowledge

What is at stake here is an epistemic break with tradition
that is seen as constitutive of new modes of being and
belonging, a view of personal transformation as linked to
the constitution of a new public culture. This involves a
series of plate tectonic movements across several different
dimensions of intimate and public life, some of which
were in considerable tension with each other. It is important here to recall the use by NGOs and the church of
such forums as seminars, workshops, training camps,
school advocacy clubs and the like. These occasions take

individuals out of their usual sets of social relations and create novel social contexts for them in which they can forge new bonds, identities and aspirations. In such contexts, the use of particular discursive strategies is decisive. One example would be the stitching together of the transformation involved in being born again with notions of enhanced agency in a changed world, as well as ideas about individual rights. This theme is not only central to most training and advocacy sessions relating to the anti-FGM campaign, but becomes part of the language of self-description of young people who speak of their decision to break with tradition, to break with the past. Such ideas form the unambiguous subtext for many of the songs and speeches involved in ARPs, as for example in the text of this song:[10]

> Decide for yourself
> Decide for yourself. Circumcision is not a must
> We want girls' development
> We want girls' development
> You girls, let us not retreat
> Let us not retreat, we proceed with Jesus
> We've refused to be circumcised
> We've refused to be circumcised
> I will not go back
> I will not go back to circumcision
> I will not go back where my mother went
> Where my sister went
> Grandmother I will not follow you

The idea of not going back, of not following the ways of the grandmothers, is explicitly linked not only to a repudiation of traditional culture, but also to specific forms of knowledge and of knowledge transfer. The future is associated very firmly with education in the minds of young people, Church members, NGO leaders and the like, and in many of the songs and dances at the ARP graduation; the refusal of FGM is linked to enhanced chances for education and for future success; and both are

often connected with opportunities to move outside the
confines of the local, to participate in the world at large.
As in this dance poem:

> I visited my neighbour when there was circumcision
>   for girls
> I wish I was told
> You girls, you study hard in school
> I wish I was told
> To go to other countries for study
> I wish I was told
> To bring degree
> I wish I was told
> N-O
> No
> F-G-M
> FGM.

All girls (and boys) who passed through ARP were
issued with a certificate which they were explicitly encouraged to see as linked to other kinds of certificates signalling
educational attainment. Stories were often told in the ARP
speeches about how girls seeking college places were pref-
erentially treated because they were able to produce their
ARP certificate. *Kapkore*, it was said, has no certificate: its
knowledge is therefore useless. The ARP certificate, on the
other hand, marked a girl out as someone on the road
towards modernity and progress, and guaranteed that she
was enlightened about the negative effects of FGM and its
associated evils, as in this oral narrative performed at an
ARP graduation:

> Welcome.
> Long long time ago, people were practising female
>   circumcision.
> Do circumcision have certificate? No.
> Circumcision have degree? No.
> But circumcision have many dangers; namely bleeding,
>   tetanus and Mr Slim.
> Do you know Mr Slim?

But I tell you Mr Slim is AIDS.
AIDS can kill the young and the old, the rich and the poor,
   the beautiful and the handsome, but it has no cure.
Can you look around the world, even our country Kenya?
We have women who are Ministers, Professors,
   Doctors, Engineers. Name them.
But they are not circumcised and why are you circumcised?
Brothers and sisters, lets us join hands together and say
No to female genital mutilation and be no in capital NO

Here, traditional culture through FGM is explicitly linked
with the past, with a lack of knowledge about the modern
world, including the evils of HIV/AIDS. Knowledge, education and informed agency are stitched together. Opposi-
tion to female circumcision is increasingly linked to a
capacity for informed decision-making, for leadership and
for critical reflection on contemporary politics, as in this
poem performed by a young boy at an ARP in 2006:

Welcome
Before you sign think first
Before you refuse to sign think again
Take time to know what you are signing;
Otherwise I stand still and say no to female
   genital mutilation

Brother, have you been raped? Yes
Sister, have you been raped? Yes
Where are we going brethren
The world is coming to an end
That is why I stand still and say
No to female genital mutilation

Stop and see the little girls in the streets
Think of starving children in North-Eastern District,
they go for long without food.
Yes, they are raped by so called Provincials.
What I hold is this.
That is why I stand still and say
No to female genital mutilation
The pastors, the priests, Reverends, Bishops,

Name them; the so-called holy people.
They are the first to betray us, imagine brethren.
God has mercy on us.
That is why I stand still and say
No to female genital mutilation

So brethren, let us sign today and say
No to female genital mutilation.
Among the first people to sign should
include teachers; the so-called holy people,
Parents and President to confirm all Kenyans and say
No to female genital mutilation

Bye bye brethren. I signed myself today to say
No to female genital mutilation

There are many themes of interest in this poem, but
prominent among them are ideas about agency, decision-
making, critical awareness and the link between anti-FGM
and regional and national politics. What is startling – at
least to me – is the explicit demand that local, church and
national leaders take responsibility for what is happening
to children, and that they should commit themselves by
signing up to the future of the next generation of Kenyan
citizens. In this context, FGM and its eradication is a central
plank on which that future will be built, and this young
boy is signing himself up to this particular vision of the
future, as well as committing himself to it. He is also using
imagined relations with various others as a means to envisage and drive personal and social transformation. Through
acts of the ethical imagination, he links his personal commitment to new relations and forms of the possible, finding
a means for dealing with the alterity of the future.

It is evident then that the future – with all that it implies
about modernity, progress and development – is tied to
new forms of self-stylization, as well as to a reworking of
self–other relations. However, I do not want to rest on this
Foucauldian point, important though it is. I am interested
in trying to understand how culture becomes subject to

contests of value, in what has to happen to make this possible. We can perhaps best approach this by recalling Benjamin's observations on how cultural objects and practices become subject to contests of value when they are removed from their context of use. It is evident that both the traditional rituals of initiation within which circumcision was embedded and the newly created ARP rituals are set within 'different informational economies' – that is, they are two different modes of managing knowledge in the context of social interaction (Barth, 1989: 641–2). Traditional initiation involved staged revelations, a set of enacted performances that conveyed the power and force of the secrets they contained (Moore, 2009a). These secrets were revealed through the manipulation of concrete symbols in context. The meanings conveyed in such enactments were never univocal: they were intentionally adumbrated rather than clearly explicated. The initiands were transformed by the rite itself and not by the knowledge it contained (Barth, 1989: 643). Hence the bewilderment of some informants on passing through the various rites that the secrets were insufficiently momentous, a residual feeling of 'what was all that about?'. ARPs, however, are part of a series of other institutionalized exchanges modelled on formal education. The emphasis here is on a store of knowledge that can be documented and acted on, where learning is cumulative and goal-oriented, where concepts link to other concepts and where systematic connections exist between different components of the knowledge system. This sort of knowledge transmission individualizes knowledge: you can internalize it, carry it with you, convey it to others (Barth, 1989). It implies a quite different kind of capacity for action in the world because it is a type of knowledge that can and will have an effect regardless of context. This makes sense, I think, of the oft-repeated 'complaints' against *kapkore*, which is that it 'has no certificate', it cannot be transferred, it cannot be carried into new domains, it does not guarantee the future, it is not applicable to the modern world.

I am suggesting that these two rather different kinds of knowledge have very different 'technical means of reproduction'. This is a familiar point and has been made before with regard to literacy, texts and schools as institutions. Again, I want to go beyond these familiar claims. Benjamin's point was that changes in the technical means of reproduction change the cultural object's relationship to value because that value no longer emerges in the context of use, but has to be assigned within the context of public presentation (Benjamin, 1992: 218, 234). This makes cultural objects something around which contests of value can take place; before that the values are immanent in practice and are not subject to contestation in the same manner. The model of knowledge that has developed in Marakwet in the context of formal schooling, biblical exegesis, NGO modelling and managerialism, human rights discourses and government policy is one which, amongst other things, treats culture as a particular kind of object of knowledge, one which can be subject to new forms of agency and governance. Through the processes of public presentation and contestation, culture has become reified, disembedded from a life-world of revealed practices, and has become reworked as an object in the world made up of sets of interconnected values, attributes and activities. It is commonplace in the valley now to hear people, mostly those of the younger generations, saying, 'Well, we can choose which bits of our culture to keep. We don't have to retain the bad parts like female circumcision, but we can keep the good parts.' Choosing the good parts has become emblematic of modern ways of thinking and doing as people increasingly engage with a process of self-fashioning cast in the idiom of new forms of knowledge.

The term culture as it is currently used in the part of Marakwet where I have worked is a curious one. For one thing, when discussing questions of culture, the abolition of female circumcision, differences between neighbouring groups, cultural politics in Kenya and so on, speakers will often use the English word culture, even when they are speaking in Marakwet or Kiswahili. This is even true of some individuals who do not speak English. The term *ng'alebo ken* (traditional or customary practices) is rarely taken as a direct translation of the English term, and has the connotation of practices in context. There is insufficient space here to go into the history of the emergence of the notion of Marakwet culture, in the anthropological sense of distinctive life-ways bound to emplacement and identity, but in earlier periods boundaries between local groups were frequently fluid, and variations within them common. The delineation of groups and boundaries began in the colonial period, and has slowly been firming up since the middle of the last century. Contemporary Kenyan politics, with their inequalities of resource and opportunity, have significantly expanded the occasions and reasons for asserting boundaries and distinctive identities. This has led to violence in Marakwet, and in the larger Kalenjin areas, most recently and notably after the national elections in 2007. Contemporary understandings and deployments of culture in Marakwet are thus not the product of localized traditions, but a consequence of national politics, Christian and NGO advocacy, international legal instruments and human rights discourses, as well as new forms of knowledge, agency and self-fashioning. For many younger people, in particular, discussions on these matters and their aspirations for the future are explicitly transcendent of what we might term the 'local'. Their hopes, desires and satisfactions reside in a complex mix of being both themselves, and being other to themselves, new ways of imagining self–other relations.

— 3 —

Slips of the Tongue

There is no ethics without the presence of the other but also, and consequently, without absence, dissimulation, detour, difference, writing.

(Derrida, 1974: 139–40)

'Half-London' is a small shop or duka on the unmade road between Tot and Chesegon in the Kerio Valley in northern Kenya. I first travelled that road in 1979, when Police and Blondie were all the rage in the UK and Manu Dbango was popular in Nairobi, before 'world music' became the ubiquitous signifier we now know. Dukas were not so evident as they are now, but they nonetheless had wondrous storefronts, depicting their commerce and contents. Dazed goats with legs of improbable proportions indicated a butchery, while agricultural implements and cans of margarine denoted something of a more general nature. At that time names were less important as signifiers: a descriptive term often sufficed. Travelling the same road again in 2005, Half-London caught my eye. What was half-London about it, and what did the signifier London mean? On the outside now, a drawing of a larger-than-life mobile phone and an advertisement for a network provider. Perhaps the promise of connection meant that one was no longer in Kenya, but somehow halfway to London.

'A Good Man is Hard to Find'

Tony Simpson was so struck by a similar claim in Zambia that he entitled his ethnography of a boys' Catholic school *'Half-London' in Zambia* (Simpson, 2003). Re-reading his book made me wonder what, if anything, might connect these acts of imagination, and what should I be making of my own status in Kenya as another sort of half-London? Simpson describes how the students call the school 'Half-London' because for them it is not in Zambia, or even Africa, but imaginatively located in another country where they might remake themselves through education in ways that would transcend the felt limitations of their circumstances and realize their aspirations (Simpson, 2003: 1–7). Drawing critically on Foucault's aesthetics of the self, Simpson argues that the students engage in performances and productions of self that seek through comportment, dress, language and orientation both to accept the regime of the Catholic mission school and to hold up that regime to ridicule, even to critique and transcend it (2003: 44, 82). The daily timetable enacts a range of qualities relating to self-presentation and performance invoking 'a whole micro-penalty of time (lateness, absences, interruptions of tasks), of activity (inattention, negligence, lack of zeal), of behaviour (impoliteness, disobedience), of speech (idle chatter, insolence), of sexuality (impurity, indecency)' (Foucault, 1977: 181; Simpson, 2003: 97). Yet, Simpson resists the easy elision of Foucauldian discipline and forms of subjectification, arguing contra the Comaroffs and, by implication, much of the literature on historical transformations of subjectivities in Africa, that the architecture of the school and its forms of regimentation do not generate a 'cogent vision of subject and society' (Comaroff and Comaroff, 1991: 33; Simpson, 2003: 82). His subtle analysis emphasizes the multiplicity and plurality of discourses and processes of self-fashioning and subjectification, rather than simply relying on a dichotomy between a dominant mission discourse and acts of resistance. Simpson reveals how different spaces within the school, and different contexts for the production and performance of self, provide prototypes for, and possibilities for, action, as well as for the creation and evaluation of value, understood both as personal worth and social standing (Simpson, 2003: 61).

The mutually constitutive relations of power and knowledge may be particularly salient in disciplinary institutions such as prisons and schools, but Simpson's careful discussion of how the students view the Catholic brothers who form the majority of teachers at the school discloses the means through which the students seek knowledge of the brothers, interpret their aesthetics of self, and reflect on their ontological nature and moral character (2003: 70–3). In such a context, non-knowledge, or lack of knowledge, is a powerful constitutive element of self–other relations. It leads through circuitous routes to questions of ethics, ontology and morality through such ordinary interrogations as 'what kind of people are they?', 'are they like us?', 'how should we interpret their actions?', 'what is it that they are concealing from us?'. Unknowing engages with the ethical imagination. Simmel famously argued that it was the very situated character of self–other relations that necessarily made our knowledge of others partial (1950: 308). In the context of the school, knowledge production – of all kinds – is caught up in explicit and implicit oscillations between self and other. This is as true of the Catholic brothers as it is of the students themselves, and is a consequence of a mutual desire both to identify with and to distinguish oneself from the other.

In school, the students were required to dress and behave in certain ways which they associated, in overt narratives, with education, civilization, aspiration, modernity and the like. These associations were given explicit moral worth and were underpinned in certain circumstances by a broader distinction between 'Africans' and 'wasungu' (whites), one which was haunted during Simpson's fieldwork in the 1990s by a sense of failure most evidently epitomized by the collapse of the Zambian economy and the HIV pandemic (Simpson, 2003: 2–3). Many analysts, inspired by theorists from Fanon (1986[1970]) to Mudimbe (1988) have drawn on theories of abjection and alienation to characterize the construction of the figure of the 'African' as other, and also to discuss its racialized overdetermination within relays of power, exclusion, exploitation and hierarchy. The power, significance and persuasiveness of such analyses are evident, and while not in any way wishing to dissent from them, it seems worthwhile exploring the contentious mutuality of identification and desire at play in this context, which cannot, as Simpson so brilliantly demonstrates, be captured by an analysis which proceeds from the assumption that the categories 'African' and 'wasungu' are already self-evident or suspended in a particular relation of hierarchy and exclusion.[1]

Subject positions never entirely belong to the individuals who identify with them, because they are the result not only of personal fantasies, disciplinary discourses and institutional, familial and national locations, but also and most crucially of entanglements with the personal, institutional and discursive structures of others, and above all with their fantasies of otherness. Otherness is a resilient and intoxicating site of power and desire (Moore, 2009a). This is true both for the brothers, with their desire to dedicate themselves to God and to mission work, and for the students with their desires for aspiration and self-realization. Multiple versions and conversions of self and other circulate around and through these desires. Much of the literature about power differentials and hierarchies in colonial and postcolonial contexts fails to acknowledge the conscious and unconscious processes at work in constructing the other – and their secrets – as an object of desire. The desire for the other, the desire to be the object of desire for the other, is a process at work in all circumstances, but one that finds specific valence and character in particular contexts (Moore, 2009a).

If subjectivity – and thus forms of subjectification – are always produced through forms of knowing and unknowing, this, as indicated in the quote from Derrida that opens this chapter, both provides the grounds for the ethical and at once reveals the contradiction inherent in its constitution. Ethics is about a relation to self and to others, but because it is impossible to know either oneself or an other completely, it must be one that is premised on difference, on dissimulation, on absence. Hence Simmel's point that it is impossible to imagine any social interactions or social relations, indeed any society, without 'a teleologically determined non-knowledge of one another' (1950: 312). In the interplay between knowing and unknowing, what remains is the practice of judgement, the exercise and demonstration of moral subjectivity, the management of self in relation to others, an ethics (Moore, 2009a).

One of the definitions of a 'good man' employed by students in the school was of someone who had nothing to hide, whose life was open to inspection (Simpson, 2003: 53). This evaluation of moral worth certainly exhibits continuities with Zambian value systems (the students came from many different ethnic groups), where concealment is associated with potentially nefarious activities, especially witchcraft, but it was powerfully reinforced, as Simpson makes clear, by Christian ideals. The values and ideals of Christianity, however, and their associated aesthetics of self, were a site of contestation in the school. Many students were Born Again or Seventh Day Adventists (SDA), and they held strongly to the view that the real truth of God was known to them, personally experienced, and made evident in all aspects of life and worship. Consequently, they held negative views of the moral worth, faith and worship of the Catholic brothers, and in particular their devotion to the Virgin Mary which they regarded as dangerous idolatry.

Conflict between and within the Christian communities represented in the school is not surprising, and stems ultimately from the personal relation to God that all believers claim, even if the character of that relation and the form of the claim itself vary across different versions of the faith. The result is a contestation over revealed truth and the forms that it takes in the world. This process ties Christian subjectivities and modes of subjectification both to particular forms of knowledge and to changing, but historically specific, sets of meanings and values. Truth, value and faith are, however, not simply established through knowledge, but also through forms of unknowing: experiences, events, statements, texts and others that require interpretation, evaluation and judgement. Meaning does not inhere in the world, but has to be made historically, personally and socially present. This is not just a consequence of modernity or of the particular ethics and aesthetics of religion, but something that has a long history in Africa, where a concern for the relation of the visible to the invisible is intrinsic to art forms, ritual practices, the creation of value and the exercise of power.[2]

The Real of Fantasy

As a name for the school, Half-London is a fantasized point of interconnection within a social imaginary, understood as a set of cultural representations and symbols, values and normative understandings, that make the position of the individual and the nation intellectually and emotionally plausible within an imagined global space.[3] This imagined space of the wider world necessarily transcends the confines of the ethnic group, the school, Zambia and Africa, and is actively envisaged as constituted through sets of interconnections and disconnections: forms of knowing and unknowing, practices of moral agency and their failure, self–other relations, and modes of belonging and not-belonging with all of their potentialities. As such, it engages with a multiplicity and plurality of discourses and practices of self-fashioning and subjectification, conscious and unconscious attempts to locate the self and the lived realities of the intersubjective self (family, community, nation, Africa) in space and time. It is not just a matter of appropriating images from elsewhere, of mimicry, hybridity or even of resistance, but rather an active means of participation, a form of agency. The interconnections between personal fantasies and social imaginaries have to be analysed within specific social, economic and political circumstances. In short, fantasy, like meaning, has a history and one that is too often neglected.

We can explore how forms of subjectification and aesthetics of self operate at the intersections between personal fantasies and social imaginaries by turning to another context in contemporary Africa. Brad Weiss discusses how young men in Arusha in Tanzania insist on the absolute veracity of the Quran, not just as a sacred text, but as an encyclopedia of empirically identifiable knowledge which further scientific research will reveal as correct (2009: 200–5; see also Kresse, 2007; 2009). In this regard, these young men have much in common with Simpson's Born Again and Seventh Day Adventist students, for whom history and theories of evolution are intertwined problems that run counter to the expressed truths of the Bible (Simpson, 2003: 149–50). What these sacred texts provide is a sense of revealed truth, and with that comes certainty and the possibility of hope. Part of the force of possibility, of potentialities, is encapsulated in the way that the stories of the Bible literally empower a process of transformation, of new life, made evident in the manner in which young Seventh Day Adventist preachers actively remodel the narrative of their lives on those of exemplary biblical figures (Simpson, 2003: 152). In a similar vein, Weiss discusses a young man, Ahmed, who had been a self-declared thug and school drop-out, but who decided in 2000 to return to Islam and become a devout Muslim, praying five times a day. Ahmed spoke of his return to faith as finding 'the right way', proudly exhibiting texts published in Kuwait on the proper meanings of Islam and how to pray, saying that although he had known these rites from childhood, he found particular satisfaction in seeing them published as an imported text in English (Weiss, 2009: 211).

What is powerful for both these young men is that the truths of the Bible and the Quran are made manifest by the fact that they find their lives in the text. These sacred texts literally speak to them of what has happened in their lives and of the exemplary lives they should seek to live. This makes the texts of immediate relevance to their lived experience of the world, connecting their personal experiences and their lives to ultimate truths and the reality of God. These forms of self-fashioning are additionally powerful, both intellectually and emotionally, because they link the desires of self-realization to forms of legitimacy and authority that transcend context. In their aesthetics of self, their claims about connections, belongings and truth, these young men locate themselves in relation to specific forms of knowledge and the space of the wider world, both enlarging the world of the self in space and time, and mapping the lived realities of the intersubjective self (family, Zambia/Tanzania) onto a broader canvas that includes global communities of the faithful. As Keane argues, the very power of Christianity lies in the opportunity it provides to 'enter into a vastly expanded historical narrative' (2007: 115).

The fantasies and identifications of specific social imaginaries intersect with personal fantasies, lived experience and individual emotions and affects. How should this be accounted for theoretically? What terms and concepts might be appropriate? Examining the conceptual and theoretical repertoire deployed in the literature – hybridity, mimicry, resistance, alienation, abjection – it becomes evident that each term carries specific spatial and temporal assumptions, but more problematically that they are routinely used in ways that assume that we know the character, significance and meaning of the interrelations they presuppose. Looking at the Zambian and Tanzanian material, it seems patent that to use a term like hybridity to capture the specific character of the moral and emotional engagements these young men have with the world would be a serious misrepresentation of their experiences and intentions, but also of the processes of self–other relations at play, and the manner in which the potentialities of belonging and not-belonging, of knowing and unknowing are played out in the contemporary moment in Zambia and Tanzania.

Analyses of social change and transformation which focus on modernity, and its latest incarnation 'globalization', frequently draw on the trope of hybridity to capture the particular processes of mixing, mimicry, identification and resistance that seem to typify encounters between different world-views, systems of power, and distributions of resources, as I argued in Chapter 1. Hybridity as a term, however, seems an imprecise formulation – culturally, symbolically and historically. Its advantage is that it appears to capture differences in reception and response to external influences of all kinds, but its weakness is that it gives little insight or understanding into how or why these specific differences should be generated, except via an unexamined notion of the particular 'capacities' of previously differentiated entities. Hence, Fardon's (2000) claim that 'mestizo logics' entails no logics at all because it just claims that things are mixed. Friedman goes further, suggesting that hybridity as a term that designates an in-between state located somewhere between the western and the non-western or pre-western reflects a set of western preoccupations and categorizations (2000: 640–1). This view is given further specificity by Dirlik, who argues that the 'formulaic litanies' of hybridity and in-betweenness betray signs of theoretical or analytical exhaustion, and as theorists we need to be aware that we may be adhering to 'colonial spatializations' that are obstructing our ability to engage with the changed circumstances of the present (2002: 613–14).[4] In short, hybridity as an analytic category does not provide us with sufficient purchase to understand the contemporary claim implied in being Half-London.[5] The phrase 'half' is a misleading one if we read it as implying an actual condition of creolization or cultural mixing or as a state of in-betweenness understood as a liminal position between western modernity and cultural traditions (see also Werbner, 1997).

Terms such as mimicry, resistance and abjection have a long history in African studies (e.g. Magubane, 1971; Fanon, 1986[1970]; Mitchell, 1956; Wilson and Wilson, 1945), and as descriptors of particular kinds of identifications, events, structures and processes they clearly have purchase, but, when framed as all-encompassing analytic concepts, they are effectively contentless.[6] For the young men in Zambia and Arusha, the truth of their realities is incontestable; their fantasies of their relation of self to revealed truth, of knowing and unknowing, belonging and not-belonging bind them into located social imaginaries that connect via complex overdeterminations to broader horizons. There are undoubtedly aspects of mimicry, resistance and abjection at work in their identifications and lived situations, but the whole of their experiences, aspirations and circumstances cannot be grasped by labelling them using one or more of these terms. To say that a particular individual or group is mimicking or resisting a behaviour posited as 'external' or 'coming from outside' does not give us much purchase in trying to understand how personal fantasies and affects actually intersect with social imaginaries under specific social, economic and political conditions, nor does it tell us anything about the experience, meaning and affect of the process of mimicry.[7]

A fantasized relation to knowledge – that is, to meaning and representation in the world – and to how they are created and what might be made of them, is part of all processes of subjectification: who am I for the other and for myself? what can I know? what should I do?[8] This links the aesthetics of self to ethics, but it also binds the ethical imagination and the exercise of interpretive judgement to the embodied, sensory, affective and emotional aspects of subjectification. Weiss point out that this is a very important element not only of religious experience in Arusha, but also of popular culture (Weiss, 2009: ch. 7). Hip-hop and rap are global mass-mediated cultural forms, and ones that are very popular across East Africa (Behrend, 2002). This signals an immense interest on the part of urban youth, particularly men, in the aesthetics and politics of American hip-hop, including the images of performers and their self-presentations. However, it has in addition produced a thriving African rap scene where the lyrics often have an explicitly religious theme, with many songs based on recognizable narratives of greed, losing one's way, the indulgence of alcohol and sex, followed by recognition of errors, knowledge, truth and finding God. This focus on religion, God and morality is effortlessly linked with elements of the 'progressive politics' of rap found in many other contexts: that is, its condemnation of racism, exclusion, urban violence, poverty, illegitimate power and state venality. However, terms like mimicry, hybridity or appropriation as analytic constructs seem to glance off the contemporary situations in East Africa. American hip-hop and rap have certainly revitalized local music scenes, and opened up new spaces of representation, taste, style and pleasure, but the musical forms that are produced are not perceived or intended as mimicry, as ostensibly hybrid forms or even as appropriations. As Weiss makes clear, hip-hop and rap are 'political' not necessarily because of Black Power or identity politics, but because they engage with productive moments where the reality of the experience of urban living is revealed and enacted. Rap is thus a means for 'telling it like it is', but also a space of ethical judgement, a grounded reflection on the reality of life and the truth of circumstance.

This immediacy of experience is captured in the lyrics of two young rap artists: 'We have ears, but we don't hear. Prophets guide us but we don't follow.' Weiss demonstrates how the authenticity and reality of this truth is revealed through the body, where the malfunctioning of the contemporary body is seen as evidence of evil and a failure to recognize the rightness of God's creation, and yet the lyrics go on to suggest that with a renewed bodily connection to divinity the body offers a means to correct those failures, since it has 'a head to think with and eyes to see' (2009: 217). As Weiss persuasively argues, the real and ways of representing it are mutually constituted, and rap is a form of cultural engagement that explicitly refers in its lyrics, and in the values associated with it in the urban milieu, to the importance of thinking and knowing, of being aware, of making interpretive judgements as part of a moral agency that actively seeks to extend the self and the moral community of which it is a part into history (2009: 212).

Connected Worlds

What the analysis of religion and rap reveals is that processes of subjectivity and subjectification are always more than local. Subjectification is both a form of connection and a form of agency (Weiss, 2009: 128). Urban East Africans, like millions of people around the globe, are consumers of mass-mediated technologies, with the internet playing an increasingly important role by connecting individuals through social networking sites and providing access to downloaded material.[9] However, it is important to be clear that in urban contexts in East Africa, access is strongly correlated with class and with employment. For those on low incomes or those who are unemployed, newspapers, television and the radio (and to a lesser extent cassettes) provide the only regular means of access to mass-mediated popular culture and news. Television and radio are public media in the double sense that much of their reception takes place in public spaces, in bars, barber shops and mini-buses. Newspapers and glossy magazines cost money, but circulate through many hands. In recent years, there has been an explosion of glossy magazines aimed at niche markets, and although these are well beyond the means of most urban residents, they are often shared and, indeed, sold second-hand.

Popular culture and news media make a variety of worlds instantly mediated and instantly present. As a process, this is about connection, but also serves as a claim of coevalness, co-presence. Its immediacy is profoundly felt. University students and young professionals whom I interviewed in Nairobi in 2009, like Weiss's young men in Arusha in Tanzania, talked of finding 'lessons for living' in certain television series and films. These lessons were not necessarily positive, in the sense that they were not based on affirmation, appropriation or mimicry, but they were often seen as 'educational' in the sense of providing new languages of self-description, ways of imagining and handling intimate relations (often through examples of how not to do it), additional images of self-presentation, mechanisms for resolving moral puzzlement,[10] examples of how to interpret meaning in the world and the efficacy of human action in it, and how to create and live a life of value. Lisa Rofel uses the term 'public allegory' to describe how people use the media, public discourses and images to reframe aspects of self and its relation to the world – how, for example, by watching television shows people 'learn the "art" of longing' (Rofel, 2007: 6). Such 'lessons' or 'arts' of living do not proceed through appropriating particular aspects of another culture or mimicking a specific behaviour. The protagonists are not trying to be the same as the images or individuals they see or hear or read about; rather they are trying to see themselves in them, exploring affective dispositions, thinking through the potentialities that are offered, extending self and community into history and meaning. As Argenti says 'The mimetic – what imitates – is not imitative, *it is new*' (2007: 28).

The theoretical challenge then is how to account for processes of social transformation. As Robbins asserts, we still need to develop a 'viable theory' of how cultures change (2003: 5). The difficulties inherent in this task are evident in the way that disciplinary presuppositions and pre-theoretical commitments keep emerging in forms of explanation. For example, a number of scholars have argued that mass media provide an opportunity for viewers and listeners to explore cultural differences (e.g. Larkin, 1997; Barber, 1997), but while such an exploration is undoubtedly part of the pleasure audiences derive from mass media and popular culture, we should not imagine that this is the main experience or purpose of viewing or listening. In a similar vein, a number of analysts have suggested that mass media offers a set of spaces for emerging cosmopolitan practices, as a way of attempting to dislodge pre-theoretical assumptions about the local or parochial character of cultural and social practices (e.g. Abu-Lughod, 1997; Foster, 2002). Weiss critiques both of these views, pointing out that they are based on the assumption that sets of images/sounds/performances/texts embody 'cultures' in some way, and that audiences experience and describe their responses to these reifications as a series of interpretative contradictions (Weiss, 2009: 172–81). In both cases, the project of anthropology once set loose in the world is rediscovered as a structuring or explanatory principle of that world.

An analogous problem is at work in the way that most studies in the human and social sciences configure situations of 'contact' or the 'impact' of modernity/globalization/capitalism as overdetermined by states of suffering and exclusion – assumptions that often resurface in theoretical discussions about abjection and alienation. At this juncture, it is important to be very clear that while suffering, pain and immiseration are an all-too-overwhelming reality of daily life for many people around the globe, as are violence and forms of exclusion and neglect, the argument made here is that we should not develop theories in the human and social sciences that presuppose the dominance of abjection and alienation, nor should we develop theories of the historical transformations in subjectivities and processes of subjectification that foreground these states to the exclusion of others; not least because to do so undermines our theoretical capacity to account for alienation and abjection when they do occur as salient conditions. More importantly, it excludes from analysis the ambivalent character and power of identification, recognition and subjectification, and rather than treating alienation and abjection as dynamic processes of engagement with the world – however painful and overdetermined by power – it renders them as immutable states of being that effectively cast many individuals and communities as victims.

The melancholic nature of much theorizing in the social and human sciences is perfectly comprehensible because of the ethical commitment many practitioners have to 'telling it like it is', documenting and analysing the horrors and miseries of the contemporary world, explaining how the privilege of some creates the misfortune of many, how power distorts and extracts the value and vitality of lives. This is one of the most valuable contributions the human and social sciences make to the analysis of the contemporary. But, the apocalyptic character of much writing about power, particularly in my own discipline of anthropology, not only reveals the depth of disquiet about the predations of contemporary capitalism and its seeming omnipotence, but also the anxieties of privilege on the part of anthropologists and our complex identifications and dis-identifications with global power regimes and their activities.[11] It is, in addition, a product of profound empathy and identification with the people we work with; a consequence of the fantasies that motivate the sociality and conviviality of the fieldwork situation. The desire for knowledge of the other, the forms of knowing and un-knowing, of belonging and exclusion that invigorate the fieldwork context, all that makes us 'Half-London', inevitably colour our analytic and conceptual preoccupations (Moore, 2009a).

In the context of Africa, recent analyses of transformations in subjectivities have focused extensively on the depredations of power, the occult, witchcraft, illicit power and extractive and exploitative accumulation as part of a renewed attempt to analyse the continent's engagement with postcolonial modernities (e.g. Nunley, 1987; Geschiere, 1997; Comaroff and Comaroff, 1999; 2000a; 2000b; Ferme, 2001; Moore and Sanders, 2001; Roitman, 2005; Argenti, 2007). Mikael Karlström acknowledges the innovative appeal of this work and its importance in the field, but also criticizes it for an excessively narrow focus on power, domination, conflict, exclusion and suffering. He argues that such processes, structures and relays most definitely cannot be neglected, but neither should life and what people make of it be reduced to them (2004: 609). He argues for a complementary approach that engages with how people have creatively imagined their modernities and futures across time, and sought to enhance their moral capacities and maintain versions of moral communities. He suggests that people's active and collective appropriation of the potentialities of modernity should not be reduced to 'responses' to western models of progress, modernity and capitalism (2004: 607–8).

Karlström's point is similar to that of Steven Feierman (2001), who argues that despite the creativity of theories of multiple modernities, transformations in subjectivities and the imaginative remaking of selves, there is still an implicit assumption that the macro-historical narrative invoked is grounded in Europe or the West, and that Africa and Africans are reduced to responses, resistances and appropriations. What is missing is the history of the transformations in meaning, fantasy, subjectivity and power in Africa, the narratives of the longue durée that arise in Africa and provide their own encompassing horizons, their own extensions of selves and communities into history. Histories of what we might want to call 'hybridities' existed in Africa long before the Europeans, especially in those regions where rulers were not autochthones or where trade had transcontinental links (Fardon, 1988; Bayart, 2000; Geschiere and Nyamnjoh, 2000). In addition, as

Lisa Rofel has so persuasively argued for China, we need to recognize that formulations of change or transformations in subjectivities that are essentially based on how a specific locale has 'indigenized' modernity, globalization and/or capitalism are unduly narrow and reductionist. Globalization is not 'exterior' to these societies, but 'interior' to them, part of their lived relation to the world (Rofel, 2007: 11; Diouf, 2000; Tsing, 2005: 58).[12] What needs emphasis is not only the historical specificity and heterogeneity of the practices cultivated and advanced in the name of modernity, neoliberalism and global capitalism, but the fact that their character is unjustifiably shrunken by referring to them or analysing them as multiple (or plural) versions of an originary model (Chakrabarty, 2000; Yang, 2000; Yanagisako, 2002; Tsing, 2005).[13]

There is a clear conceptual and emotional connection between the predominant 'response mode' of much writing about modernity/globalization/neoliberalism and the overwhelming analytic focus on participation through exclusion, alienation and abjection. Theories of subjectivity in the human and social sciences are predominantly framed within a discourse about the relation between domination and freedom. This has resulted in an overriding focus on how 'inner processes' are shaped amid 'violence and social suffering' (Biehl et al., 2007: 1); the gloss for which, as Tanya Luhrman has pointed out, is the 'subject's distress under the authority of another' (2006: 346). The result is not only a focus on the negative aspects of the impact of war, terrorism, economic reform and new technologies, but an account of the social and of social relations that emphasizes fragmentation, disorientation, 'a world in pieces'. Paradoxically, this continues to be the case even when the analysis is focusing on the creativity of agents' responses, their strategies and coping mechanisms. The emphasis, as Sherry Ortner suggests, is on crisis; the crisis of the postmodern consciousness and the crisis of orientation inherent within a world that defies interpretation (Ortner, 2005: 44). This crisis of subject, and of the subject's relation to world, figures in a very general form across the human and social sciences,[14] raising questions about overdeterminations and linkages between the degree of 'crisis' in analysis and the degree of 'crisis' in the world (Moore, 2006; see below, Chapters 6 and 7).

In anthropology, attention to the analytic preoccupation with crisis reveals that the concept of subjectivity routinely deployed is at once very loose and very narrow.[15] The term subjectivity is generally used to refer to inner states or perceptions that engage with affect, cognition, morality and agency (Biehl et al., 2007: 1; Ortner, 2005: 31). Within this broad frame, writers may take a number of theoretical positions, but two broad trends can be identified. The first is broadly cultural. As, for example, in the case of Ortner who defines subjectivity as 'the ensemble of modes of perception, affect, thought, desire, fear and so forth that animate acting subjects. . . . as well the cultural and social formations that shape, organize and provoke those modes of affect, thought and so on' (2005: 31). Ortner's attention, via a re-reading of Geertz, is on what the subject thinks and feels, and on how culture and discourse shape feelings, fears and hopes in different contexts (Luhrman, 2006: 347–9). The second is predominantly experiential and focuses on the subject's perception of their personal interrelations and situations, as well as the intersections between the subjective and the intersubjective. 'Experience is intersubjective . . . it involves practices, negotiations, and contestations with others with whom we are connected. It is also the medium within which collective and subjective processes fuse, enter into dialectical relationship, and mutually condition one another' (Kleinman and Fitz-Henry, 2007: 53). Kleinman and Fitz-Henry additionally define experience as 'the medium through which people engage with the things that matter most to them, both individually and collectively, whether a national identity, a collective memory of suffering, a personal aspiration, a health condition or the preservation of a native language' (2007: 54). Notions of historical contingency and heterogeneity are present in this conceptualization of subjectivity[16] – as they are in Ortner's theorization and others like it – but the processes through which subjectivity is constituted, an actual theory or account of how the personal connects with the social or the cultural is unspecified except as something that takes place within the realm of experience. But experience itself is a loose term in which specific discourses, practices and affects dissolve rather than crystallize. Experience acts as the grounds for motivation, providing impetus for thinking, feeling, evaluating and justifying (Kleinman and Fitz-Henry, 2007: 61). It also acts as the context of or medium for intersubjective relations, but what this entails is never explored, leaving a banal assertion that 'the subjective is always social and the social, subjective' (Kleinman and Fitz-Henry, 2007: 64). Intersubjectivity thus becomes an empty concept, a form of social relations plus thoughts and feelings, combined with a degree of self-reflexivity about the self and its relations to the world.

Attention to the experience, thoughts and feelings of the acting subject is an ethical imperative across the human and social sciences, and is part of a more general recognition that people's causal ontologies, their accounts of how things come to be as they are – through such diverse mechanisms as cognitive mapping, narratives, moral and philosophical discourses – have a direct impact on their interrelations with the worlds they inhabit. As an analytics, this is a form of social and cultural constructionism, albeit a necessary one in the human and social sciences where analysis has always to make room for the fact that agents create their worlds. However, as an account of the interrelations between subjectivity and intersubjectivity, and/or of forms and processes of subjection, it is severely under-theorized. One reason for this is the resistance to theories of intersubjectivity and the dynamic unconscious in much recent writing on subjectivity, with the exception of work directly inspired by psychoanalytic theory.[17] For example, while Ortner says that she does not exclude unconscious dynamics (2005: 34), Kleinman and Fitz-Henry describe psychoanalysis as 'a sectarian view' which has 'long been overworked and overreached as an explanatory framework' (2007: 52). Werbner in his discussion of this matter (2002) does draw attention to the importance of historicizing intersubjectivity through an examination of the ways in which subjectivity and intersubjectivity are linked, but the actual character of that linkage is never explored. In the same volume, Nyamnjoh employs Mbembe's notion of 'conviviality' in an attempt to transcend the antinomy between the autonomous/individual subject and the social collectivity. He examines the conscious discourses and practices through which individuals come to be who they are through relationships with others, the way that 'conviviality' situates individual aspirations in relation to cultural solidarities, the mechanisms through which the actions of the self always have to take account of the actions of others such that interdependence is the very ground of agency (Mbembe, 2001; Nyamnjoh, 2002: 111–15).

In all these approaches the emphasis is on thinking, feeling, rationalizing, experiencing, acting, but always within the frame of the creative acting subject. The value of this is incontestable, but it still engages with the relation between subjectivity and intersubjectivity, the psyche and the social at the level of discursive practices, without exploring the specific grounds for transformations in subjectivities and in the forms and mechanisms of subjection, except as a consequence of 'external forces'. The constraining tropes of 'interior' and 'exterior' are here at play once more, a strange unrecognized apprehension that in the case of Africa, for example, subjectivities are always transformed by what comes from outside, that nothing new arises in the continent itself (Moore, 2009b). But also present is an equally disabling assumption about the 'new'. Hence Werbner speaks about 'a current postcolonial phenomenon' where 'subjects are compelled to be aware and concerned about their interdependence, their mutual entanglement', as if intersubjectivity had never before been about interdependence and mutual entanglement (2002: 2). The result is that a residual discourse of hybridity inserts itself into many analyses, suggesting that those who are the subjects of study are somehow hybrids born of a relation between autonomous, (liberal) individualism and social collectivities, while those who conduct the analysis are not (e.g. Durham, 2002).[18]

Part of the difficulty here seems to be a surplus of agency – combined with a surplus of early Foucault: subjects are thinking, acting and speaking in ways that are both always consciousness and intentional, and are presented as constituted through discursive regimes which in their turn are understood primarily as cultural contexts and relays of power. Given the extensive critique in the human and social sciences of cultures as sets of reified, coherent and located entities, this might be best understood as a form of haunting, a residual identification that extrudes into analysis. For subjects are not just discursive effects: they can never be fully determined by discursive regimes, but equally, there can be no radical creation of the self ex nihilo. The social always precedes and exceeds the subject, providing limits as to what will be considered an intelligible subject within a given historical moment. The subject always has a history, but because it is necessarily formed in relations of interdependence, this history must be simultaneously personal and social/cultural. Intersubjective relations are formative, but these relations – and their affects – are not always available to conscious knowledge, they are not always explicit, they are not necessarily formed in language and there may be many slips of the tongue. Hence, we cannot unproblematically base our theories of subjectivity on the experience of the conscious subject or on their conscious meanings and intentions. This is most evidently the case when we consider the embodied nature of the subject, the fact that bodies have histories which can never be fully grasped within language and the symbolic; they can never be completely captured by historical narratives, there may be additional slips of the tongue and more. We cannot reduce analysis to subjects who endow meaning through acts of consciousness. It is a paradox of human life that cultural identities only emerge through forms of identification with social values and moral norms which subjects may then seek to contest or transform. This means that we have to acknowledge the limits of cultural determinism, but also to try and theorize the nature and consequences of those limits, but we can only do so if we move away from the structure/agency dialectic and make room both for the dynamic processes of the unconscious, and also for the radical potentiality in the histories of fantasy and their transformative possibilities.

Fundamentally, we can say that fantasy has a history because you can never completely know yourself and nor can you ever completely know the other. The relation between self and other is thus set up in fantasy, based on a series of identifications and their circulations. The self–other relation is one that takes place within the relational character of being human and thus it is always shot through with social imaginaries and relays of power. The 'you' and the 'I' are imaginary positions, partially formed in language and partially not. But, the mechanisms and forms through which I recognize myself and the other are not mine alone: they are always relational – that is, fantasized, social and affective. In this logic, the relation between self and other, between subjectivity and intersubjectivity, is historically specific, taking particular forms at particular times. It may be a fundamental aspect of human relationality – there is no self without relations with others – but it is not an ahistorical, transcendental, universal relation. It is always a matter for investigation, and one that inevitably requires ethical commitment.

— 4 —

Other Modes of Transport

As we have seen in the previous chapter, self–other relations are always acts of imaginative identification, and as
such they are historically specific (Moore, 2007: 139).
Intersubjective relations are the grounds not only for self-
making, but for participation in knowable social orders,
for making connections with historically and socially constructed others across space and time. This suggests that
we need theories of identification, connection and belonging that depart from existing formulations with their over-
commitment to understandings of identity grounded in
difference, where difference is both a defining feature of
self-expression and of group membership. In particular, we
need to rearticulate the connections between identity and
cultural difference. This task involves a number of challenges for social and cultural analysis, but here I want to
focus on just two. The first is to ask what alternative theories of connection and relationality might look like and
how they might differ from earlier theories. The second is
that, given that self–other relations develop in dynamic
matrices constituted through fantasized relations to knowledge, that is, to meaning and representation, how should
we understand these fantasized relations and forms of

knowledge? What is the nature of the connections made, how do they arise, what transports them and how do people imagine them? In this chapter, I explore transformations in gender and sexual subjectivities as a device for drawing out new theoretical approaches to these challenges.

Relational Subjects

One of the curious features of self–other relations is that they are scalable; that is, they can have different spatial scales within the same temporal frame (Harvey, 2000). However, the forms of knowledge on which self–other relations depend are not all of the same type or character: some of them are premised on detailed empirical knowledge of shared intimacies and spaces, while others are mediated by more distant institutions, structures and imaginaries. The other with whom the self shares a relation could be in the space of the home, the village, the city, the nation or the diaspora, and possibly all of those simultaneously (Harvey, 2000; Boellstorff, 2005). Novel forms of belonging not only involve novel performances of self (Weiss, 2009), but also new ways of imagining our relations to our bodies, to others, to objects and to the wider social and cultural worlds we inhabit. The result is that more distant and fragmentary engagements with others are caught up in the relays of affect, emotion and desire that characterize our more intimate, somatic self–other relations, and simultaneously our most intimate relations are animated by more alienated forms of otherness, and the pleasures and desires of estrangement. The various ways in which we engage with changing worlds and seek for an active and collective appropriation of their potentialities thus draw attention to the fact that the self–other relation being envisaged here is not one based solely on a dyadic exchange, nor even on a set of proximate, intimate relations, as psychoanalytic approaches suggest. If it is true that the self can only be produced through intersubjective relations, social values, objects and forms of intelligibility that provide a framework or horizon for the self to be understood as such, it is equally the case that these cultural or normative frames cannot fully constrain its forms or the forms of self–other relations on which it depends (Butler, 2005: 22–5). It is the fundamentally social and intersubjective nature of self-making that accounts for the scalable capacities of self–other relations, their potentiality for making connections across geographical locations and temporal frames. Clearly, there are issues of intensity and performative engagement to be calibrated, since our most proximate and intimate relations are particularly formative, structuring not only the movement of desire and the character of satisfaction, but the rhythms and pulses of everyday life. However, imaginary identifications are frequently attached to relays of affect and longing that do not respect the boundaries of gender, race, ethnicity, religion or nation.

In order to understand how this operates, we need to turn briefly to a discussion of the subject and processes of subjectification. Much important scholarship in the human and social sciences has concentrated on transformations in selves and subjectivities, but, as discussed in the previous chapter, the resulting analyses have predominantly sought to explain how globalization, modernity, capitalism, neoliberalism or some other set of powerful external forces have 'reinvented', 'reconstituted' or 'transformed' subjectivities.[1] In such contexts 'subjectivities' are most usually glossed as 'people's understandings of self'. In reflecting on the social science literature, it becomes apparent that part of the difficulty concerns an unhappy elision between the terms self and subject, where individual selves are somehow possessed of something called a subjectivity.[2] However, selves are not subjects (Moore, 2007: chap. 2). Discourses, practices and affect provide subject positions, and individuals are multiply constituted and multiply layered subjects who take up and inhabit a dynamic matrix of subject

positions, some of which will be contradictory and conflicting. The process of subjectification is never a finished
or closed one. Culture, power and ideology may work to
produce subject positions, but they do not determine how
individuals will identify with and inhabit different subject
positions at different times, nor how they will be involved
in the transformations of discourses and power over time.

The advantages of a theory of a multiply constituted
subject is that it allows us to formulate theories of social
change and transformation that do not have to rely on
'impact' theory or on notions of hybridity that imply –
however unintentionally – that individuals are a mix of
'cultures' or of 'traditional pasts' and 'modern presents'.
This is a theory of the subject that seeks to provide a means
for understanding how a complexly-constituted self identi-
fies with, challenges and potentially transforms the various
subject positions available within particular social, cultural, economic and political contexts. It explicitly links
the dual aspects of subjectivity within one theoretical
framework, accounting both for the workings of power
and regimes of truth, and for practices of self-realization
and creativity, the techniques of the self.[3] However, it does
not reduce discourse simply to language, because it retains
complex relationships between cognitive structures, symbolic systems, objects and material conditions, while
simultaneously emphasizing the importance of praxis,
embodiment, affect and unthought and unconscious
engagement with the world. Fantasy, desire and unconscious motivation are always in play, alongside strategy,
rationalization and emotional intelligence, in the process
of making and sustaining a self through identification with
multiple subject positions which are themselves dynami-
cally related. This process of identification may be ambiguous and painful, but it also provides satisfactions, some of
which will be available to the conscious mind, and some
of which will be unconscious, tied up with affect, objects,
bodily practices and the desires and unthought behaviour
of others (Moore, 2007: 40–2).

Within this framework, individuals do not have singular identities; nor do they have identities that arise unproblematically out of social and cultural affiliations. Differences are internal to the subject, and they act as a set of relational coordinates that coexist in time, and produce the potential for further forms of identification. The analytic focus is on identifications rather than on identity, and it makes identification a process that is productive both of the specific locations in space and time that we frame as culture, and of future forms of belonging that exist as possibilities. As Rosi Braidotti has so cogently argued, these subject positions coexist in time, they intersect, coincide or clash, but they are rarely synchronized. Synchronization is itself a dynamic process which works in relation to the requirements and expectations of society, as well as in response to one's own hopes, desires and satisfactions (Braidotti, 2006: 94–5).

Connected Worlds and Modes of Transport

In order to explore the question of relational subjects further, and to suggest an alternative to the 'impact' model of globalization, it might be helpful to begin with an empirical question: why is it that projects of modernity, and indeed projects of social change and transformation in general, focus so powerfully on gender and sexuality? In this regard, Southeast Asia provides a challenging starting point because right across the region gender diversity and gay and transgender sexualities are expanding and diversifying (see, e.g., Jackson, 2001; 2004; Sinnott, 2004; Boellstorff, 2005; 2007) in ways that exceed the 'global gay' identity development trajectory formulated by Altman and others (Adam et al., 1999; Altman, 2001). Tom Boellstorff has analysed how Indonesian *gay* and *lesbi* identities have emerged since the 1970s, and how those who use these terms consider them to be 'authentically Indonesian' ways of being. He makes it clear that regardless of ethnic and religious background, it is always clear to Indonesians that these terms do not originate in locality or tradition – they do not have an originary source in tradition or ethnolocality (Java, Sumatra, Sulawesi, for example) and are not derivatives of existing and socially recognized forms of transgender practices (*warias* or *banci*). But neither can they be simply glossed as the result of globalization or the consequence of western gay rights movements. In contrast to the kinds of assumption routinely made about the emergence of new subject positions, most gay and lesbian Indonesians are not part of a cosmopolitan elite or even of the consumer oriented middle class, have seldom travelled outside Indonesia, have never seen western lesbian or gay publications, do not speak English and have rarely encountered a gay or lesbian westerner, let alone had sex with one (Boellstorff, 2005: 6–7). In fact, *gay* and *lesbi* identities are founded on rhetorics of national belonging – they are Indonesian. They are ways of understanding self in relation to others, and of drawing connections at the national level and also beyond. The question is, how do these forms of identification and belonging work? what modes of transport do they use?

Boellstorff makes it clear that mass media, starting with print media, has played an important role. Many of his informants state that they first encountered these terms and their possibilities and potentialities through the media, but this media is Indonesian and employs the national language. Insofar as images of and information about western homosexuality are available, it is predominantly in the form of gossip about Indonesian or western celebrities in the Indonesian press. Information about western homosexuality is generally fragmentary, and cannot be said to constitute an authoritative discourse. Through the 1980s and 1990s, a number of imported programmes presented gay or lesbian characters, and since 2002 several private Indonesian television stations have run programmes on *gay* and *lesbi* life in Indonesia, or have featured discussions on talk shows (Boellstorff, 2005: 68–78). Nonetheless, media coverage is still minimal, and what 'media messages' there are coexist, as Boellstroff says, in the clamour and noise of other images, identities and practices, and cannot be said to be an everyday occurrence. They certainly disseminate the idea that *gay* and *lesbi* Indonesians exist, but they are 'vague, incomplete, and contradictory as to what they might entail in terms of everyday practice. They also imply that these subjectivities are Indonesia-wide phenomena, non-ethnolocalized and bearing some kind of "family resemblance" to gay and lesbian subjectivities outside Indonesia' (Boellstorff, 2005: 77).

A number of studies in Southeast and East Asia have noted the emergence of sexual and gendered subjectivities which use terms derived from English (*gay, tom* [tomboy], *dee* [lady], *lesbi* [lesbian]). In each case the analysis emphasizes that the deployment of such terms does not indicate either that they are the direct result of western discourses or that they are seeking to mimic western identities or adapt local sex/gender systems to western categories. The West, whatever that term might mean, is not the source of cultural change and social transformation. As Mark Johnson says of the Philippines: 'The appropriation of the term *gay* and the identification with an imagined *gay* universe signal their own transgenderal projects, projects which are informed less by contemporary Western homosocialities than by local sensibilities about love, kinship, gender and gifting relationships' (1997: 183). As Boellstorff argues for Indonesia, *gay* and *lesbi* subject positions 'place the self in a dialogical relationship with a *distant but familiar other*' (2005: 71–2). In each ethnographic case, the self–other relation is an historically specific one, but interestingly they also share some similarities, and they all connect in complex, but specific, ways with economic and political change, transformations in family structures and marriage strategies, waged work, media and communication, class structures and forms of consumption. Changes of all kinds open up new opportunities for new subject positions to emerge. However, this process is not in itself new, as Megan Sinnott points out: 'The meanings of Thai terms for sex and gender categories have changed over time and are neither static nor homogenous' (2004: 4). It is, paradoxically, the comparative method of anthropology that creates the fiction that change is new and that it emerges in relation to external influences (Johnson, 1997: 233), as well as the pervasive insistence in the human and social sciences that we now live in a new era characterized by unprecedented changes in capital markets, communications, information technology, and flows of people and goods, and that it is the scale of these interconnections that accounts for the changes we observe. However, while changes in sexual subjectivities may not be new in and of themselves, we still need to account for how they arise beyond the idea that they are simply the *product* of social, economic and political change or outside cultural influences. Here Foucault's notion of problematization, as discussed in Chapter 1, is a useful way to formulate the challenges posed for self-formation and for politics by changes in gender and sexual subject positions. While specific social, economic and political processes have initiated the process of problematization within the general terrain of gender roles and sexual behaviour, they do not, as I argued earlier, completely determine its form and character. Historically specific transformations in gender and sexual practices are never a direct consequence or expression of socioeconomic and political change, but are instead a set of located and embedded responses that take particular forms. In this context, culture as a set of dynamic coordinates is key. Problematization, as Foucault suggests, nourishes the conditions in which these responses develop, and in consequence opens up further possibilities for change.

However, while problematization as a notion prevents us from reductively conceptualizing transformations in gender and sexual subject positions as the product or consequence of globalization, we still have to address the issue of why people's projects of social change and transformation focus so powerfully on sex and gender. In approaching this question, Boellstorff's work is insightful because of his insistence that subject positions operate on different scales – the other involved may be near or far – and also that they are 'inhabitable' in multiple ways – there is no single *gay* subject position to which one must adhere completely. It would be more accurate, as he suggests, to see *gay* and *lesbi* subject positions as involving several different aspects of identification, some of which are translocal and some national, some of which engage with specific cultural imaginaries and others with aspects of consumer aspirations. *Gay* and *lesbi* subjects are not defined solely with reference to sexuality, but also identify with other subject positions which are 'inhabited' by fellow Indonesians, and perhaps individuals elsewhere, who are not themselves gay or lesbian. Boellstorff explores ideas about *gay* and *lesbi* love and desire, their relationship to marriage and social aspirations, and the connection of both to the national imaginary. The meanings of marriage that circulate in Indonesian popular culture are powerfully influenced by the state and mass media. Marriage practices have undergone great change, but the dominant model of marriage is one based on monogamous love and choice. Love marriages are associated with modernity and with nationalism, partly because love and choice imply 'democracy, equality, and a horizon beyond the family and locality' (Boellstorff, 2005: 105).

Consequently, the model of love with which *gay* and *lesbi* Indonesians identify is shared with other Indonesians and is based on a notion of heterosexual marriage actualized through love and choice (Boellstorff, 2005: 104). *Gay* and *lesbi* Indonesians consistently speak of how they value same-gender love, and they see this as what distinguishes them from others. *Gay* and *lesbi* relationships can persist over long periods of time, and involve great devotion and fidelity. Romance and a long-term relationship are seen as the main aspiration (Boellstorff, 2005: 102–8). It is not the sexual act that distinguishes *gay* and *lesbi* subject positions, but the nature of same-gender love. *Gay* and *lesbi* individuals have thus performed the Foucauldian operation of decoupling pleasure from identity, sexual practices from sexual identities. Such a move makes sense because, in addition to their gay lovers, most *gay* men have girlfriends and desire to marry heterosexually. In Indonesia, men and women are not considered adult until they have married, and marriage is considered an essential step regardless of religion, ethnicity or class (Boellstorff, 2005: 109). Unmarried *gay* men and *lesbi* women often look forward to their wedding day with all the anticipation of any non-*gay* or *lesbi* Indonesian. Marriage is therefore a source of meaning and pleasure, and not just an external imposition, allowing individuals to enjoy homosexual relationships while pleasing their parents, carrying on the family name, having children and becoming full members of national society (Boellstorff, 2005: 111).[4] However, as Boellstorff makes clear, the desire to choose marriage, and the social imperatives surrounding it, do not arise from long-held kinship traditions, but from a national imaginary where love marriage is a powerful symbol and manifestation both of citizenship and modernity through the encompassing logic of the nation understood as the Indonesian family bringing together those of diverse regional origins (Boellstorff, 2005: 116–19).

What the Indonesian material underscores is that masculinity and femininity are constructed in a world of objects, constituted and experienced through a set of imaginary relations to bodies, fertility, sexuality, reproduction, and much else. In this context, *gay* masculinity is not completely separable from other aspects of masculinity and their connections to wider gender and national imaginaries. *Gay* and *lesbi* sexualities are not predominantly premised on sexual acts, but on same-gender desire, and as such, while they may not be valorized in the same way as heterosexuality, neither can they be separated from broader understandings of normative sexualities. As Boellstorff points out, this important detail is more difficult to recognize in western contexts, where sexual desire is seen to be central not only to selfhood, but to sexual identities understood as social categories (2005: 125). However, gender and sexual subject positions not only relate to each other in complex ways within gender, cultural and social imaginaries, but are also 'internally' multiplex. Masculinity and femininity as aspects of self, and between sexual partners of whatever gender, retain a relationship with each other, but also with the objects (particularly body parts and fluids) and social relationships that give them form. Whatever masculinity and femininity are for a specific experiencing self, they are always modelled on the multiple and fantasized nature of one's own and other people's experience of them, both in concrete social relationships and in more fragmentary images, symbols and affects which may arise from contexts and associations that can seem to have little to do with gender or sexuality (Moore, 2007: 158–60). Hence the ubiquity of gender symbolism, but also its rather underdetermined character. What binary categorizations of gender achieve most often is the reiterated failure of representation to capture in any lasting and fixed sense the distinctions between masculinity and femininity. Masculinity and femininity are conjoined, and gender and sexual subject positions necessarily engage with the entanglements of bodies, emotions and erotic desire. These entanglements are lived out in a material world of objects, and are caught up in representation and fantasy. Hence new encounters will open up the potential for new ways of knowing, relating and attending to self and to other, but also to persons and things. These potentialities are made manifest in concrete social, economic and political situations, where they are not best understood as mimicry or as the consequence of globalization or neoliberalism in any straightforward sense, but as authentic attempts to create ongoing ways of being. Figured in this way, *gay* and *lesbi* have to be understood in their Indonesian contexts, and gender and sexual subjectivities, here, as elsewhere, will continue to change precisely because they tie our bodies, emotions and desires to self–other relations, and to the fantasized relation to images and objects in which those relations come to us.

Sexuality Goes Global

A discussion of the Indonesian material allows us to shift frame, to begin from elsewhere, and to refigure changes in gender and sexual subject positions as more than simply a consequence of the globalization of gay identities or the impact of specific socioeconomic and political changes. It also departs from an understanding of gender and sexual subject positions as overdetermined by a model of identity grounded in difference. There is no definitive or fixed relation of difference either between Indonesian and non-Indonesian understandings of gender and sexual subject positions, or between normative and non-normative understandings: they both partake of each other and resonate to different degrees. Equally, gender and sexual subject positions are internally multiplex; there is no simple masculine/feminine or gay/lesbian identity to which one must cleave. The whole notion of a singular sexual identity to which individuals must adhere is put into question by the figure of the multiply constituted and multiply layered subject who inhabits a dynamic matrix of subject positions where gender and sexual subject positions cannot ever be experientially or analytically divorced from other aspects of identification and imagined self–other relations that have little to do in any obvious sense with gender or sexual practices.

However, what reflection on this material also suggests is that one of the reasons why it has proved so difficult to appreciate transformations in gender and sexual subject positions is precisely because of the analytical and political dominance of a very particular set of mechanisms linking gender and sexual practices to sexual identities. As I suggested in Chapter 1, the experiences and understandings we have of ourselves at specific historical moments always involve certain forms of problematization which bear on the question of how we are constituted as subjects of our own knowledge, and on the kinds of selves we are for others and for ourselves. In the last several decades, one particular form of problematization has developed the conditions in which changes in gender and sexual practices are framed and experienced as a mode of relating to self and to others. Sexuality as a mechanism for linking gender and sexual practices to sexual identities has gone global, and the social sciences are implicated in this process, acting as one of its major 'modes of transport'.

What is sexuality? This is not an easy question to answer. Most contemporary definitions favour an answer along the general line that sexuality is how people experience the erotic and express themselves as sexual beings; more broadly, it is defined as relating to sexual pleasure and to all things sexual, encompassing also the deep emotions and profound social bounds that it engenders and which sustain it. As one of the social science students I interviewed in Nairobi replied when I asked him to define sexuality: 'Not much in it, Prof, it's just sex without the "uality"!' Sexuality, however, goes far beyond this definition, and is taken to be connected in multiplex ways with issues of morality, philosophy, religion, ethics and law. In our present environment, it is everywhere.

Writing in the 1970s, Deleuze and Guattari explained the ubiquitous character of sexuality:

> The truth is that sexuality is everywhere: the way a bureaucrat fondles his records, a judge administers justice, a businessman causes money to circulate; the way the bourgeoisie fucks the proletariat; and so on. And there is no need to resort to metaphors, any more than for the libido to go by way of metamorphoses. Hitler got the fascists sexually aroused. Flags, nations, armies, banks get a lot of people aroused. (Deleuze and Guattari, 2004[1977]: 322)

The argument here is not just that sexuality is political, as in the feminist movement or in campaigns for gay rights, but that politics, and much else besides, is sexualized. But, if sexuality is absolutely everywhere, if it imbues every facet of our lives, then what is it, how do we distinguish it from other things and how do we know that the effects we see are those of sexuality and not of something else?

We could answer these questions in a commonsense way, and maintain, as the student from Nairobi does, that we know what sexuality is because it is what pertains to the domain of sex, and beyond that to the evident character of sexed bodies. When trying to unravel the complexities of sexuality, many scholars, as we know, have turned to the work of Michel Foucault. Foucault was clear that sexuality, as we now experience, understand and analyse it, slowly emerged during the eighteenth century and gathered momentum in the nineteenth, exploding onto the stage of the twentieth century with a resounding bang:

> Sexuality must not be thought of as a kind of natural given that power tries to hold in check, or as an obscure domain which knowledge tries gradually to uncover. It is the name that can be given to a historical construct: not a furtive reality that is difficult to grasp, but a great surface network in which the stimulation of bodies, the intensification of pleasures, the incitement to discourse, the formation of special knowledges, the strengthening of controls and resistances, are linked to one another, in accordance with a few major strategies of knowledge and power. (Foucault, 1976: 107)

Here Foucault emphasizes that sexuality is not a pre-existing entity, a constant, a naturally given domain or set of practices. But elsewhere he is equally firm that it is not just a product of sex itself, a way of referring to those bodily sensations, experiences and activities connected to the sex drive and human reproduction. Instead of envisaging sex as the 'anchorage point' of sexuality, he proposed that we should understand sex as something which actually takes shape and form inside the deployment of sexuality (1976: 152). His contention is that sex and sexuality, in their contemporary form, emerged at the same time. The notion of 'sex' is what made it possible to link together anatomical elements, biological functions, behaviours, sensations, pleasures and emotions to form a fictitious unity which acted, and continues to act, both as a causal principle and as a universal signifier. Sex, like sexuality, is not natural; it is a product of particular historical conjunctures. In the crucible of nineteenth-century science, both human and biological, sex was melted down into its component elements, subjected to investigation, specification and laws. Biology and physiology, along with the human sciences, were enlisted to provide the principles of normality for human sexuality.

Normality is a term that reveals how important language, power and culture are in constructing our understandings both of sex and sexuality. The historian of sexuality Thomas Laqueur contends that modern understandings of sexual difference are similarly the product of particular historical and cultural moments. In his well-known book *Making Sex* (1990), he argues that before the eighteenth century sexual difference was seen as a set of relatively unimportant differences of degree within a single or 'one-sex body', where women and men were thought to have the same reproductive structures and genitalia, the only difference being that women's genitalia were inside rather than outside the body. Bodily fluids such as semen and milk were deemed to be composed of the same matter. Women were viewed as lesser beings than men, but not wholly different in kind. The sexed bodies of women and men were in essence versions of each other, variations on a theme. However, beginning in the eighteenth century, females and males came to be regarded as different in kind, not just in body through their evident physical differences, but different in their moral aspects, and even in their very souls. Our ideas about our bodies, our sex and ourselves have changed over time, not just as a result of medical knowledge, but also because of changing ideas about what knowledge means. Ideas about femininity and masculinity colour our understanding of supposedly objective biological observations. The categories we think of as the most basic turn out to be mutable.

We might agree that anatomical difference is not something necessarily self-evident, and that it has to be read into bodies, but in the enquiry into the relation between words and things what status do we or should we accord the body? In his recent discussion of the differences between Foucault and Laqueur, Peter Cryle has suggested that one of the differences between them has to do with the assumption Laqueur makes that the body is foundational both to sex and sexuality, that while it does not remain 'untouched by words and historical circumstance', it nonetheless exists both before and beyond language (Cryle, 2009: 438). However, the problem is not so straightforward, because we cannot just move beyond the word to encounter the thing that stands behind it and then take it as foundational for enquiry. For example, in his study of masturbation, Laqueur emphasizes that while the Greeks may not have had a name for what came to be called onanism, they knew what they were talking about. In other words, they had the practice, the thing, but not the same word (Cryle, 2009: 440). This is the argument, Cryle goes on to say, that is made by various critics of Foucault who maintain with regard to the case of homosexuality that it clearly existed before the coining of the term in the late nineteenth century. So when homosexuality becomes the object of discursive concern, a new label appears, but no new practices or activities are referenced by it (Cryle, 2009: 441). It is evident that this rather misses the point of Foucault's critique, but it does usefully focus our attention on language.

The problem with sex and sexuality, indeed with all forms of knowledge of the body and its engagement with a sensate world, is that language plays a part in shaping perception, sensation, desire and affect. A pleasure named is a different pleasure, because naming, and all that might follow from that – identification, modification, supplementation – are part of the pleasure. There are certainly limits to discursive and social constructionism. The materiality of the body exists before we magic it into being by naming and labelling it, its sensations, revulsions and pleasures, but so much of what we do with our bodies cannot be separated from the words we use to describe the things we perform because language is part of the way we materially embodied beings imagine and reach out into the world. Language is, after all, a bodily action. 'Making love' and 'having sex' are not the same activity, however much they might engage with the same body parts and involve certain physiological responses.

Sexuality, with its evident links to the material body and its experiences, sensations and pleasures, provides us with a specific, if at first sight banal, version of what we might term the 'seeing is believing' problem. Much social science work on sexuality, while emphasizing the contingent, historical character of sexual identities, practices and discourses, nevertheless takes the physicality of sexual difference as foundational to any analysis. Women's and men's bodies look different, and anything else we want to say about sexuality starts from that material difference. However much we may 'queer' those distinctions, or unsettle the assumptions of heteronormativity, we find ourselves discussing whether people with particular sets of genitalia are or are not performing certain acts with their bodies and their identities, with other persons who may or may not have the same set of genitalia. From this perspective, whatever sexuality is, it can only be the particular historical sense that people make of their bodies, and their associated objects, sensations, practices and pleasures. This means that everyone everywhere has sexuality, it just varies across space and time, although it may not necessarily be designated by the term sexuality. Sexuality then becomes a plural, capacious concept that exists everywhere, even if the term for it, the word, does not. This is what Laqueur means when he says that in the history of sexuality there is an 'exigent tension' between the body and a recognizable complex of desires and practices 'loosely gathered' under the term sexuality. He goes further: 'I insist that the sexual body is recognizable as a ground for the making of culture over very long periods of time' (2009: 419–20).

Well, that would seem to be the end of it; not much more to say about it really! Why then should we be concerned about sexuality as a category of analysis, experience and identity? There are a number of reasons. First, the very ubiquity of sexuality in social science and cultural analysis raises queries in my mind. Why so much of it? Why does absolutely everything seem to be connected to it? Where does this cornucopia come from and what does it signify? Second, many disciplines in the humanities and social sciences have been concerned with the cultural and historical specificities of sexuality. Scholars have argued that western categories relating to gender and sexuality cannot be straightforwardly mapped onto categories existing in other times and places. The point, however, is not just that the concept of sexuality may have no local equivalent or that it may not designate a meaningful aspect of people's lives, but that it directs the analytical attention of the researcher towards some things and away from others (Boellstorff, 2005: 8–9). These two reasons for wanting to interrogate the self-evident character of sexuality are connected, because underlying them is the slight suspicion that the obsession with sexuality might arise on the side of the analysts rather than on the side of those who are analysed.

My third and final reason has to do both with ethics and with politics. Foucault framed the question well: '[W]hat would be the value of the passion for knowledge if it resulted only in a certain amount of knowledgeableness and not, in one way or another and to the extent possible, in the knower's straying afield of himself?' (Foucault, 1985: 8). I want to stray afield of myself, and rather than add to the stock of knowledge on sexuality and its variability, I want to question whether sexuality as a particular historical form of power/knowledge is an appropriate frame for analysis in the social sciences, whether it is the proper object of study. I want to find out how the forms of knowledge and fantasized relations of which it is composed have spread and multiplied. What have been its modes of transport?

We should bear in mind that the notion of sexuality I am referring to here is the commonsense one we think we all know, which is forged out of a long engagement with the social sciences whether we recognize it or not, and is an historical construct. Academic disciplines have had a love affair with sexuality. But academic passions are like other passions. What will happen if we fall out of love with sexuality? When we fall out of love, we often become disenchanted, the scales fall from our eyes and we see the world anew. What will this world look like? Strangely, or perhaps just perspicaciously, for a man who wrote three volumes on the history of sexuality and planned a fourth, Foucault prefigures this question. In the final pages of the first volume of *The History of Sexuality*, Foucault warned against deploying the notion of sexuality in a self-evident fashion because he argued that sexuality is not an exterior domain to which power is applied, but 'a result and an instrument of power's designs' (1976: 152), and in these last pages, Foucault actually calls for a counter-attack against the deployment of sexuality, a break with what he calls 'its ruses and seductive power' (1976: 157–9).

Why should Foucault do this? Why should he want to call for the end of the regime of sexuality and what exactly might he mean by this? He speaks in fact of the possible undoing of sexuality, of 'a different economy of bodies and pleasures', a resistance to the current mechanisms of sexuality. Now, here I suggest that Foucault is not referring to the strategies so familiar to all of us in the social sciences and humanities, the strategies of queering gender, identities and sexualities, the act of reading them against themselves, revealing their discursive constructions, their gaps, elisions and exclusions. He intends, I think, something more radical, but what exactly?

If we wanted to break with the ruses and seductive power of sexuality, how might we do this, where should we turn, how do we begin such investigations? The very 'naturalness' of sexuality makes it difficult to challenge analytically. We need a point of leverage. It may be instructive to turn in the first instance to an area where modern understandings of sexuality have been extensively deployed and very powerful, but in ways which frequently escape critical attention: international development. International development and public policy have a long history of involvement with sex and sexuality. The regulation of intimate matters touches on such pressing problems as population growth, household composition and livelihoods, the education of the young and the maintenance of the labour force. Colonial and postcolonial policy-makers exhibited and continue to exhibit an almost fetishized concern with such things as female circumcision, polygamy and, more recently, MSM (men who have sex with men). The long-standing preoccupation with population control in the Third World, and the images of excessive reproduction and ungovernable sexuality associated with it, provides an example of the ties that bind sexual regulation to forms of governmentality.

The management of sexuality has, in colonial and post-colonial contexts, frequently been associated with anxieties about morality, and public policy has regularly linked changes in sexual and reproductive practices to agendas of moral reform (Pigg and Adams, 2005: 12). In such contexts, sexuality becomes an object not just of self-improvement, but of nationalist aspiration (Pigg and Adams, 2005: 13–19). Modernization and nation-building depend on the proper management of intimate relations (e.g. Boellstorff, 2005; Gosine, 2009a). What is curious here is that development-oriented projects of sexual and moral reform are rarely talked about in the literature on globalization, despite the fact that they have undoubtedly been one of the major mechanisms for and outcomes of globalization in the last half decade. Development and development interventions and public policy more generally are concerned with social change and transformation, and they warrant particular attention because they provide an opportunity to interrogate how sexuality is deployed. A significant corpus of new research has recently emerged on sexuality and international development theory and practice (e.g. Correa and Parker, 2004; Cornwall and Jolly, 2006; 2009). This research treats sex and sexuality as neglected areas of focus in the development industry, and confronts the exclusion and neglect of non-heterosexual people in development, as well as the heteronormative understandings of gender and sexuality that underpin policies and practical applications. It also focuses on the significance of sexuality and intimate relations for the very poorest communities across the globe, arguing that more attention should be given to their well-being, which should include such things as sexual pleasure. In consequence, sexual rights are now firmly on the agenda in international development. The critical thrust of this new research is important and builds on an earlier recognition in HIV and STD prevention work of the centrality of local cultural meanings of sexuality for understanding people's behaviour, their exposure to risk and the design of appropriate and effective mechanisms for intervention and support. The governing assumption of this new research is that we need to be aware of other people's understandings of sexuality, and to recognize that the imposition of external models via health programmes and other interventions may be inappropriate and unwittingly discriminatory.

However, focusing on local cultural meanings of sexuality may not be sufficient, and is not necessarily a particularly radical or recuperative move, because, as I suggested earlier, the assumption that there exists a culturally specific sexuality which just needs to be identified for each place and time is not a priori one that can be easily maintained, and not because cultural specificities do not exist, but because sexuality may not be the appropriate framing device. Nonetheless, side-stepping the issue of sexuality is not easy, because the recognition of cultural differences requires a framing device to bring them into focus. In order to make a contrast with others, we first need to make them strange, to say that they are different. Once that process of estrangement is complete, however, those differences undergo a process of cultural translation where they are normalized through being redescribed within the comparative frame, in this case sexuality. The result, quite unsurprisingly, is that cultural differences simply serve to reveal other people's ideas about their sexualities. Sexuality thus becomes plural, but is never fundamentally questioned.

It is evident, however, that such contrasts or differences cannot be contained within an easy set of binaries: West/ non-West, scientific/cultural, modern/traditional. HIV/ AIDS prevention, for example, is now part of an enormous global industry made up of health professionals, civil society advocates, community representatives, scientists, social scientists, policy-makers and several other players besides. The medical and social scientific frameworks that underpin HIV/AIDS interventions have been developed by a global community of scientists, intellectuals and activists in a large number of countries. Development projects and programmes of all kinds have this character and are deeply entrenched in national and elite projects in many countries around the world. The result is a certain shared cosmopolitan view of sexuality (Pigg and Adams, 2005: 17). Anthropology has played a major role in developing this shared cosmopolitan view of sexuality through its theoretical work on the sex/gender distinction, its cross-cultural work on sexuality and cultural difference, its critique of the relationship between sexual identities and cultural specifics, and its reasoning about the connections between power and sexuality. The very fact that sexuality is now a global concept, but one which is firmly embedded in cultural specificities, is in no small measure due to the anthropologization of social and cultural life. I am not arguing that anthropology as a discipline set out to achieve this; rather, its preoccupation with comparison and cultural difference provided powerful political interests, including governments, NGOS and community activists with an operationalizable discursive frame.

The embedding of cultural specificities within a global conceptualization of sexuality is made possible through this anthropologization of the world, but also through the ongoing and easy appeal to the evident character of the sexed body. Many researchers have noted that there is no word for sexuality in many parts of the world, or that if individuals in particular locales wish to engage in certain kinds of discussions then they need to adopt vocabulary external to those locales. We potentially end up here talking about the arrival or construction of sexuality (Pigg and Adams, 2005: 18). However, sexuality does not just arrive as an idea; it comes as a specific set of knowledge practices, technologies and policies, all of which are premised on the specific assumption that bodies are biologically sexed, that certain practices or activities are sexual and that human sexual desire is connected to those things. These tensions arise because, while development practitioners, policy-makers and advocates recognize, for example, that sexual identities do not map easily onto sexual practices, they still want to insist that sexualities and identities are somehow connected, because otherwise how will they be able to operationalize a notion of sexual rights or sexual citizenship?

The 'queering' of the relationships between practices and identities does not resolve the problem. Queer theory, however forceful or persuasive, and despite its protestations to the contrary, can only reiteratively produce the connecting thread between bodies, sexual practices and identities. The result then is not only an anthropologization of the world, but an equally curious sexualization of it. Sex is now everywhere. My complaint – if this is what it is – is not about the proliferation of sexual practices and pleasures, but about the globalization or analytic generalization of a particular understanding of sex that has taken shape and form within the deployment of sexuality. We, of course, and many others, believe in this notion of sex because we see its effects on the world in public policy, the regulation of sexuality, the medicalization of bodies, the sexualization of identities and the existence of HIV/AIDS, population growth and many other miseries and terrors.

One of the recent figures to emerge in this newly sexualized world is the strange hybrid figure known as MSM, men who have sex with men. He appears as a sort of free-floating signifier for cultural specificity, although he never was local in any real sense being a construct of the global HIV/AIDS industry made evident in contexts from Rio to Mumbai. He arises because his sexual fluidity, moving between male and female partners, and his secrecy – he is often concealed from view within the institution of marriage – makes it difficult for agencies and governments to assess the risk he presents and to design appropriate interventions (e.g. Larvie, 1999; Gosine, 2009b). He cuts across the homosexual/heterosexual divide that is assumed within the governing frame of sexuality, but, more threatening still, he cuts the Gordian knot that ties sexual practices to sexual identities. He refuses to say that 'he's one of them'. If, as I said earlier, we understand the notion of 'sex' as something that makes it possible to link together anatomical elements, biological functions, behaviours, sensations, pleasures and emotions to form a fictitious unity, MSM is one of the key components in a particular understanding of sex that has taken shape and form within the deployment of a certain global sexuality.

MSM is a curious term, but within the HIV/AIDS industry a whole new language has emerged, some of which outsiders are already fluent in – HIV and AIDS, for example – but the rest of it, such as ART, R&R, DIC, VTCT, PPTCT, etc., remains largely arcane. It is not necessarily evident what things these signs or words designate, but what they mark is the entry of 'particular idioms of sexualness into registers of governmentality' (Khanna, 2009a: 47). A whole new world has been created, and within it is a series of new identities relating to sexual practices. We can take India, where this phenomenon has been extensively studied, as an example (see, e.g., Boyce, 2005; Cohen, 2005; Khanna, 2009a; 2009b). When a man goes to a drop-in clinic, he might be classified as a *kothi* (a penetrated male), a *dupli* (an effeminate male who is penetrated and also penetrates), a *hijra* (a third gender increasingly identified with transsexualism) or a *panthi* (a real man whom kothis identify as their lovers). These categories are indigenous and they exist – or existed in certain parts of India – but their current definition is defined by their epidemiological status, by the fact that penetrative anal sex carries more risk of transmission. Thus, these categories are medicalized versions of local forms of embodiment and pleasure defined and hierarchized according to risk. The *kothi* is now the pan-Indian embodiment of MSM, an indigenous category stretched across culturally variegated and complex terrains to solidify sexuality as a comparative frame (Boyce, 2005; Khanna, 2009a: 47–8). More worryingly, there are other indigenous terms for MSMs around the globe and this makes the MSMs in very different contexts somehow equivalent to each other (Khanna, 2009b). This is a process whereby a series of different embodiments, gender models, psychic investments, self-understandings and identifications are made 'instances of each other' (Khanna, 2009b: 50), made into a series of equivalences called sexuality.

If saying is a form of doing, then part of what is getting done in accession to these new categories of identity has to do with the self (Butler, 2004a: 173). Acquiring a sexuality in the context of the HIV/AIDS industry is not a neutral process, but one which may guarantee access not only to treatment, but also to other resources, and through community activism and NGOs to forms of power and political representation (e.g. Cohen, 2005; Khanna,

2009b). New grids of intelligibility emerge which not only reframe different embodiments, self-understandings and identifications, but reconfigure the landscape of social and physical risk. Fundamentally, this is a specific form of problematization which defines objects, rules of action and modes of relation to oneself and to others, and as such it opens up new possibilities, new ways of being, while cutting off and disabling others.

Let me proceed by way of a further example. In her book *The Empire of Love* (2006), Beth Povinelli discusses a group of Aboriginal women and girls engaged in sexual banter with each other. What makes the ribald exchange possible are the structures and intimacies of kinship relations, and the fact that women have a special relationship with others who are classified as their cross-cousin or *menggen*, a term which, in the context of marriage and marital strategies, can also be glossed as wife. Women choose one woman from among the many who could potentially be classified as their *menggen*, and it is this specific individual with whom they engage in ribald, intimate, verbal play. Povinelli makes it clear that this is a way of strengthening, or, as she says, 'sweetening', certain specific kinship relationships outside the conjugal couple, a way of constituting social dependencies and spreading the risk of living across broader networks. She asks 'Is this sexuality?' and responds in the negative, indicating that these women are not choosing between heterosexuality and homosexuality; they are not even engaging in a discourse on sexuality. What is deployed here is what could be termed an alternative economy of bodies, connections and pleasures, and one that should perhaps be understood as such and not reduced to some cultural variation on sexuality. Povinelli underscores her point by using an ethnographic vignette of a young girl declaring to a group of women that when she grows up she is going to marry her *menggen*. Her mother corrects her saying that 'girls marry boys not other girls'. The child appeals to her grandmother: 'I call her wife, I can marry her.' The grandmother

agrees: 'She is her *menggen*, she is her wife.' The girl's
mother retorts: 'That's not *menggen*, that's lesbian.' The
grandmother responds adamantly, saying: 'No, *menggen*
is not lesbian.'

As Povinelli points out, it would be easy to claim that
the grandmother was just asserting the cultural relevance
of local modes of desire and sexuality in contradistinction
to the discourses of sexuality to be found in Australian
newspapers, on the television, the radio and the internet.
In other words, that she is refusing to acknowledge a globalized, 'western' notion of a heterosexual–homosexual
boundary. But what Povinelli wants us to understand is
that the separation the grandmother seeks to make is not
between *menggen* and lesbian so much as between different ways of thinking about connections and pleasures,
different means for imagining how the body relates to and
extends into the physical and social worlds within which
it is located (2006: 65–8). In this specific context, kinship
is both a mechanism of genealogical reckoning and a way
of organizing and maintaining the practicalities of lived
relations, of connecting to those who will give you support,
food, shelter, protection. It is a way of connecting your
body to other bodies, but also to land, ancestors, ritual
events and much else besides. This is a different way of
seeing or reading the body and its connections, sensations
and pleasures – an alternative legibility, if you like.
However, this alternative legibility cannot be closed off, as
Povinelli makes clear, from what Aboriginal women and
men know of how the wider Australian society views
them, nor can it be discussed outside what they see of *Will
and Grace* on the television, or read of white paedophiles
in the Murdoch-owned press, or indeed be dissociated
from the local parties where reggae, hip-hop and wangga
are combined, or from the long history of settler interventions into social life, bodies and desires. Consequently, if
the bodies of indigenous women and men are open to
ancestors and rituals and the like, they are also open to
what Povinelli terms 'the drama of Western sexuality with

its antagonisms and phobias, opportunities and exaspera-
tions'. These different, and often contradictory, frames of
legibility set up material connections and circulations,
acting to thicken certain sets of social relays while thinning
others, opening up possibilities for action and closing
down others (Povinelli, 2006: 70–2).

In Povinelli's vignette, we see new ways of being called
into being, new forms of labelling, new ways of being
called as a sexual subject. The attempt to collapse *menggen*
into lesbian turns particular material relations, forms of
intimacy and practices of pleasure – the 'sweetening' of
kinship relations – into a form of desire, and one that has
potentially explicit sexual activity as its aim. The subject
is required to understand and experience themselves as a
subject of desire within a specific deployment of sexuality.
A shift is demanded in how individuals think their own
nature: what it is to be a woman, an Aboriginal, a human.
This is what the grandmother refuses to do. The deployment of sexuality insistently refigures certain erotic practices as sex, and this is what the mother draws attention
to. The result is a sexualization of intimate connections,
and one that from the grandmother's perspective fails to
capture the intricacies of the relationships between bodies,
pleasures and the texture of the social. What this example
draws attention to is that if we simply treat sex as something 'natural', self-evident, it stands outside the analytic
frame and occludes our ability to understand the full complexity of its construction. We always need to ask what
constitutes sexual pleasure, and what functions does it
serve. If we simply figure the individuals involved in these
encounters as subjects of desire, as involved in sexual relations which are attached to projects of self-making
grounded in difference, it is very easy to categorize their
behaviour and ascribe it an identity label. But the point is
that this is not necessarily how it is perceived or experienced. From a local perspective, the 'sweetening of kinship'
is attached both to pleasure and to care, and the forms of
self-making it advances are about the moral responsibili-

ties of a self in connection with others, not a self defined in relation to desire understood as a sexual identity. In the second volume of *The History of Sexuality*, Foucault explores how individuals are led to recognize themselves as subjects of desire, to discover in desire the truth of their being (Foucault, 1985: 5). However, his theory refers to particular historical conjunctures, and that there are modes of self-making that do not make sexuality foundational to identity, and do not even tie sexuality to ideas of self-making, to a notion of a subject as called into being by desire. I suggest that we should be wary of treating sexuality as a cynosure; we need to fall out of love a little with sexuality in the social and cultural sciences, flesh out a critical genealogy and elaborate on the political consequences of that move for our theoretical thinking. Sexuality is now a concept with global reach, but more than that it is one of the major drivers of globalization rather than simply one of its consequences. Sexuality, as an analytic framing device and as an arena of human experience and agency, does not arise naturally from the imperatives of the body, not least because sex as a particular unity of anatomical elements, biological functions, behaviours, sensations, pleasures and emotions is something that takes shape within the deployment of sexuality. My aim has been to stray afield of myself, to break a little with the ruses and seductive power of sexuality, to demonstrate once again that battles over concepts and terms, over framing devices and proper objects, are always about ethics and politics. Sexuality has nourished the very conditions in which, as a possible response, it could develop and find form. The remaking of ourselves and our relations with others in the image of sexuality is, of course, seductive, but it is also, or should be, troublesome.

− 5 −
Second Nature

'I can't get no satisfaction' was the song that catapulted the Rolling Stones to stardom. With its famous guitar riff, which Keith Richards claimed came to him in a dream, and Mick Jagger's sexually suggestive lyrics, its visceral sounds have lasting appeal. The Rolling Stones have played it on every tour they have done since they first performed it in 1965. Satisfactions have, by implication, a sensate relation to the physical world and its pleasures, evoking ideas about appetites and satiation. Perhaps it is no small irony, then, that the lyrics of the Stones song make reference to a disillusionment with consumption and consumerism. A larger irony, no doubt, is that if satisfactions are the pleasures one finds in life, one of them, for a not insignificant number of people around the globe, has been a song called 'I can't get no satisfaction'.

One of the more curious features of the social and human sciences is that we have had so little to say about satisfaction: the satisfaction of a job well done, a basket woven, a poem turned, a marriage settled, a child grown tall, a meal with friends. We have, of course, written extensively about all of these things, but not about their satisfactions.[1] In fact, as I suggested in Chapter 1, we have come late to the whole spectrum of pleasures, anticipations and aspirations. 'I can't get no satisfaction' is a good place to start because many of the satisfactions of rock music are about our embodied engagement with the sound, the lights, the images and the performers. The 'live' experience of rock music – its directness – has always been a crucial part of its appeal (Bolter and Grusin, 1999: 42). Early recordings strove hard to sound live and to recreate that sense of the bass thudding in the chest and the fine hairs contracting along one's forearms. In the early days of rock this was often achieved simply by turning up the volume, but as electric and digital sampling became more popular, the evolution of recording techniques and hypermediation turned the authentic experience of rock into immense, elaborate, carefully crafted visual and aural spectacles. The physical engagement with the music and the spectacle is an absolutely essential part of the enjoyment, which may be why those who do not enjoy rock music focus so much on the lyrics and what they mean, worrying about such things as sexual content (Bolter and Grusin, 1999: 42–3, 71). True fans of 'I can't get no satisfaction' are unlikely to be worried about sexual innuendo – which is part of the enjoyment anyway – probably uninterested in the specific meanings of the lyrics, and certainly resolutely unmoved by the fact that they contain a critique of consumer society.

Capitalizing on Meanings

What this draws attention to is how we might explore the connection between meaning and satisfaction. Finding meaning in something is one common experience, even possible definition, of satisfaction – as in understanding a text, solving a problem, probing a mystery. We invest in our meanings, and they are rarely, if ever, devoid of emotional colour and significance. It is an unpalatable fact of contemporary life that those who work in marketing are quite expert in these matters. Recognizing that consumer empowerment accompanied by mass customization and personalization has changed people's relations to brands, and discerningly aware of the fact that consumers are expert navigators of media content, and knowledgeable about their contexts of consumption, the advertising industry works to establish an emotional connection between brand and consumer (Roberts, 2006). At the core of this affective economics, as it is known, is an explicit attempt to use ideas, sounds and images to elicit emotion and make connections. For example, Coca-Cola portrays itself not as a purveyor of soft drinks, but as a company that sponsors and shapes sporting events, concerts, movies and other entertainment media (Foster, 2008a: 11; 2008b). Multisensory and multimedia experiences are devised that create and intensify vivid impressions and sensations, and connect them to stories that are compelling. This much seems obvious, but what goes a step further perhaps is that the Coca-Cola corporate website has a section where consumers can share their stories about their relationship with the product. These stories get fashioned around themes such as romance, childhood memories, an affordable luxury, good times with friends, etc. These themes attach key emotional relationships and experiences to promotional themes, with the result that people not only integrate Coca-Cola into their memories of their lives, but also frame those memories in terms of the principles or themes underlying the company's marketing efforts (Foster, 2008b: 16). Brand loyalty is the aim of what is now termed 'experience-based, access-driven marketing', the models for these marketing strategies and the emotional attachments and identifications they strive to induce are based on the entertainment industries, and their goal is not so much to hoodwink consumers as to create fans (Jenkins, 2006: 68–72).

Fandom is something very different from the old stereotype of hordes of screaming teenage girls. Contemporary fandom is now a particularly dramatic example of how individuals draw on shared resources to construct and embellish their own and collective fantasies. It is an egregious instance of the imagination running riot and producing, through its efforts, not just ideas, images, hopes, desires and satisfactions, but emerging forms of sociality. A particularly good example of this, as Henry Jenkins has shown us, is the film *The Matrix*. *The Matrix* – that is, the original movie – was a story about digital hallucinations and ambiguous 'agents' shaping reality to their own ends. Human cyborgs provided the energy for action where the lines between reality and illusion were deliberately unstable. As Henry Jenkins says, you either loved it or hated it. *The Matrix* is actually three films, plus web comics, nine short animated films, two computer games and a massively multiplayer game set in the world of the matrix. The Wachowski brothers played all these media off against each other to enormous economic advantage. They planted clues in the film that did not make sense until you had played the computer game; they drew on the back-story using animated shorts which needed to be downloaded from the web or watched on a separate DVD. Fans rushed to websites to dissect and discuss, interpreting every tiny detail, looking for clues only to find more clues (Jenkins, 2006: 96). One writer tries to explain its fascination:

> First and foremost, the film's got pop appeal elements. All kinds of elements: suicidal attacks by elite special forces, crashing helicopters, oodles of martial arts, a chaste yet passionate story of predestined love, bug-eyed monsters of the absolute first water, fetish clothes, captivity and torture and daring rescue, plus really weird, cool submarines . . . There's Christian exegesis, a Redeemer myth, a death and rebirth, a hero in self-discovery, The Odyssey, Jean Baudrillard (lots of Baudrillard, the best part of the film), science fiction ontological riffs of the Philip K. Dick school, Nebuchadnezzar, the Buddha, Taoism, martial-arts mysticism, oracular prophecy, spoon-bending telekinesis, Houdini stage-show magic, Joseph Campbell, and Godelian mathematical metaphysics. (Sterling, 2003: 23–4, cited in Jenkins, 2006: 100)

Bug-eyed monsters of the absolute first water! This commentator's satisfaction and enjoyment leap off the page.
Yet the pleasure generated by the matrix is not only a result
of immersion in, and somatic engagement with, the many
forms of media through which it can be experienced, but
also a consequence of the wide-ranging stories and narratives – often familiar – that are woven into it. Ideas about
the experience of reading, viewing images and consuming
media are part of it, as well as theories about mathematics,
religious experiences and human quests. Baudrillard's *Simulacra and Simulation* is a major inspiration, and other
texts are referenced, including the Odyssey, the Bible, *Alice
Through the Looking-Glass*, and George Orwell's *1984*.
In short, it offers enormous scope for identification on
both personal and cultural levels.

Affect marketing and transmedia storytelling make a lot
of money. *The Matrix Reloaded* (the second movie), for
example, earned $134 million in the first four days of
release, and largely because of the build-up across several
media platforms (Jenkins, 2006: 96–7). But cynicism about
economic motives should not distract us from what is happening here, and there are a number of important things
that deserve our attention. Media convergence makes the
flow of content across multiple media platforms possible,
but the sharing and reusing of digital assets – graphics,
animation – means that comics, animation, the game world
and the film world now look like they are part of each
other. This visual cross-over allows you to move from very
different contexts and activities, but still to be in the same
'world'. The apparently interconnected nature of that
world – its authentic wholism – is shamelessly exploited
by the producers who increasingly drop elements – characters, scenes, minor narratives – into films to create open-
ings that will only be fully exploited in other media, like
games (Jenkins, 2006: 106–9). Consequently, the reach of
a film like *The Matrix* is extraordinary, and its capacity to
create strong emotional attachments immensely enhanced
by its repetitions and ramifications across space and time.

However, the sheer complexity of this world, its cinematic, sensate character, shot through with allusions and clues, means that it cannot be mastered by any single individual. You need to share, compare notes, learn from others, cooperate, agree to archive, debate and discuss (Jenkins, 2006: 133–4). This, of course is what the fans do and in the process they and their quests are part of an emerging field of social relations: a dynamic social matrix.

What is significant is how engaged fans are in creating worlds of meaning. Where once activities such as computer gaming would have been dismissed as the province of 'sad anoraks', participation in a wide range of cross-media platforms is now becoming ubiquitous for those who are connected, and an increasing part of everyday life, work and leisure. Clearly, there are many millions of people around the world who are not on the internet, cannot afford to go to the cinema and have never seen a computer game in their lives, but because the speed and quality of information transfer is not proportional to its costs, and because multinational media companies work to exploit global markets, the spread and reach of these technologies is impressive and significant. However, their reach is not just a function of their distributed, interconnected, global nature – for which the internet is iconic – but of the fact that the character and nature of these technologies means that they are able to create and develop spaces and opportunities for emergent forms of sociality, and for groups and individuals to develop and enhance their cultural and cognitive competencies (Moore, 2010).

Entertainment is not the only context in which these processes unfold. For example, mountain biking is an exceedingly popular leisure activity, but mountain bikes did not emerge from the research and development lab of a major bike manufacturer. They were first developed by enthusiasts in California who wanted to race along mountain trails. The first commercial bike came out in 1982, and by 2000 mountain bikes accounted for 65 per cent of bike sales in the USA, a market then worth about $58 billion (Leadbeater, 2005). There are many other examples: users started kitesurfing, they write their own news, they help manufacturers design cars, they provide much of the content of the most successful computer games, collectively develop software and online tools, and a great deal more. User communities are everywhere involved in innovation and design (von Hippel, 2005). But user communities are not just consumers, they also want to be creators and producers, and what they create are not just products, but new lifestyles, leisure activities, ways of connecting to each other and to their object worlds, new forms of desire and satisfaction (Taylor, 2006). Of course, the inputs of intelligent consumers allow companies to tailor their products to consumer needs and to enhance profits, as well as drawing consumers as creators closer to the brands through affective ties. The social sciences, as producers of knowledge about these processes, also find their research methodologies and theories incorporated into design, management and consumer strategies. The advertising and consultancy industries are particularly adept at deploying ethnography and psychology. The result is that user empowerment and community building are inescapably entangled both with social science theorizing and with the activities of capital.

This is particularly evident in user-created digital worlds, like that in the massively multiplayer online game Second Life, which depend for their success on the innovation and creativity of their residents. In Second Life you build yourself – your avatar and its alternatives – and your home, you can purchase items from in-world stores and spend money in clubs (Ondrejka, 2004). Linden Lab maintains the basic platform – a landscape with land, water, trees and sky – a set of basic building tools, and the means to communicate, modify and control movement and interaction. The rest of the world is the result of millions of hours every month of individual and collective effort by the residents. However, since Second Life's currency, the Linden dollar, is freely convertible with the US dollar, people can work in this virtual world, create objects over which they retain intellectual property rights and earn 'real' money (Boellstorff, 2008: 11–12). Consequently, individual entrepreneurs and even corporations transact and produce objects for sale 'in-world', but 'branding' is equally important: companies have a presence there, bands launch their albums and universities offer courses. In 2006, a company in Washington, DC, with the rather wonderful name Electric Sheep, was set up to help Fortune 500 companies and others engage customers and communities in Second Life. One of the organizations to hire Electric Sheep was the New Media Consortium, a non-profit group whose members include Harvard, Yale and Princeton Universities (Terdiman, 2006).

Yet, despite these obvious and inevitable linkages between capital and user creativity and community building, we need to be analytically attentive to the specific forms of entanglement they create. For example, modern computer technologies cannot be subsumed within a general framework of alienation and exploitation because they proffer opportunities for customization and personalization that provide sources of pleasure, as well as resources for the creation of new distributed forms of global sociality. We need to make a definitive move away from a particular line of thinking in the social sciences and the humanities that has a very impressive intellectual genealogy beginning with Walter Benjamin and the Frankfurt School, but which also draws on older notions of Romanticism and Idealism. This is the idea that technology and mass production undermine the authenticity and value of cultural products, because in the modern world we are driven by consumerism, imitation and superficiality, and cultural difference has become a commodity like any other. Global capitalism offers us Thai food, Rai music, Bedouin carpets, Aboriginal art and Maasai blankets, and we can purchase all of them. Cultural elements and products are decontextualized, detached from their authentic moorings and set adrift on a sea of individual choice wherein everything has its price.

Mixing, hybridity and creolization as descriptions of what is happening to contemporary cultures in the world, and as analytic terms, necessarily invoke their imaginary counterparts tradition, authenticity and specificity, because the former can only be defined in relation to the latter (see Chapters 2 and 3). Consequently, the spectre of threat and loss still haunts many discussions about culture, both inside and outside the academy, as I suggested in Chapter 1, and at the root of many of the anxieties expressed is the assumption that culture as a commodity cannot be squared with cultural as tradition, and in particular that global media and information technologies are creating hypermediated spaces that somehow threaten the authentic experience of culture and community. I want to suggest that this view is misleading because it is based on a very narrow perception of how social worlds and cultural meanings are created and maintained, and because it offers little purchase in trying to analyse cultural change and transformation (Moore, 2008).

We might begin by first addressing the question of whether commodification and technological mediation are necessarily impoverishing of cultural meaning, and whether by extension they necessarily undermine cultural experiences. Let me offer you an example. Tchaikovsky's ballet, first performed in 1892, is a story of a young girl whose Nutcracker Prince accompanies her, once released from his spell, to the Land of Sweets, which is presided over by the Sugar Plum Fairy who shows them a series of dances. *The Nutcracker* is a regular Christmas treat for many families in Europe and elsewhere, and ballet is one of the canonical art forms of European culture. In the 1970s, an advertising copywriter in the UK allowed his mind to drift through a series of linguistic associations – nutcracker, nuts, nutter, fruitcake[2] – and produced a television advertisement for a 'fruit and nut' chocolate bar made by a well-known UK brand, set to the music of one of the dances in the

Land of Sweets. The advert featured a well-known comedy actor of the time, and subsequently became a 'classic', a piece of popular culture iconic of the 1970s in the UK. Advertising and ballet: a mix of 'high' and 'low' culture; a travesty; a banal use of a memorable tune; an example of how commodification undermines the authenticity and value of culture? Is there anything positive to be said about it? Well, in 1992 and again in 2007, to great critical acclaim, Matthew Bourne took the slickness, the colours and textures of the 1970s, its brands, rock operas, music videos and television motifs, to produce a wonderful confection. He produced a version of Tchaikovsky's *Nutcracker* in which all the dances in the Land of Sweets were danced by characters dressed as well-known types of sweets from the 1970s: Humbugs, Liquorice Allsorts, Gob Stoppers! Clearly, each generation and each set of audiences find their own values and meanings in *The Nutcracker*, their own understandings of disappointment, desire and yearning, and of how they are at play in the narrative and in the performance. Values and meanings are far from static. But the set of associations Bourne sets in train does more than repurpose Tchaikovsky's original, bring it up to date and make it more relevant for contemporary audiences. Bourne uses the brands, colours and media images of the 1970s to intensify the audience's attachment to the story, to enhance the wish-fulfilment and fantasy aspects of the Land of Sweets, and to make the experience of the ballet more sensate, immediate and compelling. As one commentator said, 'if you watch this on video be sure to have a bag of sweets to hand because otherwise the temptation to lick the television screen can get overwhelming!'[3]

Language, Representation and Affect

What the example of Bourne's *Nutcracker* does is to draw attention to how, in many contexts, technological mediation enhances and magnifies meaning and affect, by 'extending' and 'supplementing' sensations, feelings and emotions, as well as processes of identification and narration. We all know that reality is not just about the physical world we perceive, but of how we think and feel about it, and how we orient ourselves within it physically and psychologically. What Surin terms 'the decisive moments of physical and affective communication that precede and exceed interpretation – the sensation that comes before logic, but is somehow logic's operative basis, its sine qua non' (2001: 205). An experience that is gut-wrenching, an apprehension that there is something more to a situation, the desire to lick the screen. Moments when affect, emotion and sensation are tied to logic, language and thought, but not necessarily in ways that are fixed and not necessarily in ways that always provide for clarification or elucidation. Language and affect do not always work in concert, and meaning may not necessarily depend on either, but may arise from their tensions, displacements, interruptions and absences.

Where can we find these processes at work? Well, pretty well anywhere where the struggle for representation is at play, the desire to understand, to capture in words or images or sounds those aspects of being human or being alive in the world that seem to be present in, but to go beyond the immediacy of, any situation. There are many things that we cannot securely or completely grasp in representation and that failure – that gap – is often filled with a variety of objects and technologies, ways of extending our reach beyond what we can see and know.

The most powerful and the most virtual of all our technologies, and the one which has the greatest impact on our selves, and on the nature of our social ontologies, is language. Language is the technology that is most a part of us, demonstrating that a rigid distinction between subject and object is never possible. Its virtual character is truly magnificent. We can use it if we wish to refer to our gods, to talk of those long dead, to construct something as fragile and as material as an identity, to capture the beauty of a fleeting day, to imagine the future and to create social relations. The materialization of language in writing only enhances our capacities to do these things; from lists to letters and novels, we extended our ability to create and maintain social relations and meaningful worlds.

However, language as a form of representation, as a technology for describing and knowing the world, has its limitations. Social science and philosophy have had a long struggle with the conundrum of how to explain in language cultural phenomena that are not themselves in language. This is not a problem about postmodernism or late capitalism; it is a problem about cultural mediation of all kinds. As Roy Wagner has argued: '[I]mage, as a means of construing action, power, or effectiveness, is profoundly different from verbal explanation . . . An image can and must be witnessed or experienced, rather than merely described' (1986: xiv). His point is that images – and by extension symbols and sounds – do not always convey meaning in the way that language does. The affect of an image or symbol or sound may have little to do with its content. Content and affect cannot always be logically or straightforwardly related within the realm of language or signs because an image's or a sound's affect is not necessarily semantically or semiotically ordered. Affect may work within or it may work against language.

One way of demonstrating this is to consider the issue of song. In the formal and generic sense, a song must always be 'motivated by what its words express', but, as we all know, 'it is not by attending to words alone that we make sense of or attribute meaning to songs' (Kramer, 2002: 63). 'Heidenröslein' is a well-known song composed in 1816 by Schubert to a text by Goethe. Ostensibly, as Lawrence Kramer says, it is about a flower, and, by extension, about a girl being deflowered. The song invites appreciation, but does so without making a statement. Its meaning is about recognition, both a familiar aesthetic pleasure and connections to certain emotions, situations

and relationships. Kramer argues that it conveys and
evokes ideals of community, purity, authenticity and sim-
plicity, but if it does so it does not achieve it via direct
reference. There is an expression of feeling that is linked
not to action or narrative, but to atmosphere, and in this
context the exclusion of specific meaning, of ostensible
reference, is intentional because it frees the music from any
one particular set of circumstances. It transfers affect to
the voice, and beyond that to a potential for imagination
and fantasy that is not already occupied by specific ostensible meanings (Kramer, 2002: 59–60). Meaning loss is
necessary for the song to work.

However, in other contexts, it is not just that meaning
is conveyed by atmosphere or the evocation of feelings and
ideals, but that it is powerfully dependent on the physicality and materiality of the voice. A very powerful example
is provided by the singing of traditional ghazals. Ghazals
are a poetic form that speak of the pain and loss and
beauty of love, where the beloved may be an earthly sexual
lover, but is often in fact God. Ghazals belong to a great
metaphysical tradition and there are many different levels
at which they can be interpreted. Exegetical meanings
clearly exist on one level and are important for certain
forms of interpretation and pleasure. However, what is
equally important, and especially for those listeners for
whom many of the metaphysical, spiritual and esoteric
meanings might be obscure, is that as a form of devotion,
the narrative of the ghazal, its lyrics, are subordinated to
the sound of the voice. The sensuousness and vibratory
fullness of the voice is felt in the body of the listener, physically, emotionally and symbolically condensing and per-
petuating an experience of love, implying a directness of
material connection with God, moving beyond the terrain
of language to connect to the bliss or rapture of oneness
with the beloved (Kramer, 2002: 51–2, 63–6).

What these examples suggest is that cultural meanings
work on a number of different levels which are never
entirely separate, but neither are their relations predeter-

mined. Linguistic reference provides one set of meanings, with their attendant pleasures and satisfactions, but there are meanings which can exceed or escape representation in language and which do not necessarily work through direct or ostensible reference. Much of what we think of as meaningful is somatic, sensate, carried by affect, and is a consequence of certain material connections, of how we are positioned within any particular environment and what we make of the connections between objects, bodies and technologies in that environment. Deleuze explains rather well how it happens in cinema:

> There are Lulu, the lamp, the bread-knife, Jack the Ripper: people who are assumed to be real with individual characters and social roles, objects with uses, real connections between those objects and these people – in short, a whole actual state of things. But, there are also the brightness of the light on the knife, the blade of the knife under the light, Jack's terror and resignation, Lulu's compassionate look. These are pure singular qualities or potentialities – as it were, pure 'possibles'. (2005: 102)

Deleuze makes a very particular distinction in his analysis between the images and their affects as they unfold in specific narrative sequences in a particular film – that is, the specific meanings that may rise from their particular deployment in a particular context – and the singularity of the possibilities contained within the images – that is, the potential they have for entering into virtual relations with other images and other forms of affect. Potentialities are presented, such as brilliance, terror, decisiveness, action and compassion. They are proffered in a particular way at a particular moment, in a particular film, and we do two things with them. First, we use them to interpret the particular narrative sequence with which we are presented. We make the image/narrative sequence our own by limiting and temporarily fixing the potentialities. Second, we carry the potentialities presented with us into other contexts, other films, and they form part of the mechanism through which we elicit and limit meanings in those contexts. These potentialities are the stuff of culture, but they are not in themselves meaningful, they have no deeper meaning. These potentialities may never enter language directly, and yet they are much more memorable than the actual narratives or plots or interpretations. I'm sure, for example, that many of you remember the woman in the shower, the knife and the scream, but how many of you remember the details of the plot of Hitchcock's film *Psycho*?

The potentialities Deleuze refers to are quite different in character from the notion of the alternative meanings that may be given to any sign by virtue of repetition, of deferral of meaning or of performative context; that is quite different in character from all the variations of poststructuralist reference. Deleuzean potentialities are materially present in resonance, in interference and in affect. Thus meaning is not something to be decoded; it does not necessarily inhere in the image, object, sound; it is not the result of a particular interpretation, but of a particular engagement with the world. What Deleuze signals is a particular approach as to how we might introduce intensity and affect into cultural theory (for a critique, see Chapters 6 and 7).

Art, Aesthetics and Affect

The relationship between language, meaning and affect is part of a larger problem about representation and its failures (Moore, 2007: ch. 9). The desire to make representation and the world coincide, to bring things into being, to make evident what is felt and apprehended beyond what is immediately sensible, is one of the purposes of objects and technologies. The making of art forms is one such instance. The struggle for representation takes different forms and has different purposes across cultures and through historical time. Classical realism, for example, is not something that art forms in other cultures have sought to achieve. Aesthetics have no universal standing. However, the engagement of human technologies with representation, and the effort to bring forms closer to movement and action in life, to resonate and interfere with the work of affect, is one explanation for the productivity of cross-cultural exchange, for why mediation and remediation enhance cultural capacities and are productive of new cultural forms and new cultural ontologies (Moore, 2011). A familiar example is that of Picasso and his use of African and Oceanic art, and the subsequent influence of these art forms on the revolution that became modern art. It is often said that Picasso and his contemporaries had no interest in the religious or cultural symbolism of African and Oceanic art, or in the social contexts in which they were produced. Picasso said as much. So that far from enhancing cultural capacities or imaginative possibilities, modern artists simply valued these objects superficially, stripping away their cultural relevance, and exploiting their expressive style. When cultural meaning is removed, what is left but the empty form?

When we look at *Les Demoiselles d'Avignon*, one of the earliest of Picasso's major works to show the influence of non-western art forms, it is immediately obvious that we do not remember or value Picasso because he was an expert on African art. He and others effected a revolution in representation that had a profound impact not just on ways of seeing, but on the nature of the materials used for artistic expression and on the function of art itself. The inspiration he found came not from any understanding of African cultures or social systems, but, as he said, from an engagement with the objects themselves, a sensate experience that was more apprehension than comprehension. He reflected on his reaction to the objects and where it led him: 'And then I understood what painting really meant. It's not an aesthetic process; it's a form of magic that interposes itself between us and the hostile universe, a means of seizing power by imposing a form on our terrors as well as on our desires. The day I understood that, I had found my path' (quoted in Meldrum, 2006).

What Picasso intuited is that African masks and other ritual objects are often about the management of power, an intercession in the relation between the seen and the unseen, an attempt to impose form on our terrors as well as our desires. How they do it or why they do it was not Picasso's concern, but he used the marvellous austere beauty of those objects to enhance his own imagination, to make something more of his own world, something resolutely modern. New technologies not only make new ways of seeing possible, but they are productive of new relays of affect and intensity which in turn produce new cultural forms.

The problem of form was something that the painter Francis Bacon often spoke about. He was fascinated by certain images – the Cimabue *Crucifixion* and Velasquez's *Pope Innocent X*, for example – which he painted again and again because he said 'they breed other images for me' (Sylvester, 1975: 14). Bacon painted *Three Studies for Figures at the Base of a Crucifixion* in 1944, inspired by Picasso's depiction of the suffering human body, saying 'there's a whole area there suggested by Picasso . . . of organic form that relates to the human image but is a complete distortion of it' (Sylvester, 1975: 8). Bacon was always interested in the relationship between media and form, and he wanted his ideas to be inseparable from his use of technique. Talking of his work, one critic referred to a piece that had paint on it so thick that 'it had a texture like rhino's skin' (Sylvester, 1975: 32; see also Stephens: 2008: 94). Bacon himself engaged with the visceral qualities of paint as a medium and said 'There is an area of the nervous system to which the texture of paint communicates more violently than anything else' (Sylvester, 1975: 18; see also Walsh, 2008: 85). Bacon made a distinction between painting and illustration, between an attempt to capture intensity and feeling in a specific form and the use of paint to capture a story, a narrative, something already within representation: '[T]he moment the story is elaborated, the boredom sets in; the story talks louder than the paint' (Sylvester, 1975: 22).

'One wants a thing to be as factual as possible and at the same time as deeply suggestive or deeply unlocking of areas of sensation', was how Bacon put it. He derived inspiration for his figures from great works of art, as discussed above, but he also found inspiration from film images and photography – including photographs of Nazi leaders, Muybridge's sequences of *The Human Figure in Motion*, African big game, figures in the street during the Russian Revolution, an image of a motorcyclist prone besides his crashed machine, and positioning in radiography. Bacon sought to bring painting closer to movement and action in life, to the materiality of affect and sensation, to organize optical phenomena in a way that creates sensation, provokes thought and feeling. He wanted to capture the emotional force through manipulating the space–time dimensions of the image. The search for intensity dominates his work, and intensity results in a degree of distortion of the image because you cannot get intensity from what is seen naturally. In a way, all of Bacon's art is about the search for intensity, the desire to get beyond depiction to a different order of understanding about the bestiality of humanity, the violence it has wrought on bodies, psyches and selves. As he said, the job of the artist is to 'unlock the valves of feeling and therefore return the onlooker to life more violently' (Sylvester, 1975: 17). It is what makes Bacon a great twentieth-century artist, a commentator on the brutality of his times, and yet much more than that.

The search for intensity is about finding a form of representation that proffers new ways of seeing, but which captures the materiality of affect and sensation. The quickening of the pulse in response to certain objects or images is not just about how they convey affect to us, but about how we respond to their materiality, how we develop an affective relation with them, and how that relation will animate, extend and intensify the meanings we attribute to them on other levels. One place we see this most dramatically in ethnographic material is in relation to initiation rituals. For example, in northern Kenya where I have been working, these rituals unfold in several stages, but at each stage initiates are subject to spectacular performances where singing, dancing, painted bodies, masks, imaginary animals and powers, as well as ordinary household objects, are all used to emphasize that masculinity and femininity are constructed in a world of objects. Objects, songs and dances set up a series of concrete, imaginary and yet physical connections between bodies, fertility, sexuality and production. Diverse aspects of life are connected not by ideas or by language necessarily, but often by rhythms and sounds, such as when the pounding of grain is linked to the act of sexual intercourse. The physicality of that thrusting, thudding sound is picked up in the dances and linked to other ideas about the continuity of the human and the divine.

The result is an experience of the materiality of consciousness, of the way that thoughts, feelings, desires, hopes and expectations are connected to the bodies of women and men, and also to other objects in the world, including the landscape and the environment. Initiation rituals turn children into women and men, they impart knowledge, provide new ways of seeing, and they do so partly through instruction and exegesis, but much more importantly and more powerfully through engagement with a world of objects and their associated technologies (Moore, 2009a). The girls and boys who go into those rituals already know about bodies and sex and reproduction and household objects, but what the ritual does is make new connections between those things and through dramatic performances speed up those connections and relays, intensifying them, distorting them and making them new. It is quite something to be part of. Many young women and men say that after initiation sex is better, and you can see why because the act itself, the desire and the enjoyment, is now linked indissolubly to an enlarged and intensified world of the imagination.

Inside the World of Objects

It is through culture that we humans are already virtual, and that virtuality is part of our cognitive and sensate relation to the world of objects and to our own bodies. Virtuality is that cultural capacity that allows us to represent the world and to act on it, to be effective in it, but it is the self's location within a physical body that means we need to attend to the way bodies are constructed in a world of objects, where affective, material, symbolic and discursive connections are set up, experienced, performed and reflected upon. Virtuality is a human mode of being that we simultaneously embody and enact in different modes or registers: linguistic, material, affective, symbolic. When Francis Bacon complains that he loses the form the paint contains if he allows himself to be swept up by narrative, he is talking about shifting between different modes or experiences of virtuality. In human ways of being, the subject–object distinction can never be absolute (Moore, 2007). We are born into cultures, and their virtuality becomes part of our experience of embodiment, of relating to self, to others, to physical and conceptual environments, to all the ways in which we register our effects on the world and its effects on us. These things are not absolutes; they can be changed through time, and life courses and interactions, and anthropology has gathered many thousands of such examples.

For example, the Malanggan are funerary sculptures from New Ireland, off the coast of Papua New Guinea. They are made to be destroyed, and one way to do that is to put them into the hands of European traders (Strathern, 2001: 1). Consequently, they are to be found in almost every ethnographic museum in the world. They are bodies made up of parts of humans and animals, and are wonderfully described by Alfred Gell:

> The purpose of a Malanggan is to provide a body or, more precisely, a 'skin' for a recently deceased person of importance. On death the agency of such a person is in a dispersed state. In our terms, indexes of their agency abound, but are not concentrated anywhere in particular. The gardens and plantations of the deceased, scattered here and there, are still in production, their wealth is held by various exchange partners, their houses are still standing, their wives or husbands are still married to them, and so on. The process of making the carving coincides with the process of reorganization and adjustment through which local society adjusts to the subtraction of the deceased from active participation in political and productive life. The gardens are harvested, the houses decay and become, in time, particularly productive fields, and so on. That is to say, all this stored 'social effectiveness' of the deceased, the difference they made to how things were, gradually becomes an objectifiable quantity, something to which a material index may be attributed. This is what the Malanggan is; a kind of body which accumulates, like a charged battery, the potential energy of the deceased dispersed in the life world. (1998: 224–6)

The Malanggan embody a life force, as well as being a vehicle for thought. Marilyn Strathern points out that each one is composed of elements of previous Malanggan. They replicate figures or motifs produced for past clan members, so that they contain elements that are passed down through the generations, as well as some that may have come in from other local groups. As objects, they are created from elements dispersed across space and time, and will be again when they are disposed of or destroyed because at that moment individuals will acquire through payment the rights to reproduce elements of the designs in the future. What the Malanggan do, however, is more than just represent personal and clan relationships across space and time; they act, as Gell suggests, as a moment of capture for social effectiveness, for actions that have been taken in the world, for the way that bodies and objects, persons and things have affected each other, and have produced material productive effects – food, sex, exchange and fertility. It is perhaps this capture of affect that makes them so appropriate as funerary items, representing the leaking away of life, the waning of affect. We are part of the world of objects and they are part of us, but the struggle for representation is itself productive of affect and this is why, as they decompose or are destroyed, elements of the Malanggan will be transformed across space and time and reappear in other sculptures to capture future affects, engaging with emergent forms of sociality.

Humans use objects and technologies to extend our reach across space and time, to create new forms of self, of social relations and social ontologies. Many of the relationships we have are virtual – our relation to ancestors, spirits and our own imaginations. New technologies enhance our capacities for virtuality and for making social relations. They not only make new ways of seeing possible, but they are productive of new relays of affect and intensity, which in turn produces new cultural forms and cultural capacities, as I have already suggested. We can explore this further by turning to Japanese popular culture as an example of how objects, technologies and selves become involved in extending emergent forms of the social across space and time, providing opportunities for enhancing cultural capacities.

Since the early 2000s, the global value of sales of Japanese animation and character goods has exceeded $80 billion. Many of the most successful children's series worldwide, such as Pokémon (Tobin, 2004), and their associated products come from Japanese production houses, as does almost all of the animated content for the most popular computer games and films. This has not just been as a result of concerted marketing by Japanese media companies and their global partners, as Henry Jenkins explains, but has been fuelled to a very large extent by anime and manga fans, who have used newly available technologies – most of them made in Japan – to build and expand globally distributed communities based on the desire for and engagement with these materials (Jenkins, 2006: 160–1).

There is currently a great deal of debate, inside and outside the academy, as to whether Japanese animation is actually Japanese in content and character. Critics point out that the characters do not look Japanese – they are, at the very least, 'white' by default – and that most of the viewers who enjoy anime and manga have no sense that it is Japanese. Perhaps the creators and producers of games software intentionally make the characters look non-Japanese because they know that their market is global? Yes, to a certain extent, but, as Koichi Iwabuchi (2002) makes clear, the popularity of these products is probably dependent both on a pleasure to be found in things Japanese and Japanese culture itself, as well as on the fact they are racially, ethnically and culturally disembedded to a certain extent.[4]

Anne Allison is one commentator who has argued that the attractiveness of Japanese products is that they encompass the consumer in a world that is both imaginary (imaginary places, creatures and adventures) and real (activities, exchanges, purchases, social relations, quests). The imaginary aspects involve and provoke strong emotional attachments with resonances to childhood and also to traditional Japanese culture. Allison suggests that this is because aspects of Japanese culture involve 'a tendency to see the world as animated by a variety of beings, both worldly and unworldly, that are complex, (interchangeable), and not graspable by so-called rational (or visible) means' (2006: 12). Susan Napier shows that the traditional arts of Japan, like Hokusai's woodblock prints and manga, but also theatre and dance, have always produced wonderful images of other worldly characters, including ghosts, ogres, goblins and demons, that are at once grotesque and uncannily beautiful (2007: 160). Drawing on aspects of

Shintoism and Buddhism, this animist sensibility, Allison argues, must not be understood as a timeless component of a stable and homogenous Japanese culture, but as an evolving aesthetic, investing objects – including consumer items – with human, non-human and spiritual life in a way that re-enchants the lived world (2006: 12–13). In this world, familiar forms break down and recombine, using human, machine and organic parts, and can thus be reassembled into new hybridities and possibilities. The attraction is a world of polymorphous perversity or, more prosaically, a set of tensions and possibilities between the fantastic and the real, the foreign and the familiar, the strange and the everyday. As Allison says, it is a fantasy world but one that people also want to inhabit, to become fluent in and to be at home in. It is a world where the boundaries between play and non-play, work and leisure, the actual and the virtual are pleasurably blurred. But of crucial significance is the fact that for fans, and particularly for those young enough to have been entirely or largely brought up in the time of Google, 'worldliness' – knowledge of things beyond your own domain, engagement with difference – is a desirable quality; more than that even, it is cool (Allison, 2006: 275–7)! The engagement with cultural difference provides its own satisfactions, and not least because it is productive of new relays of affect and intensity (Moore, 2011).

Fans get together in many ways, online and off, but in the United States the anime and manga conventions are huge affairs which last for several days, during which time many participants can be in costume as one or more characters. These occasions also involve Japanese food, tea ceremonies, exhibitions of martial arts and swordsmanship, and language lessons. Guest speakers include academics, industry people, voice actors, manga writers and artists and musicians. All this activity is combined with the opportunity to buy the most recent anime and manga paraphernalia, to gossip, network and hang out (Napier, 2007: 152–4). Many participants at these conventions are actively interested in Japanese culture, and speak and/or read Japanese. As one would expect, fans have a wide variety of ideas about, interests in and experiences of Japan, but many insist that their interest in anime led them to an interest in Japan and Japanese culture (Napier, 2007: 185–7).[5] Clearly, we cannot make much progress with our analysis if we just dismiss these people as doing nothing more than playing games or see them as deluded or as geeks with reality problems. We need to proceed from the fact that their interests in Japan are genuine, but that their relation to Japan and things Japanese is an imaginary one – as indeed are all forms of identification.

As Allison argues, modern media and information technologies are not only a key component of the manner in which life is constituted in this interpretive community (2006: 12–13); they are the platform that makes this world possible, and the new forms of distributed global sociality on which it is based. Yet, in one sense modern media and information technologies are no different from other forms of technology which may also involve multiple media and multiple forms of mediation, as in African initiation rituals, for example. They are certainly no different in consequence of their virtuality or as a corollary of the fact that they allow new combinations and relationships to exist between the human and the non-human. Human culture understood not just as relations between people, but as the relations between persons and things, the human and the non-human across space and time, has always been virtual. Seen from this perspective, the virtual worlds enabled by modern information technologies are just another means of enhancing a very familiar and well-worn set of cultural capacities.

Relations With Self and Others

We can examine this more closely by returning to the digital world Second Life, where the only game to be played is one of learning to live in the virtual environment in such a way that it becomes second nature to its inhabitants, an actual second life. There have probably been no human cultures in which individuals and groups did not use some form of technology – be it masks or spells or paintings – to prosthetically extend the reach of the human body. The virtual worlds of modern technology allow us to produce bodily capacities – such as the ability to fly or to suddenly materialize in a certain place – that are well beyond the body's organic, physiological constraints, but the use of technology to supplement the body is not new, and neither is its virtuality. Where there is innovation is in two areas: first, computer-mediated modern information technologies massively enhance this cultural capacity for 'extension' and 'supplementation', as well as the possibilities it provides for sharing with others and thus creating new forms of sociality; and second, they magnify the intensity of affect in a particular way which has consequences both for the way we experience and create culture, and for the manner in which we analyse it.

The virtuality of Second Life is like the virtuality of all culture, human created. This accounts for the fact that when interviewed many participants in Second Life refer to two things: first, its familiarity; and second, that in the virtual world they can be more nearly themselves. Artifice and fabrication are a defining feature of all forms of human sociality. In Second Life, as discussed earlier, its inhabitants first construct themselves: they name and clothe their avatars, build their houses, make money, attend courses, go shopping, hang out in clubs, get married, have children, pursue affairs and get divorced. In this space, one interacts with others from all over the world while constructing objects (houses, bodies, clothes, accessories), identities and social relations. Avatars can fly, teleport between any two points instantaneously, and one can view one's own body and the world either from a disembodied camera view or from an embodied perspective through one's virtual eyes. The result is a significant ability to collapse space and time and to alter one's perspective on, and physical engagement with, the world. Unsurprisingly, Second Life acts as a space for fantasy and wish-fulfilment, and participants often speak about its beauty, seduction and freedom. It is a place where one can have the body one has always wanted, the house of one's dreams, and the kind of social life that is rarely possible in real life (Jones, 2007: 31). In consequence, it is a space for the enactments of desires, hopes and satisfactions, and, as such, it is full of sexual activity and conspicuous consumption, thereby revealing that the virtual is always haunted by the actual.

Every user inhabits at least one avatar. The Second Life platform allows inhabitants to change every aspect of their appearance as often as they wish. You can choose the width of your lips, the parting in your hair, whether you are a wolf, a vampire or a winged Hermes. Residents lavish time and money on their avatars (Boellstorff, 2008: 129). However, total control over the body takes some level of expertise, and within Second Life there is a significant market for avatar bodies, body parts and accessories. One can buy skin, hair and genitalia, as well as clothing, jewellery, and wings! The more 'life-like' the body parts, the more expensive they are (Jones, 2007: 55). Every part of the constructed self is essentially for sale. The avatar is tailored to the wishes of the user, and can run, dance, swim and fly, touch other virtual bodies and, if so desired, have sex with them. Avatars are depicted in rich graphic formats and engage in ongoing social relationships in-world. A strong sense of place, of dwelling and of interaction is the result. This does not mean that the online world mimics physical reality, but it is nonetheless a distinctive material and social reality, filled with other objects and avatars with whom one interacts (Jones, 2007: 56). As Boellstorff suggests, participation in this world is not so much about sensory immersion, as social immersion (2008: 116).

The relationship between avatar and self is a complex one. Many users have more than one avatar, known as alternatives (alts), who may even encounter each other in-world. From the earliest days of cyber-sociality, there has been a recognition that technology allows individuals to have distinct and multiple identities in-world. The gap between virtual and actual selves is often experienced as empowering, and sometimes leads to changed behaviour in real life as a result of gaining confidence or learning to establish new kinds of relationships (Boellstorff, 2008: 120–1). Jones argues that the virtual body always reflects aspects of the authentic self, and that an individual's fantasies and desires mould the appearance, interactions and social relations of the avatar, with the result that the avatar as representation is both a reflection of self and the performance of a desired self (Jones, 2007: 57). Interestingly, Boellstorff suggests that the advanced degree of possible customization of avatars tends to mean that inhabitants interpret appearances as indicative of authentic selfhood, while simultaneously realizing that selves might have multiple manifestations in the form of several avatars (2008: 129–30). Some Second Life residents speak of their virtual world self as 'closer' to their 'real' self than to their actual world self (Boellstorff, 2008: 121–2).

The self-authenticity many residents refer to and experience is about a self in social interaction, a form of relationality, which, like all self–other relations, is constructed in fantasy (see Chapter 3). This is one of the reasons why social interactions in Second Life can both transform actual world intimacy and social relations, and yet create real forms of online intimacy (Boellstorff, 2008: 156). It is notable in this regard that nearly half of the respondents interviewed by Jones reported 'playing' a different sexual or gender identity at least some of the time (Jones, 2007: 68). Avatars are defined by difference from their creators; they can accomplish feats no human can – fly, teleport and sprout wings – they may become rich and powerful, engage in sexual behaviours no human could, be part animal/ robot/human. Avatars have life histories: they change and develop over time, become involved in specific relationships and develop a distinctive personality. The avatar is a creation and an object of desire, and thus acts in part as other to the self of their creator, as well as being an aspect of self. This circulation of self–other relations, as well as their construction and reconstruction in fantasy, accounts both for the seduction of the virtual world and its power to mobilize new modes of belonging, of relationality and of self-styling.

Desirable intimacies often take sexual forms, but for most residents of virtual worlds non-sexual friendships are the most important aspect of their online lives. 'Friendships are the foundation of cyber-sociality; the friend is the originary social form for homo cyber' (Boellstorff, 2008: 157; see also Boyd, 2006). Contrary to many discussions on this topic, it is not immersion in the physical reality of the virtual world that is compelling – although the gorgeous graphics and excitement of Second Life are compelling – but the new forms of self–other relations that are possible, the spaces and opportunities for using technology to create new meanings, new ways of belonging and of being human. 'What makes these virtual worlds real is that relationships, romance, economic transactions, and community take place within them – in short, that they are places of human culture' (Boellstorff, 2008: 245).

It is easy to dismiss people whose marriages break up because they are having an affair in an online game, or those who gather in Tokyo's parks to re-enact scenes from a film, or adults who dress up as cartoon figures and go to three-day conventions to discuss imaginary worlds, as individuals who do not know the boundaries between the virtual and the actual. But contemporary information technologies do not work just because they allow people to be escapist or to confuse the relationship between the virtual and the actual – although this may well be the case for some individuals. They work because of the satisfaction that arises in the tracking back and forth between the virtual and the actual, the way that the tension between the virtual and the actual creates spaces for our hopes and desires. What is so extraordinarily compelling about the virtual worlds proffered by modern information technologies is the way that people are using them to bind themselves to new interpretive communities, working out new ways of seeing and doing, innovative means of relating embodied experience to what cannot be perceived directly by the senses, forging new forms of social relations, creating new possibilities for the emergence of the social through the recombination of the human and the non-human. Through the integration and intensification of affect, and the new distributed forms of sociality they make possible, they are allowing individuals and groups to rework the virtuality which has always characterized being human. They are, in sort, allowing us to develop new cultural ontologies, new ways of being humanly cultural.

– 6 –

Arts of the Possible

How, in his own words, could a 'skinny kid with a funny name' find his place in the American dream and rise to become the President of the United States?[1] Barack Obama's campaign rallying cry, 'Yes, we can!' was, like all good political slogans, thin, specifying little and yet saying everything. 'Yes, we can!' Can do what? Erase the stain of race from the history of America, build an inclusive society, provide jobs and homes, stop unjust wars, ban torture, rein in the vaunted rapaciousness of capitalism, make the world a freer and a safer place? The hopes not just of one nation, but, it would seem, of many nations and many individuals all came to rest on one man. What audacity! What hope! The transformative power of such hope won President Obama the 2009 Nobel Peace Prize. The committee's citation was succinct: 'Only very rarely has a person to the same extent as Obama captured the world's attention and given its people hope for a better future.' Hope may be inspiring, but is it enough to bring about change? More cynical commentators thought the award premature, asking what Obama had really achieved in office, a concern that was unwittingly echoed by the head of the Nobel Committee, who said that Obama had won the prize because they wanted to support what he was 'trying to achieve'.[2] And it was a thought that reverberated through Obama's acceptance speech, in which he pledged 'to reach for the world that ought to be'.[3] I want to take the opportunity provided by Obama's meteoric rise, and the force with which his success unleashed an outpouring of aspiration which banished – if only temporarily – an apparently deeply entrenched pessimism about politics around the globe, to think about the relation of hope to politics and the political, as well as its present relation to social theory. We need to attend, I suggest, to Karlström's reminder that 'most popular imaginaries . . . contain visions of light as well as murk, hope as well as fear, aspiration as well as anxiety' (2004: 596). If we are going to theorize states of alienation, abjection and pessimism, we also need to theorize 'sources of hopefulness'. Now, if hope springs eternal, in Pope's sonorous phrase, so does cynicism. In fact, insofar as one can speak accurately of 'theories of hope' in philosophy and the social sciences, they have a propensity to emphasize hope's connections to delusions, fantasies, longings and daydreams. Writing on this point, Vincent Crapanzano quotes Søren Kierkegaard, who puts it rather wonderfully:

> It is indeed beautiful to see a person put out to sea with the fair wind of hope; one may utilize the chance to let oneself be towed away, but one ought never have it on board one's craft, least of all as pilot, for it is an untrustworthy shipmaster. For this reason, too, hope was one of Prometheus's dubious gifts: instead of giving human beings the foreknowledge of the immortals, he gave them hope. (Crapanzano, 2003: 19)

Of course, we all understand that Obama was not *stricto sensu* the origin of the wave of hope his election released, but rather the consequence or product of it, perhaps even its pilot. From an anthropological perspective, hope, with its links to memory, aspiration, desire and anticipation of the future, is necessarily culturally and historically specific (Crapanzano, 2003: 15). There can be no universal category or experience of hope *tout court*. But beginning with the United States, the hope that Obama speaks of and that he engenders is not his alone. His speeches and references are in the great tradition of American political oratory: 'this nation under God, shall have a new birth of freedom – and . . . government of the people, by the people, for the people, shall not perish from the earth' (Lincoln's Gettysburg address, 1863); 'And, so my fellow Americans, ask not what your country can do for you; ask what you can do for your country. My fellow citizens of the world, ask not what America will do for you, but what, together, we can do for the freedom of man' (JFK at his inauguration). Promises and aspirations, some would say dreams, are the currency of presidents, especially those who are newly elected. But, one of the striking features of this American rhetorical form is the repeated theme established through historical time of the inclusivity of government, the direct address to 'we the people', an older form of 'yes, we can!'. Obama's rhetoric, and thus much of his emotional impact, harks back also to revivalist preachers and to the great abolitionist Frederick Douglass, and his inheritor Martin Luther King. The linkages between race, freedom, equality and aspiration are not new in American politics. Given the history of the United States, the particular character of the hope there – the great cry for freedom that strikes so deep a chord in that place – should not surprise us.

Is Obama deluding himself and are we all deluding ourselves about the possibilities of change? Can one person really make a difference, govern differently, reposition American power, give up the delusions of grandeur and military might? How much do politicians really change anything? There is, after all, nothing new under the sun. Perhaps our desires are out of step with reality. It is not just, as Crapanzano reminds us, that hope has important interlocutory dimensions (2003: 16), but that it draws on deeper moral roots connecting both to individual agency and collective notions of the good life. In addition, capitalism and democracy are terms with multiple histories, emotional, intellectual and practical, and intertwined in those histories and woven into their institutional arrangements are organizing metaphors of hope, possibility, vision and goals (Appadurai, 2007). It would therefore be perfectly proper to argue that Obama's move for change is less about transformation than it is about possibilities, imagined realizations, the perfectibility of systems that have not yet delivered on their promises. However, Obama's more stringent critics would go further, pointing out that his substantial defeat in the midterm elections in 2010, the continued prosecution of war, the appeasement of Israel and the light-touch regulation of financial services and banks are all just a continuation of the same old politics – often with the same personnel – and gives very few reasons for hope (see, e.g., Ali, 2010). Obama himself seems undeterred, and used his State of the Union Address in February 2011 to detail his plan 'to win the future'.

There are two important elements in all of this which bear further thought: the first is the relation of hope to what is proximate, realizable, just within reach; the second is the connection between aspiration and spirituality, the notion of a world that is going to come into being under God's aegis. Arguably, it is the perceived link between these two elements which has prevented hope from becoming a serious subject of study or category of analysis in social theory – the idea that hope is not practical, that it relates to things that cannot be realized and which may in the proper sense of the phrase be 'other-worldly'. Bearing this in mind, let us in the course of this chapter explore two problematic issues and their interconnections. The first concerns how we go about changing the world we live in, changing capitalism. How, why and when can hope provide models for social transformation? What are the links between hope and the alterity of the future? In exploring this question, we address the relation between hope and the political, between ideas and social transformation, asking both about the ideas and social imaginaries of ordinary people, and about the theories and preoccupations of social theorists. The second issue is about the kind of humans/subjects/selves we envision as pursuing the changes or transformations we seek to analyse. What capacities do they possess to drive change? How does agency link to the ethical imagination, and to new forms of the political? In this context, we are enquiring into theories of the subject, and the manner in which hopes and desires are created by shifts in subjectification.

Hope as a category of experience and/or analysis has not featured prominently in social theory for at least a couple of decades or so. In my experience, reading Fredric Jameson, David Harvey and Giorgio Agamben back-to-back does not generally make one's spirits soar! As I discussed in Chapter 1, a number of commentators have remarked on the melancholia of the intellectual Left in its various manifestations around the world and across the disciplines. This depressive state is not perhaps surprising, given that recording the retreat of collective politics and the rise of social inequality in some parts of the globe, while documenting the emergence of spaces of exclusion, conflict and immiseration in others, is not the most cheerful of experiences or occupations. Some have suggested that this despair has deeper roots deriving from a failure to identify new models of social transformation after the demise of Marxism, and even more worryingly the failure to find political and ethical critiques of contemporary capitalism which would have sustained moral purchase (Harvey, 2000; Zournazi, 2003). What seems at issue in these concerns is how to develop and defend a notion of the 'good life', how to develop forms of critical thinking that might open up new possibilities, might eschew negativity in favour of the 'arts of the possible'.

This is no easy task because particular lines of intellectual enquiry arise at specific historical moments, and consequently there are always concerns about forms of theorizing and the specific historical conditions in which they find favour and purchase (Moore, 2006). David Rieff, for example, has wondered whether multiculturalists realize how often their language of 'cultural diversity', 'difference', 'the need to do away with boundaries' resembles the discourse of multinational corporations (Rieff, 1993). Slavoj Žižek (1999) has suggested that postmodern theories of a subject divided by race, gender, class, sexuality, etc. are only possible in the context of global capitalism where differences are themselves commoditized, and, rather than subverting capitalism, such theories actually become an obstacle to social transformation.

In a similar vein, feminist and political theorists have argued that postmodern theories of gender, class and race are 'merely cultural', that they lack a clear relation to social and political transformation based on economic equality (e.g. Butler, 1997; Fraser, 1998). Some have suggested that they are predominantly a preoccupation of western, white elites with little relevance for those suffering exclusion, discrimination, violence and immiseration (e.g. Fraser and Nicholson, 1988: Lovibond, 1989; Mohanty et al., 1991), and that while theories of difference certainly underpin a form of politics that seeks 'recognition' and 'social justice' for specific groups, as has been noted in several chapters, they do so without necessarily demanding or entailing structural change and/or radical reform (Fraser, 1997; Phillips, 1997; 1999). Injustices of distribution and of recognition clearly interconnect, but in the complex multicultural societies of the contemporary world questions of recognition have often eclipsed issues of redistributive justice, and a focus on identity politics has all too often led to increased separatism and intolerance (Fraser, 2000; Phillips, 2007).

Again as I argued in Chapter 1, some of the malaise of the intellectual Left can be attributed to the fact that in the context of the proliferation, hyper-commodification and politicization of differences, social theorists have not been able to develop theories of difference that provide

sure ground either for political change or for sustained
moral action and ethical critique. What might be the
reasons for this? Paradoxically, it is partly a consequence
of the overdetermination of difference, where theoretical
models have insufficient distance because their pre-theoretical assumptions mimic the processes they wish to
analyse. To be effective, critical theories have to stay close
to the actualities of the situation they want to critique –
and this is most especially true when the hoped-for outcome
of critique is political or social transformation – but if the
relation between analysis and the world it engages is too
close, then theoretical purchase is lost and critique becomes
a form of description or documentation (Moore, 2006).
When critique collapses in this way, melancholia is the
inevitable result.

The relationship of concepts to empirically existing conditions – the fraught character of representation – is one
of the things at issue here. The practice of social science
requires an ethics and a politics of engagement precisely
because it both responds to and brings into being its object
of study. Current theories of globalization, for example,
are less about a generally agreed-upon set of technological,
social, economic and political developments than a set of
practices, a way of trying to grasp the social world and its
future (Perry and Maurer, 2003: x). The difficulties this
presents are not just confined to matters of definition or
debates between various academics, but are also about
how the different understandings of globalization held by,
amongst others, business leaders, financiers, media moguls,
religious believers, internet socialites, civil society advocates, artist provocateurs and ordinary people both respond
to and produce the character and content of globalization,
as concept and as experience. Terms such as capitalism and
globalization are concept-metaphors (Moore, 1997; 2004)
and they retain an indeterminate status both as theoretical
abstractions and as a set of processes, experiences and
connections in the world. This is true both for social scientists, whose theories are inevitably influenced by their

experience of living in the world they seek to analyse, and for the rest of the world, whose lives are increasingly influenced by concepts and theories originating in the social sciences. One of the most powerful examples of this is probably the notion of gender; nearly every country in the world now has gender policies.

The meanings and entailments of terms such as capitalism and globalization are not static: they change in response to global consumerism, transnational communities, mass media, flexible capital and virtual economic transactions. Our shifting understandings of these terms are driven by these material changes, but it is also the case that alterations in the way these terms, entities or processes are perceived and understood propel further changes in material conditions. The notion of capitalism both within the academy and outside has changed dramatically in the past 20 years, and yet, since it is impossible to adequately specify in any comprehensive or complete way the referents of such a term, it continues to function as an abstraction that guides our imaginative relation to lived worlds. We all clearly recognize that the way we think about things has an impact on the way we live in the world. Thought is a form of agency. Worlds and their futures are created by the actions of human beings in specific contexts, and representation is an indissoluble and crucial aspect of those actions. These representations do not just provide the grounds for action, but are forms of agency in themselves (Keane, 2003).

This much seems self-evident, and would be banal if it were not for the problem of how critical thought and forms of self-representation are linked to individual agency and collective action. At the root of this problem is the question of the conformity of the subject to social norms, the degree of autonomy or distance the subject has from the social and its sedimented distributions of power. To what extent, and in what manner, do individuals and communities bring about social change? Is thought or critique enough to bring about change? In the contemporary moment, it certainly seems insufficient to envisage the history of thought in Weberian terms as based in a developmental model of rationalization. What we might want to retain from the Weberian vision is a sense of the uneven distribution of modes of thought and/or specific 'orientations to the world' across different institutional spheres, social spaces and political geographies. What seems most urgent is to link shifts in conscious, willed agency to more inchoate emotions and sentiments that may or may not have clearly delineated languages of self-description and self-objectification. In this regard, hope and its cognates – aspiration and desire – force us away from a history of ideas too strongly attached to rationalities and ideologies. What we observe are shifts in forms of subjectification linked to emergent publics and new forms of sociality rather than to ideational forms.

Of Markets and Gods

In my discipline in recent years, it is in economic anthropology and the anthropology of finance that we have seen some of the most sustained attempts to elaborate on hope both as a descriptive and as an analytic category. What this work emphasizes is the temporal character of hope, the fact that hope gives social reality an historic character, inserts it into history. The analytics here recognizes a distinction between hope as longing, fantasy and desire – what Keats so evocatively referred to as 'a hope beyond a shadow of a dream' – and other forms of hope. By focusing on the difference between hope as 'ultimate end or goals' and hope as 'means or method', the analysis seeks to differentiate between unrealizable aspirations, on the one hand, and types of orientations to the future, on the other, associated with outcomes that are realistically and/or potentially in view (Crapanzano, 2003: Miyazaki, 2005). This latter set of possibilities invokes hope as capacity, aspiration, speculation, reconfiguration: the hope of think tanks, NGOs and entrepreneurs (Appadurai, 2004). Of course, a distinction between hope as a means to an end, a method, and hope as an end in itself, an existential state of longing outside the realm of the possible, cannot be maintained in any rigorous sense, if for no other reason than because it is often through the act of hoping that new possibilities come into view, the identification of new ends or goals makes new means possible and vice versa.

Hope as an animating force in providing reorientations towards possible futures and outcomes focuses attention immediately on how such a process involves the deployment of knowledge and the engagement of forms of agency. Hirokazu Miyazaki (2006; 2007) explores these questions in his work on Japanese traders in global financial markets. His starting point is that hope becomes a subject for social theory precisely because it has a capacity to 'reorient the directionality of critical knowledge'. He describes how one trader, whom he names Tada, employed a range of economic concepts and neoliberal ideas to analyse his present and to reorient his knowledge towards a possible future. In 1999, disillusioned about his future, Tada had reportedly turned to his Excel spreadsheet to try and calculate his worth. He modelled a number of scenarios involving variations in earning potential, income, pension and age and found like most of us that he could not afford to retire. This action was, in part, prompted by a popular discourse, well reported in the media in Japan at the time, about how calculations of personal worth and the value of one's labour spread through a lifetime of work were evidence of a strong individual's rationality, their ability to take risks and their self-responsibility. These qualities were explicitly imagined as the personal elements or aspects of wider neoliberal and economic reforms, which would depend for their realization on a new generation of winners and risk-takers whose efforts would secure the future, a type of individual quite different from the traditional Japanese corporate salary-man of the past, whose successes had depended on collective decision-making mechanisms based on group-oriented values.

According to Miyazaki, the recourse to what looked like a simple piece of sensible retirement planning was understood by Tada himself to be evidence of his wider personal goals of objectivity and logicality, which he felt characterized his management of trading strategies within the group for which he was responsible. He had developed over time the idea that all his traders would interrogate their trading strategies through extensive computer simulations in order to identify their weaknesses, and that over time this would allow all the traders in the group to emulate the team's most successful strategies. Tada's ultimate goal was to invent 'an automatic trading machine' which, with the help of computer simulation, would outperform the entire team. Tada's own trading strategies and his managerial supervision of the strategies of others were the means of collecting the data necessary to build this machine. They were therefore not merely ends in themselves, but a means to reorient knowledge towards the future. All attempts to predict markets – and Tada would not be the first person to dream of transcending human error and/or limitations through technology – involve positing a link between present actions and future consequences, but Tada's machine, if it were ever to exist, would of course do away with all such links, and the future would become simply a repetition of a continuous present.

However, when Tada calculated that he could not afford to retire unless he raised 210 million yen (at the time about $1.8 million), he decided to leave his employment with a major securities firm and go to work for a small investment fund. Shortly after he made this move, he began to realize that the management of risk, and thus the determination of success, in the venture capital business depended more on evaluating people and their trustworthiness than on analysing publicly available information on market performance. His determined logicality was not of much use in a context where risks were more volatile, involving deals with individuals and business ventures of unproven worth. He arrived paradoxically at a situation in which a commitment to logicality and objectiveness had induced him to leave his secure employment, but to prosper in the new environment would require him to shift his method from one based on a reliance on logicality to one based on trust. By the summer of 2001, some of Tada's schemes had not gone well; he had lost money, including some of his own savings. In this context, logicality once again emerged in his account as a method for securing a hoped for future. He blamed himself for not being logical enough in entering this new arena of trust and risk; he had trusted the wrong people, and now felt that he should dedicate himself to devising a method to calculate other people's trustworthiness.

It is easy to be cynical and dismissive about these various rationalizations and baffling attempts to make money, but seen from another vantage point, Tada's major life choices involved a sequence of shifts in agency, in self-stylization and in the deployment of critical knowledge, adding up to a series of considered attempts to link the present with the future, through personal and social transformation. Tada's decisions exhibited, I suggest, an obstinate search for a style of being, a means of projecting himself into history. By 2005, Tada had recovered from his losses, but interestingly, despite his success, he had lost faith in the system:

> There is something wrong with today's economy. The basis (of an economy) should be barter. Capitalism is a fraud. It depends upon people's greed. . . . People have begun to sense the limits of this system, but once you're in it, you can't exit from it too easily. . . . But greed destroys civilization. It has already created all kinds of challenges. We are facing important choices. For example, there are environmental problems. Should we make the Earth unlivable? (Miyazaki, 2006: 161)

In his analysis of this moment, Miyazaki rather wryly points out how well Tada's disillusionment resonates with the lament of the intellectual Left and their/our incapacity to imagine alternatives to capitalism, but also how well his sustained attempts to reorient his critical knowledge to bring a desired future into being echoes the attempts of social theorists to resuscitate hope as a method for devising new analytic models and forms of critical practice (2006: 162–3). Tada's hopes, like those of the social theorists, are based on the view that ideas generate concrete effects, and that critical thought is a form of agency. In both cases, what gives hope is a process of moral empowerment that seeks to overcome failure based on the capacity to creatively engage with the alterity of the future.

Yet, in Tada's pensive reservations concerning greed and its unbridled effects on the environment, we see perhaps several things in play. Tada is continuing to orient himself towards his understanding of the future through the deployment of critical knowledge, but the character of that knowledge has changed once again – in response, it would seem, to broader discursive shifts. When his story begins in 1999, neoliberalism and the mantra of free markets are at their zenith. By the time he reflects on his efforts and their moral value in 2005, his views, despite his success, are tempered by emerging popular critiques of capitalism and its wanton destructiveness. It would be more accurate to speak of several different types of critical knowledge that coexist, but come into play at different moments. As Tada shifts over time from one form to another, or gives one more weight than another, he moves along an uncharted course from hope as a method – a means to secure a possible future, one that is realizable, but just off the page – towards hope as a goal or ultimate end, a revision of capitalism which is urgently felt, but not very likely to happen any time soon.

Faith and Reason

Part of the difficulty here concerns different forms of knowledge and how they relate to people's understandings

of time and of temporal processes. If hope inserts agency
into history, through the deployment of critical knowledge,
as Miyazaki suggests, then how and why does the shift
from hope as realizable, as method, to hope as an ultimate
goal, an ideal, a vision, come about? Or rather, what is the
relationship between the two moments or types of hope?
What might be the connection between the temporal frame
and orientation of critical knowledge in the present and
longer-term change in the world?

Jane Guyer has recently explored this question by
examining how neoliberal economics and evangelical
faith are based on similar temporal structures and frameworks. She argues that in both cases the strategies of
the present have very little impact on outcomes in the
future. Neoliberal policies are based on the goal of freeing
up markets for innovation, and the movements of such
markets are calculated using increasingly sophisticated
mathematics and model building, accompanied by a wide
range of financial instruments – futures, options, currency
swaps – that seek to manage and to take advantage of
market risk (Guyer, 2007: 412). What gets lost in this
process, however, is the link between the short term and
the long run, between what can be done in the immediate
term by individuals and institutions, and final outcomes.
Markets may go up and down, but in the long run, provided there is no unnecessary interference, neoliberal
theory presumes that the market will deliver growth. The
market is self-regulating, it is not to be interfered with,
we can devise ever more sophisticated methods for
knowing it, but we cannot and should not seek to control
it. Reasoning from experience as a way of understanding
markets would only result in 'erroneous rationalism', in
us being 'the captives of the ideas we have created', in
Hayek's phrase (cited in Guyer, 2007: 412). The market
is autonomous, moving towards convergence at some
unknown point in the future when final or 'marginal utilities' can be calculated, but this is not strictly speaking
something that is thought to be under human control,

although human actions may certainly cause catastrophic short-term effects and distortions.

If this disjuncture between the short term and the long run exists, what consequences might this have for our distinction between a hope that is realizable and one that is not? Is it just a matter of the application and/or directionality of critical knowledge, as Miyazaki suggests? Or, is it a question of the accuracy and power of our models? If you want to change the world, it may not be enough just to act on the world as one knows it because that knowledge could very likely be imperfect, erroneous or incomplete. The problem begins, perhaps, with the limits of what can be known. Prometheus did not give humans the foreknowledge of the immortals, and so humans do not know how the long run will come out, but nor do they know how the world works unless they make sense of their experience of the world and create models of it. The ability to make and remake the environment is one of the defining characteristics of being human. There are certainly different kinds of models at work here, those based on direct sensory experience of the world and those based on technology and expertise, new ways of seeing and doing. But, for most people, experience, knowledge of the world as lived, is not a good guide to the character of the divine, to the intricacies of mathematical modelling and computer simulation, to the long-run movements of markets, or the replication of stem cells. There are individuals, like Tada, who have expert knowledge and command of technologies and prosthetic practices, but are they more effective at realizing individual hopes or collective aspirations? Do their more sophisticated models give them greater control over the world, more reason to hope?

The short answer is that they may do so, especially in the short term, but that they may not do so in the long run because they are not necessarily designed for that purpose. For example, mathematical economics is a powerful modelling tool, but in the long run it is not a description of economic value; rather, it is a metaphor for it, a model of it. When Isaac Newton invented the calculus to solve problems in mathematics and physics, he thought he was discovering God's mysteries, and the notion of infinity allowed him to connect the mysterious convergence of the stars with numbers and mathematical reason (Thornton, 2007: 438). Contemporary economics, science and biology have built into their theories ideas about infinity, the end of time, the final frontier, the secret of life, intelligent design. We know that there are mysteries out there, things we can posit, but do not know and cannot control. We know that our representations create the arc of the world we inhabit, but we also know that there are things that exceed them, forces at work in the world that are not human and may never be fully comprehended. This does not mean, of course, that we do not seek to explain them or influence them, because we most certainly do all the time. Paradoxically, many of our models, particularly those concerned with having an impact on or changing the world, posit an organizing point, or force, or end point that animates the agency of the short term and encourages the development of models for action, but which does not connect in any empirically specifiable way to life as it is lived in the shorter run.

It is not just that contemporary living is increasingly dependent on ways of knowing the world that are not experientially based, but that in the context of increasing sophistication in instruments and technologies of knowing and seeing, the requirement for faith has not diminished: it continues to animate a quest for knowledge and comprehension, and to underpin forms of agency and engagement with the world. We can see this in Tada's faith in the possibility of mirroring the market's perfection through the development of an 'automatic trading machine' which would transcend the knowledge and actions of humans. A similar act of faith is evident in his later desire to devise a method to calculate people's trustworthiness. In both instances, Tada seems to have been engaged in an imaginative act of purification, where it would be possible to perfectly understand the workings of the market if human experience, error and inconsistency were to be erased. Caitlin Zaloom recorded similar practices of decontamination in her study of futures traders in a London firm where the definition of a successful trader hinged on a practice of disciplined submission to the market. Traders were explicitly trained to leave all affect and individuality outside the space/time zone of trading. This included such private distractions as personal problems and financial difficulties, but also events in the public arena, including the impact of their trading on world markets. Perhaps more surprisingly, it precluded any narrative of gains or losses. Traders were trained to forget about the consequences of each trade, and in particular how to take a loss, exit from it and move on to the next trade. Traders who lacked discipline were at risk because they personalized their success or failure, bringing their desires and convictions into the market, investing in particular positions and thus failing to exit from them quickly enough, instead of following the objective movements of the market. Traders who could not divest themselves of a personal history, those caught up by the affect of engagement, were likely to suffer further losses as the market punished them for their lack of discipline and objectivity. So extreme is the denial of experience and of the materiality of the world that traders here, as elsewhere, count their gains and losses in ticks, a measurement that separates transactions in the market from money and the exchanges required for the necessities of everyday life. Money is dematerialized to conform to an economic logic that exceeds human experience (Zaloom, 2005: 258–61). The market is elusive, it is a dematerialized presence on the screen, and yet its existence is imagined as going beyond the material. The market possesses a truth: it is always right. It is spoken about as the highest authority; as one of the managers was reported as saying: 'We don't know value. Only God knows value' (Zaloom, 2005: 251).

The reference point for many of our actions and knowledge practices often lies in a final utopian moment in the
distant future, and this is both enabling, because it animates agency (hope as an ultimate goal), and disabling,
because it evacuates the possibility of a realizable near
future (hope as a method) in favour of a model of coping
with the present while wishing for a change that will sweep
everything before it. Guyer has recently discussed how a
commitment to the immediacy of the present combined
with an orientation to a very long-term horizon has evacu-
ated the field of the near future – the middle range – as a
field of intentional action. It has been eclipsed by an
amalgam of 'fantasy futurism and enforced presentism'.
Guyer has in mind here the way that immiseration, debt,
crushing work routines, declining healthcare systems and
much more have eroded many people's ability to envisage
and plan for the future, to hope within the arc of their
lifetimes for a change for the better, to take charge of their
fate. This has been accompanied by an exponential increase
in membership of evangelical and prophetic movements
around the globe, as well as a turn towards other forms
of spiritualism (Guyer, 2007: 426). The rise of such religious movements is often said to be connected to poverty
and disadvantage, and also to popular longings for a different kind of world, for a more meaningful life, but these
alone are not sufficient explanation for a dramatic turn to
what has been termed post-secular spiritualism. Belief in
end times, for example, is about a mode of being rather
than a literal belief in the end of the world. It is about
re-enchantment, about new forms of the ethical imagination, of identification, technologies of self and modes of
being in the world. These are very particular forms of
satisfaction and they arise in contexts where religious and
prophetic movements are resolutely modern in their epistemological claims and in their use of new technologies.
What modern religious and spiritual movements comprehend is that identification and the cultural production of

collective identities are powerful tools for mobilization. What is mobilized here is a form of self-stylization, a transformation of self that allows for its insertion into history – apocalyptic though that temporal frame may be – and finds through the agency which results a form of moral empowerment, a reason for hope.

Guyer suggests that the rupture that emerges between enforced presentism and fantasy futurism is one that is located not at the level of the system, but at the level of the subject. Indicative of this is the idea of a present that is dominated by events, events that are reconfigured as involving violence, rupture, exclusion, exception. In such accounts, lived time gets squeezed out, it is impossible to create a sense of continuity and community with a predictable future when your life is governed by events that are not of your making. However, as Joel Robbins points out, we need to enquire how and why the world has come to appear to us and to others in this way; we need to reflect on the fact that in this moment we are inclined to rely on thinkers who focus on events and exceptions and are attracted to framing these phenomena in messianic terms – thinkers such as Agamben, Badiou, Žižek. Once again, in this moment we need to be alert and ask ourselves whether this form of critical thought, with its commitment to a kind of standoff between the present and the future, generates the sort of critical thought that will open up novel models of the good life, and engenders the kinds of plans and interventions that will move us, however slowly, towards an improvement in our current circumstances. Will it provide a method for hope, for something realizable, just off the page (Robbins, 2007b: 434–5)?

I think that Robbins's question is an urgent one, and not least because the default position in these theories is one of abjection. The entanglements of the pleasures of self-stylization and self-transformation with the perils of the market and messianic thinking should not blind us to the pleasures, desires and satisfactions at work in these contexts. New theories, new ways of being and imagining engage with the ethical imagination and through imagined relations with others – God, the market, *homo economicus* – lead to novel ways of approaching social transformation. It is a curious feature of many contemporary theories of self-stylization and self-transformation that they are themselves modelled on a specific theory of social change. Management techniques and business schools focus on the production of skilled, flexible, networked, globalized selves, generating a model of the type of enhanced and dynamic citizen that fuelled part of Tada's hopes for the future. Like Tada, this subject is self-willed. In earlier forms of its instantiation, management techniques emphasized rationality and objectivity, but these gradually morphed through ideas about leadership, responsiveness and emotional intelligence into a subject that is produced in and through environments where learning is a continuous activity, with an emphasis on knowledge produced through affect and fantasy, and 'a commitment to tapping the fruitfulness of the contingency of the event'. Through this form of 'instrumental phenomenology', subjects emerge as part of a world that is uncertain, indeterminate and risky, but also creative, entrepreneurial, connected and full of potential. It is a world 'continuously on the brink', not of apocalypse, but of becoming (Olds and Thrift, 2005: 274–5).

This notion of a subject that is finely tuned to the capitalist marketplace, constituted through the modes of its insertion into history, made real by its complicity with the alterity of the future – 'tapping into the event', 'going with the flow', 'moving with the times' – draws attention to the fact that, while we must always attend to cognized models and the interpretive talk the ethical imagination makes possible, we need to pay heed also to the importance of affect, performance and the placement and use of the body. If we return briefly to the world of financial traders, we note not only their construction of the market as an authority, perhaps even a God, but the complex procedures of mental and physical discipline required for trading, and for interacting via technology with the market. Zaloom records not only the paring down of the self, the preparation for engagement with the market that requires a stripping away of thoughts, identifications and desires, but the constant physical readiness required to monitor and register its every movement, its mood, its character. Traders become immersed in the flow and movement of the market (Zaloom, 2005: 261–7). 'You are part of the market, you notice every small shift, you notice when the market becomes insecure, you notice when it becomes nervous' (Knorr Cetina and Bruegger, 2002: 180). The market becomes a life form, a living environment which the trader never completely inhabits, but cannot afford to be separate from. The market, as mediated through the computer screens and other technological devices, becomes a complex other with whom the self is strongly and obsessively engaged (Knorr Cetina and Bruegger, 2002: 162). Through its object forms, it provides evidence of its agency and capacity, threatening not just to 'punish' those who do not maintain discipline, but also responding to inattention and failure with terrible violence. As suggested by one trader describing his losses: 'I got shafted, I got bent over, I got blown up, I got raped, I got stuffed/the guy stuffed me, I got fucked, I got hammered, I got killed' (Knorr Cetina and Bruegger, 2002: 176). This is a form of self–other relation that permits no easy separation between subject and object, between self and other. Financial trading is an institutional context which depends on specific rearticulations of the self, on shifts in forms of subjectification. But such shifts are only partly self-willed; they are also fuelled by fantasy and affect, by processes of visceral identification, desire and longing.

Political Ecologies and the Hopes of Democracy

There is no small irony in the fact that the financial crisis of 2008 ushered in a new wave of thinking about economic actors, agency and rationalization. Suddenly, the super-rational, maximizing calculators were replaced both in academic discourse and in the public imagination by a vision of individuals – and anthropomorphized markets – as driven by affect and emotion, most evidently panic and anxiety, but also more worrying atavistic emotions, such as greed. All at once, visceral politics were on the agenda, and expanded notions of motivation and agency foregrounded sensation rather than logic. We can readily understand the errors of under-resourced families desperate for cheap credit and the promise of being able to own a home, but how might we explain the cavalier miscalculations of investment bankers and other financial brains? Of course, long before the credit crunch arrived, the rational, self-interested character of *homo economicus* was already being undermined by different groups of social scientists. Behavioural economics, for example, and theories such as 'nudging' – encouraging consumers and citizens to act in certain ways – had been widely discussed by academics and policy makers well before the financial world tilted on its axis (see Lunn, 2008; Thaler and Sunstein, 2008; Ariely, 2009). The reality is not only that people often act against their own self-interest – that is, irrationally – but that economic decision-making is strongly influenced by other people. It should not be a surprise then to discover that economic theories are themselves influenced by broader ideas about how people conceptualize and relate to their environments. For example, Richard Bronk's *The Romantic Economist* (2009) discusses the links between Romanticism and economic theories, demonstrating how sentiment and imagination provide a guide for thinking about the connections between people and their worlds, and in consequence proffer a more useable set of economic theories.

If 'a sense sublime of something far more deeply interfused' has begun to penetrate economic theory, this is true also of theories of the subject more generally in the social sciences and humanities. Subjects quite suddenly – but not at all surprisingly – have become relational, affective and ecological. These ideas are not entirely new either. Theories of the embodied, sentient actor long predate the most recent discussions on affect and emotion which anyway draw on earlier philosophical discussions about vitalism, as well as on Deleuzean-inspired notions of becoming, via circuitous routes that go back to Spinoza and move forward by way of Bergson, William James and Merleau-Ponty. These complex genealogies are important, because there is no single definition of affect or unified theoretical approach. But what is attractive about philosophies of affect – and runs like a golden thread through them – is their inflection towards freedom, autonomy and singularity, and their consequent move away from social construction, normativity and constraint. What they share is a commitment to 'eschew the politics of negativity' and melancholia characteristic of poststructuralist and deconstructionist theories (Braidotti, 2002; 2006), and a desire to embrace 'an optimism of the intellect' (Harvey, 2002: 17). The hopeful promise they convey, as I argued in Chapter 1, is the capacity of embodied experience and affective states to refuse and/or exceed social subjection and social constraint (Hemmings, 2005). The implication is that there is a part of us that is not captured by the system, something that both comes before and exceeds language, social norms and social structures; and therein lies the possibility for change and transformation.

Academic theories of affect, and their associated theories of the subject, have little direct impact on the lives of ordinary people, except and insofar as aspects of behavioural psychology and behavioural economics are incorporated into social practices and social discourses, via such routes as marketing, consumer participation, social policies and media content design. However, their underlying philosophical assumptions are evidently lifted from the world and returned to it. Affect theory has found particular purchase at a time when alternatives to capitalism seem elusive – as discussed earlier – and when the political will to address issues of common humanity – climate change, environment, unjust wars – has seemed sorely lacking. For example, relational views of the political subject make much more sense when we are confronted by a particular kind of collective politics, one in which 'we are all in this together'. Given the extent and the scale of social inequality around the globe, this togetherness is a sham, but it is a powerful sentiment. It links national imaginaries – 'we the people' – with those of humanity on a planetary scale. This was one of the reasons for Obama's enormous appeal ahead of the 2008 election, with his implicit message, 'together we can change capitalism'.

Politics have always been about affect: the power of the crowd, the charismatic leader, the rumour mongers. A number of commentators have made much of the emergence of new forms of citizenship tied to specific modes of affective politics. These emergent publics are bound up with technological developments and new political imaginaries because new means of connecting people create new interpretive communities, make new ways of seeing possible. These emergent socialities take many forms, supplementing existing ways of addressing and participating in the political, creating new forms of political ontology. Political and social theorists emphasize that today's younger generations are much less likely to engage with traditional political channels and institutions, and are much more motivated by 'ad hoc, contextual, and specific activities of choice', such as new social movements, internet activism and transnational policy networks (Norris, 2002: 222). In the identification and mobilization of these political choices, the media and other forms of technology play a crucial role. As the domain of the political shifts and expands, new political ontologies emerge as a consequence of shifts in subjectification, and these plate-tectonic movements are not just in the character of subjectification, but in its processes also, and the ways it engages the ethical imagination, providing new horizons for self–other relations.

It has been said that one of the effects of the hypercommodification of difference within contemporary capitalism has been an explosion of identity movements – ethnic, regional, indigenous, religious, gender-based – each following the logic of self-willed subjectivity, autopoiesis in its collective manifestation. The broader context is a set of interconnected processes where the amplification of demands for recognition connect to the possibility of proliferating identifications, which in their turn are undergirded by the media, and other new means for the construction and circulation of images, fantasies and ideas. Mediation speeds up and intensifies emotional attachments to identifications, while new technologies of self-extension, new ways of seeing and doing, make them more sensate, immediate and affective (Bolter and Grusin, 1999). The emotional and affective dimensions of self-recognition and self-identification have shifted the grounds for political engagement, and technology has provided novel spaces for building, narrating and regulating particular futures based on new forms of relationality and technologies of self.

Consequently, technologies provide for new forms of sociality based on affirmation and radical/intensified relationality, as I argue in Chapters 5 and 7. The affect expressed through, and made possible by, these intensified forms of relationality opens up emotional and cognitive vistas of possible futures, ways of overcoming failure. They generate horizons of hope. But they also provide, through their collective agency and imagination, a sense of empowerment, a form of critique, a way of speaking back to power. This is reflected not just in the forms of political agency pursued, but in the kinds of knowledge that are sourced and authorized. Conventional channels of information dissemination are distrusted, circumvented and parodied. Henry Jenkins has argued that recent research suggests shown that young people under the age of 30 find that the entertainment media rather than traditional journalism more fully reflects their perspectives on current events. The suggestion is that they get the majority of their information about the world from music videos, rap songs, live sketches – such as *Saturday Night Live* and *Bird and Fortune* – stand-up comedians and the plots of prime-time dramas and gags on sitcoms. Politics has become a form of popular culture, where fan expertise is applied to civic responsibilities (Jenkins, 2006: 235; see also Corner and Pels, 2003; van Zoonen, 2005).[4]

YouTube, for example, is a space in which new forms of cosmopolitan citizenship are emerging, where participants are both producers, consumers, critics and distributors, and where they can represent themselves and engage with the self-representations of others. In this space, popular music plays a particularly crucial role – as it has arguably always done – moving and intensifying reactions, connections and sentiments, and linking the experience of individuals directly and sensuously to that of larger social and political collectivities (Burgess and Green, 2009: 81). The financial crisis of 2008 produced a huge number of remixed songs and parodied musical forms which were uploaded to YouTube. For example, a video appeared there in 2008 of two masked musicians, one with the face of Gordon Brown and the other with that of George Bush, performing a number entitled 'The credit crunch anthem' to the tune of 'Candle in the wind'.[5] The song located responsibility for the financial crisis in the sub-prime catastrophe in the US, parodied UK government responses, criticized them for bailing out the banks using public funds, and quite straightforwardly suggested that the 'fat cats' would prosper at the expense of ordinary families and taxpayers.

Goodbye Bradford & Bingley[6]
And though I never banked with you at all
It's nice to know my taxes will save you when you fall.

And you were very generous
Self-certified mortgages you gave
£50 billion in personal loans that can never be repaid.

And it seems me banks live their lives
Throwing caution to the wind
Never banking on liquidation when the rain sets in

And I would like to know who
Is gonna feed my kids
My credit burned out long before the repayments
    ever did.[7]

As important as the lyrics was the tune of the song, and
its own history, most especially the way it had served to
connect the emotions of many individuals to the collective
outpouring of grief after the death in 1997 of Diana, Princess of Wales. The clear sentiment was of another 'national'
institution biting the dust as a result of the indifference
and callousness of those in power. Interestingly, the words
of Elton John's repurposed song for Diana – 'And your
footsteps will always fall here / Along England's greenest
hills. / Your candle's burned out long before / Your legend
ever will' – referenced not only the great nationalist hymn
Jerusalem, but William Blake's original poem with its reference to the overweening power of industrialization as
against ordinary working people, and the now largely
forgotten fact that thousands of millworkers adopted the
song as a socialist hymn in the early twentieth century.

A conscious knowledge of the full history of the song
was not necessary for its appreciation and enjoyment. The
credit crunch anthem might be a clear example of 'we
the people', but its political message was plain. As one
blogger noted: 'Here's some advice to avoid recessions
like the credit crunch / don't borrow money if you can't
pay it back!' Another 'credit crunch song', posted in Sep-
tember 2008, elicited the following comment: 'This should
be played instead of a report on the 10 o'clock news.'[8] In
January 2009, Astroturf posted a song titled 'Lehman bros
and financial crisis revisited song'.[9] It explicitly referred to
the tide of hope that had carried Obama into office, and the
failure to carry through on that promise: 'So Barack came
in and easily took the crown / But markets shrugged and

still came tumbling down'. It generated a debate about responsibility for the deficit and the relative economic performance of Democrat versus Republican administrations. More poignant were the themes of loss of trust in the government, in its ability to protect its citizens, and in the capitalist system more generally. What songs such as these show is that popular music is a good way to convey issues and people's responses to them, a way to galvanize critique and find a voice, a means of expression which derives from and generates affect, and through technology and ease of access spreads quickly and exponentially. It should be said that political satire is one of the oldest genres of expression, and has often been viral in nature, as in the case, for example, of sixteenth- and eighteenth-century satirical pamphlets in England. What is new is the reach of such satire: its easy, multi-user production, its immediacy and scale. As a form of political critique, YouTube is magnitudes faster than troubadours and pamphlets. What is different also is the multiply mediated, participatory culture of contemporary politics.

The shape of what counts as 'the political' is changing. Politics now intersect with and are continuous with the production of new social imaginaries which are themselves not so much about ideational forms or ideologies as about emergent socialities. Information technologies provide us with further examples. In Egypt in April 2008, young activists used Facebook and SMS messaging to organize protests against rising food prices, high rates of inflation and unemployment. The government moved swiftly against them and this made international news. One of the attractions of the April 6th movement, as it came to be called, was that it was not part of mainstream party politics. Interviewed at a protest, one young man said: 'I am involved in no parties, never. I just go to Facebook events, wherever they are. I'm in the Facebook party' (Shapiro, 2009). Forms of social networking such as these, and the exchange of views and information on blogs, have changed the dynamics and organizational forms of political action.

In November 2008, a Facebook group in Saudi Arabia helped organize a national hunger strike against the imprisonment of political opponents and in February 2008 activists in Colombia used Facebook to organize demonstrations against the FARC insurgency.

Governments cannot ban sites like Facebook without alerting a large group of people who use those sites for mundane activities – like posting images of their pets – and whom these governments cannot afford to radicalize (Shapiro, 2009). However, political protests such as the April 6th movement tend to lack unified leadership and organizational structures, making it easy for governments to move against them, but also, and perhaps more worryingly, for interested others to capture them. Washington took a keen interest in the April 6th movement because State Department officials believe that social-networking software, such as Facebook, has the potential to become a powerful pro-democracy tool. The State Department even created its own group on Facebook, called Alliance of Youth Movements, and in December 2008 it brought together a group of international online activists with representatives from Facebook, Google and MTV for a three-day conference in New York (Shapiro, 2009). The subsequent result is an alliance between 'individuals from technology companies, media, the NGO community and digital activists from around the world', providing 'a global network that aims to support and sustain campaigns for nonviolent social change that harness 21st century tools to safeguard human rights, promote good governance and foster unprecedented civic empowerment'.[10]

What gives this form of politics traction in people's minds, what gives them hope, as opposed to the old form of politics, is that this is citizenship as a form of shared sociality in contrast to the traditional hierarchies of political representation and control. In this form of politics you represent yourself and your shared convictions with others. This is politics as inclusion, rather than as exclusion and exception, and it is seductive. Suddenly, instead of disillusionment with politics, a paralysing apathy, there is a community of like-minded people, who share ideals and feel that they can make a difference. Such connectivity often takes concrete form, when mobile phone footage or user-produced material suddenly erupts onto the international stage through YouTube or social networking sites, alerting hundreds of thousands of people across the globe to political oppression, violence and human rights violations. Once again, emotion and affect are harnessed to political agency through the stimulation of information and powerful images. The comments generated by these materials – through blogs and other participatory means – from concerned political agents from around the world increase the sense of belonging, of being part of something bigger: 'we the people' on a planetary scale.

The internet is routinely used now by individuals, human rights activists, NGOs, government agencies, political parties, environmental activists and constituencies of concerned cosmopolitan citizens of all kinds. But, there is no easy correlation between freedom of expression, access and dissemination, and actual political freedoms. Commentators have suggested that this is because the collectivities that gather on YouTube or Facebook or other internet sites are ill-equipped to deal with the power of the state, and are temporary in nature, forming and disbanding as political issues come and go. A politics of fashion. This may seriously underplay the importance of these forms of political mobilization and critique, but it does emphasize that 'voice' is rarely enough to bring about change.

For example, when Neda Agha-Soltan was shot during protests in June 2009 following the Iranian elections, images of her death were uploaded to YouTube and broadcast all over the world. The video has been seen by more than 2 million people. In June 2010, Iran jammed satellite broadcasts in an attempt to stop people from seeing a new film telling Agha-Soltan's story on the Voice of America Persian TV network. The 70-minute film, made by Mentorn Media for HBO, rapidly went viral in Iran in the run-up to the anniversary of the disputed 2009 elections that triggered the protests. But, leaving aside government anxieties about the possible impact of the film, reports suggest that in 2010, only one year after images of the mass protests against the elections were beamed around the world and across cyberspace, public dissent and demonstrations had all but disappeared in Iran. The state acted swiftly to maintain control over internet and social networking sites. To date, hundreds of civil society activists remain in jail, at least nine have been executed and more than 250 have been tried and convicted.[11] A very small proportion of those who saw the video of Agha-Soltan's death are currently actively pursuing an interest in political reform in Iran. She was nominated *Time* woman of the year (2010), and commemorative jewellery has been made honouring her, but none of this has so far resulted in significant political change. In fact, Iran is arguably more closed than before.

More recently, events in Tunisia and Egypt in January and February 2011 showed that successful political protests are those that link online activism to ordinary offline organizing (Radsch, 2011). In both countries, sustained street protests by hundreds of thousands of people, many of whom were without smart phones, internet connections or Facebook accounts, backed up by well-coordinated internet and mainstream media coverage, generated a huge outpouring of public rage which built into a momentum for genuine change. Both the President of Tunisia, President Zine al-Abidine Ben Ali, and the President of Egypt, Hosni Mubarak, were forced out of office. Blogging, networking and SMS messaging had been used for political protests in Egypt for several years, and were particularly successful in reporting police brutality and torture and sexual assault, stories that would otherwise not have come to light. Photosharing via Flickr allowed activists to get photos out fast, and Facebook and Twitter were powerful citizen tools for disseminating information (Radsch, 2008; Etling et al., 2009; Fahmi, 2009; Fahmy, 2010). Many bloggers were between 20 and 35 years old, and internet users found citizen journalists and internet information to be more truthful and reliable than mainstream media in a situation where the media was strictly controlled. However, as the failure of the original April 6th movement demonstrated – although the members of that movement were to play a significant role in the events of 2011 – digital activism is not enough unless it is linked to mass protest and broad public support, and change did not come about in Egypt until that moment arrived (Radsch, 2011). Equally important, however, was the role of the Al Jazeera network, where many well-informed Egyptian and other Arab journalists covered, recorded and supported the street protest and the digital activism. Al Jazeera continued to broadcast around the world when the internet and mobile phones were blocked. As one analyst opined, Al Jazeera acted 'like a real political party in a place where political parties have little or no legitimacy' (Echchaibi, 2011). The outcome was a shift in media influence between the Arab region and previously dominant western media. In short, digital activism and social media did not bring about the revolution as some claimed, but they did play a major role in coordinating and informing tens of thousands of citizens, articulating their aspirations, fears and hopes, as well as influencing how the outside world saw these momentous events.

Interestingly, the state's ability to co-opt and control new information technologies is widely discussed in relation to oppressive regimes, but it is equally problematic elsewhere. Building on the lessons learnt in the 2004 presidential campaign, Barack Obama and his team made very good use of social networking sites and SMS messaging during his 2008 campaign, raising more than $650 million, and creating many different media outputs that were viewed millions of times. His dedicated YouTube channel contained more than 1,800 videos and more than 50,000 images regularly updated via Flickr (Thompson, 2005; Harris, 2008). Internet campaigning is, of course, cheap.

But, the real breakthrough is not just in terms of viral marketing strategies; it is in the way imagined relations with others provide novel forms of social transformation. For example, John Edwards – a Democratic candidate for the presidential nomination early on in the 2008 race – would reportedly routinely whip out his mobile phone at campaign rallies and ask people to punch in a short code accompanied by the word 'today'. This harvesting mechanism produced lists of mobile phone numbers to which his staff could send fundraising appeals. More importantly, it sent an obvious message, 'I now have your number on my phone', a tangible connection between candidate and supporter carrying, albeit unrealizable, expectations about social relations, even a form of intimacy.

Power – political and corporate – is now fully behind affect. Emotionality – the ability to convey affect – is currently the pre-eminent sign of credibility and integrity in public life (Thrift, 2008: Part III). It works through an ideology of relationality and belonging: 'We are in this together'; 'I am one of you'. The withdrawal of emotion or the inability to demonstrate it is instantly interpreted as a sign of mendacity or of indifference to the public, a refusal of a relationship. Today's new citizen consumers are more socially connected, but as Henry Jenkins (2006) and others have noted, they are simultaneously more fragmented, attached to niche communities of like-minded individuals where their views or preferences are reinforced rather than challenged. The manipulation of affect, and sentiments of belonging and identification, are massively enhanced by new technologies, and intensified in ways which make them very difficult to resist. The management of affect is now a form of governmentality – as it has always been in certain times and places – and while we recognize that the shape of the political is shifting, and new political and social imaginaries are emerging, bringing with them forms of political ontology, we should perhaps be wary of appeals to hope, and a little more sceptical of the limits of the arts of the possible.

What Obama understands is the importance of the internet for building a political brand, creating a sense of connection and engagement, and driving forward new mechanisms to allow people to self-organize and do the work of the party. In 2008, more than 2.9 million Americans signed up to get an 'exclusive' text message from Obama revealing his choice of vice-president. Nearly 900,000 MySpace users called him 'friend'. My.BarackObama.com, built by Facebook co-founder Chris Hughes, encouraged visitors to set fundraising goals and set up groups – they eventually numbered more than 35,000. Obama targeted niche communities online and through their social networks – Glee (lesbian, gay, bisexual and transgender), BlackPlanet, Eons (baby boomers), MiGente (Latinos) and many more – creating a sense of outreach, connection and identification: 'You are one of us' (Harris, 2008). In July 2010, Obama hit 10 million Facebook followers, pipped at the post by Lady Gaga who managed it two days before![12] That's a 10-million-person contact network ready and waiting for his re-election bid in 2012. A real cause for hope.

− 7 −
New Passions for Difference

In this chapter, I begin by discussing how theories of affect intersect with new developments in biology and informatics. My focus once again is on questions of social change and their links with recent theories and critiques of the acting subject. While the philosophical antecedents of affect theories are very varied (see Thrift, 2008; Braidotti, 2010), what connects them is an affirmative politics that not only situates the human subject among the vital forces in the world, but locates it within sets of complex relationalities – networks, rhizomes – that cannot be figured through linear causal explanations. The discursive tropes and imaginative parameters of affect theory link humans with other living things, and with the natural world, by focusing on the sensations, emotions, feelings and intensities that are not captured by power and systems of signification. They thus reconnect the human subject to the material world and its potential for change and transformation. I explore how ideas about self–other relations – here understood across the human/non-human, subject/object, human/machinic, human/inhuman interfaces – influence our ideas about the acting subject, and ultimately the kinds of people we would like to be, as well as our visions of the good life. I suggest in the course of the chapter that we should see these theories as instances or examples of the ethical imagination, a way of rethinking self–other relations animated by the hopes, desires and satisfactions of social and cultural theorists. There is much to recommend these theories, but I return to the question of how readily they can take account of people's own projects of self-making, including their desire to transform the conditions that make them. My repeated question is what significance and value should be given to people's own theories of self-making and social transformation, given that we know they play an important part in driving social change?

Hope Springs Eternal: Affect and the Resurgence of 'Life Itself'

As we saw in the last chapter, politics is about passion. It is not just about refiguring society or the way we live and are governed, but also the kind of people we are allowed to be. Those who are denied self-representation, those who are represented by others, have through history very often been denied the category of human or been seen as less than human (Spivak, 1988; Butler, 2004b: 140). It is not just a question of who will be heard, but of the ability to claim membership of the category human, to be within the definition of what Paul Rabinow (2003) has termed 'anthropos'.

What does it mean to be human? The category of the human has in some recent debates on political ontology and power seen a reduction to the notion of life or life itself. Giorgio Agamben discusses how the invocation of states of emergency suspends the citizenship rights of subjects, changing their ontological status, and forcing them into a zone of suspension where they are neither political subjects within the community, nor yet truly outside the rule of law. They are suspended between life and death, not so much outside representation as disallowed within it, reduced to 'bare life' by being excluded from meaningful social existence (Agamben, 1998). This form of exclusionary power is not unique to our times, but the reduction of the socially constituted human to biological life is given powerful new force by the development of biotechnologies which extract information and resources from the human body reconfiguring its values and orientations. Genetic materials, for example, can now be mass-produced outside the organism and this is only one of the many ways in which human life can transcend human limitations, and indeed the category of the human itself. The state plays complex new roles in the management of these fresh resources and the knowledge and power regimes that govern them, giving novel meanings to established notions of sovereignty as the control over life and death (Franklin and Locke, 2003; Biehl, 2005). Modern biopolitics entails a very particular configuration of the relationship between the life sciences, biotechnology, capital and regimes of governance and regulation, as life itself is extracted, patented, mediated and interpreted. Capital invests in the labour performed routinely by cells, proteins and DNA (Clough, 2007: 25), and seeks to capture through patents and intellectual property rights the essence of vitality, the ceaseless, restive capacity of life generation (Parisi, 2004). This makes some bodies more valuable than others, and distinctions of ethnicity, race and gender become further commoditized at the sub-individual level (Clough, 2007: 25–6). Additional distinctions get drawn between lives or forms of life that are valuable and those that are not (Franklin et al., 2000). Biopolitics moves beyond established modes of governing bodies and populations (Foucault, 2007; 2008), and becomes a fetishized form of biosecurity; what emerges are new configurations of inclusion and exclusion, well-being and immiseration. The 'new biopolitical body of humanity' takes shape within a political form where the drive to enhance 'life itself' is matched only by the capacity to destroy it (Agamben 1998: 9; Mbembe, 2003).

'Life itself' is a curious term, acting as both supplement and remainder. Its introduction into social theory comes by circuitous routes, but the timing is of course not coincidental. Technological innovation has produced new forms of knowledge through experimentation with the structure and organization of bodies, matter and life, introducing what has been termed a post-biological threshold into 'life itself' (Clough, 2008). Through digitization and other information technologies, biological materials are transformed into information. Stem cells and other biological materials become data banks of potentially profitable information which are stored, distributed and commercialized just like other information-based resources (Thacker, 2006; Cooper, 2008). Biology is no longer contained within the walls of the body: it has spilled out into the world in new forms, complicating the relations between human and non-human. The distributed and intermediated nature of entertainment, social interaction and community building increasingly means that the self/subject is similarly no longer confined to the physical individual, but is mediated by and distributed across the human/non-human interface, as we saw in Chapter 5 (see Turkle, 2009). One of the key developments here is the way that new technologies allow us to record and visualize the interiors of bodies, but also to categorize and re-categorize the information we uncover. Technologies of security and surveillance record bodily affects, and deploy neural imaging, iris recognition and a host of other techniques designed to distinguish those who are acceptable from those who are not – a biopolitics of racism that goes well beneath the skin (Clough, 2008: 19; Amin, 2010).

Part of what has happened here is a shift in our understanding of biology. As Sarah Franklin has so cogently argued, the decoding of the genome promised us the 'blueprint' for life, but what we got was the more complicated science of epigenetics. Most biological accounts of 'the crucial pathways that determine one biological form or another' recognize that gene expression is not determined by the underlying DNA sequence because non-genetic factors play a crucial role in gene expression (Franklin, 2006: 169–70). What this has focused attention on is cellular potential: life's in-built potential for differentiation. Transbiology – stem cell science, regenerative medicine, tissue engineering – is the domain of practice that will create 'new health and wealth products harnessing the pluripotent power of recombinant regenerativity' (Franklin, 2006: 71). How exactly cellular potential will create new goods and markets is not necessarily known, but the drive is one of directed hope. The promise goes further with synthetic biology, where the combination of biology and engineering is poised to design and build new biological functions and systems that are not found in nature. In both cases, the desire is to harness the generativity of life, to mimic nature, only better. Scientific breakthroughs and new technologies are always animated by the circulation of hopes, some futuristic, some outlandish and some that will come to pass: can we transplant human hearts, enable 65-year-old women to have babies, implant parts of pigs into human brains? Science is very often poised between fact and fiction. New research requires imagination to direct its efforts, but we do not always know where discoveries will lead. This makes science an unstable endeavour, as much driven by affect as by reason.

However, the biological sciences are not just engaged in trying to mimic life – in the sense of creating it or supplementing it or regenerating it – because biology has always meant both 'the thing itself' and the 'knowledge of what it is'. Consequently, we need to remind ourselves of the overdetermined mechanisms through which biological knowledge, biotechniques and biology 'itself' reshape each other (Franklin, 2006: 168). Life is changing as it gets remade, but the structure of biological knowledge comes more closely to resemble biological processes or 'life itself'. The mimetic enfolding of biological knowledge with 'life itself' is driven by developments in technology which have made informatics constitutive of contemporary understandings of matter and life (Thacker, 2004). The recognition of matter's capacity for self-organization – that is, its capacity to make forms – propels a search for the smallest form – the cell – from which all of life can be generated. This generative reduction can be seen in other areas of science. Ben Anderson (2007) points out, for example, that nanotechnology both reduces life to matter, to atoms and the different relations between them, while simultaneously offering the promise of new, altered and apparently limitlessly generated materialities.

This strange amalgam of reduction and limitless alterity has quite recently become a feature of the social sciences and humanities. The figure of 'life itself' has emerged in the form of affect, bound up with processes of becoming. Affect as a term and as an analytic concept has many different philosophical and disciplinary roots or points of emergence, as I suggested earlier, but it does herald – in its most positive form – some kind of rapprochement between the social, human and natural sciences, while simultaneously, of course, undermining these distinctions. Practitioners in the social sciences and humanities, like those in the natural sciences, emphasize that the phenomena they study are relational, indeterminate and subject to constant processes of differentiation.

> Advances in the fields of genetics and biological sciences, mathematics, quantum physics, the physics of small particles, neurosciences, narrative analysis, media and information theory have contributed to this epistemological shift. In its wake, a common ontology linking the social and the natural, the mind and body, the cognitive and affective is beginning to appear, grounded in such concepts as assemblage, flow, turbulence, emergence, becoming, compossibility, relationality, the machinic, the inventive, the event, the virtual, temporality, autopoiesis, heterogeneity and the informational. (Blackman and Venn, 2010: 7)

What is significant about the 'affective turn', as it is often termed, is that it wishes to signal not just new theories, but new ontologies, as the above quote demonstrates, while simultaneously embedding humans in the world in such a way that they are not different in kind from any other natural phenomena. This is achieved by a strange process of analytic reduction from human, to the body, and on to autonomic responses that precede cognition and perception, and finally to the circulation of intensities and potential energies. It is these energies and intensities that constitute affect. What drives intellectual interest here is a reworked vitalism, a commitment to the world's 'striving potential', to an 'expressive multiplicity', 'to the constitutive power from which the lived world unfolds' (Colebrook, 2010: 77–9). There are several ways in which theories of affect are enfolded and animated by hope, but one of them is the manner in which such theories are based on 'multiple articulations of excess embedded in the category of the "not-yet"' (Anderson, 2006: 748).

The 'not-yet' finds expression in affect theory in the entwined notions of relationality and indeterminacy, and central to both of these is the pivotal philosophical commitment to the virtual. 'The body is as immediately virtual as it is actual. The virtual, the pressing crowd of incipiencies and tendencies, is a realm of *potential*' (Massumi, 2002: 30; emphasis in the original). As described in Chapter 1, the capacities to affect and to be affected are the stuff of everyday life, but they are not held to reside in or be possessed by a body or subject. Instead, they move through relations, shifts, pulses and intensities, sometimes described as viral or imagined as contagious. Affects encompass the human and the non-human, life and matter, they function through non-lineal connections and combinations, circulating, finding expression and being qualified in context. The movement of affect is therefore indeterminate, vital, open to diverse possibilities, always part of a series of virtual tendencies, incipiencies, potentialities that ceaselessly generate differences and divergences in what becomes actual. Humans are not only corporeal and material, but they are, in their relations with the world, a form of potentiality actualized. This applies not only to humans as part of the larger category of 'earth' others – human and non-human – but also to individuals, each of whom is a 'singularity, a particular actualization of potentialities (Braidotti, 2010; Colebrook, 2010). Humans are at one with the world, and through their embodied relation to it, affects function as the inbuilt potential for generativity and for change. The model for this is modern biology:

> Behaviour can no longer be localized in individuals conceived as preformed homunculi; but has to be treated epigenetically as a function of complex material systems which cut across individuals (assemblages) and which transverse phyletic lineages and organismic boundaries (rhizomes). This requires the articulation of a distributed conception of agency. The challenge is to show that nature consists of a field of multiplicities, assemblages of heterogeneous components (human, animal, viral, molecular, etc.) in which 'creative evolution' can be shown to involve blocks of becoming. (Ansell Pearson, 1999: 171)

Within this general framework of human subjects as actualized potentialities, there is no generally agreed-on definition of affect – across a diverse range of literatures a variety of interpretations and approaches are collectively assembled and offered – but one evident principle is that embodiment involves a generative capacity as opposed to a finished form.

> A germinal or 'implicit' form cannot be understood as a shape or a structure. It is more a bundle of potential functions localized, as a differentiated region, within a larger field of potential. . . . The playing out of those potentials requires an *unfolding* in three-dimensional space and linear time-extension as actualization; actualization as *expression*. (Massumi, 2002: 34–5)

The notion of 'expression' Massumi employs draws directly on biological metaphors, specifically the notion of gene expression and the multiplicity of potential biological forms within a specific environment. However, Massumi's underlying logic lays emphasis on the autonomy of affect.

> Affects are *virtual synesthetic perspectives* anchored in (functionally limited by) the actually existing, particular things that embody them. The autonomy of affect is its participation in the virtual. *Its autonomy is its openness.* Affect is autonomous to the degree to which it escapes confinement in the particular body whose vitality, or potential for interaction, it is. Formed, qualified, situated perceptions and cognitions fulfilling functions of actual connection or blockage are the capture and closure of affect.... Actually existing, structured things live in and through that which escapes them. Their autonomy is the autonomy of affect. (Massumi, 2002: 35; emphasis in the original)

The continuity – the ceaselessness – of affective escape is the guarantee both of vitality and of changeability. However, in Massumi's work – as elsewhere in writing on affect theory – it is not evident how the generative capacity of human embodiment and the autonomy of affect is to be analysed in specific contexts, whether physical, environmental, social or cultural.

Consequently, although theories of affect reconnect the embodied human subject to the material world and its potential for change, it is not always obvious how we should reconceptualize human agency as part of a more generalized redistribution of agency among heterogeneous components. One enormously influential body of work that has sought to address this question is actor network theory (ANT). ANT has been particularly influential in sociology and anthropology, where it has reanimated work on the agency of non-human actants. The scholarship of Bruno Latour (1993; 1999; 2005) has been foundational to this approach, and its resonance with the philosophy of Gilles Deleuze probably owes much to their joint inspiration derived from the sociology of Gabriel Tarde (Candea,

2010). ANT suggests that there are no differences in the abilities of technology, humans, animals and non-humans to act.

> For the thing we are looking for is not a human thing, nor is it an inhuman thing. It offers, rather a continuous passage, a commerce, an interchange between what humans inscribe in it and what it prescribes to humans. It translates the one into the other. The thing is the nonhuman version of the people, it is the human version of things, twice displaced. What should it be called? Neither object nor subject. An instituted object, quasi-object, quasi-subject, a thing that possesses body and soul indissolubly. (Latour, 1996: 23)

Anthropology has taken up this approach as a way of arguing against approaches to material things that privilege language, and as a means to explore the intelligence of things (e.g. Miller, 2005; Henare et al., 2007), as part of a larger project of criticizing subject–object dualisms from a number of perspectives (e.g. Strathern, 1988; Moore, 1994; 2007; Keane, 1998; Gell, 1998).

A focus on the agency of humans and non-human actors in hybrid networks forcibly returns us to the question of shared worlds and to how we as humans share those worlds with a variety of non-human others. From this perspective, it is possible to reconceptualize affect as a translocal or background process that potentializes difference across space and time. It is, by definition, non-deterministic and non-linear; it is the potentiality of form that works as a set of intensities that come before, yet set up, and are realized in, specific encounters between bodies, between the human and the non-human, life and matter. 'Affect is as good a general term as any for the interface between implicate and explicate order. Returning to the difference between the physical and the biological, it is clear that there can be no firm dividing line between them, nor between them and the human' (Massumi, 2002: 37). Things, like humans, have affects. It is in the nature of our encounters in the world that they involve many things that are non-human. At the core of the idea of encounter is the notion of contagion implied in the very term affect, the relational connection and movement between things. The effect of such movement combined with intensity is a series of actualized forms, understood not as objectified, but as affective in their own right, as singularities (Massumi, 2002: 252). The result is a decentring of the human subject, a recognition that the subject is formed through a series of encounters which it does not author or control. In fact, it is no longer the origin or the only source of agency. Agency becomes a distributed capacity which no longer coincides with the human subject. The consequence is a foundational break – not just epistemological, but ontological – in the understanding of what it is to be human.

The Triumph of the New or the Remaindered Subject?

What is productive about theories of affect is their attention to somatic experiences and forms of communication that are outside or below the registers of language, their insistence on how bodies keep in touch with other bodies, and with the different elements of the material worlds they inhabit. Particularly appealing also is the potential affect theories offer us for thinking humans and other living creatures within the same frame, their insistence on shared worlds. As Rosi Braidotti, among others, makes clear, we have now to contend with biotechnological societies in which the post-human – everything from the machinic distribution of consciousness to the remaking of human life outside the human body – is part of the worlds we inhabit and share. Consequently, we have an ethical requirement to rethink what our 'bodily materialism' means in this new context (Braidotti, 2006: 33). I have no quarrel with any of this, but like many critics (e.g. Hemmings, 2005; Navaro-Yashin, 2009), I am dismayed by the idea that in attending to such matters we should eschew previous theoretical stances completely. Many versions of affect theories emphasize contingency and indeterminacy, and champion this as though no other theoretical work on this topic had even been done. Equally, they emphasize that embodied experience has the capacity to transform, as well as exceed, social subjection, but this is hardly a new realization in the human and social sciences. While affect theories reasonably critique poststructuralism and social constructionism for their over-dependence on language and signification, as well as their inability to address the residue or excess in life that is not socially produced, it is not as though existing work on embodiment, desire, emotion and sensation has never made these arguments before. What might arguably be new is not affect – its existence, its forms, its potentialities, its capacity for creating relations – but, as Braidotti suggests, the way in which new developments in biology and informatics have the capacity to alter the kinds of relations we have with the others – human, post-human, inhuman – with whom we share our worlds.

However, even allowing for this, we do need to question the degree to which we should celebrate affect as the sole solution to these challenges. Should the critique of humanism and the philosophy of the subject be pursued to a point where we want to shift from a subject-oriented philosophy to an object-oriented one (Latour, 2005; Henare et al., 2007)? from a focus on language and signification to a non-representational theory (Thrift, 2008)? from a concern with human subjectivity to the autonomy of affect (Massumi, 2002)? We might readily agree that the analysis of affect should not be constrained by the frames of subjectivity, human agency and language, but should we have to choose between ostensibly competing paradigms, between subjectivity and affect, as though they cancel each other out (Navaro-Yashin, 2009: 14–15)?

This is particularly pertinent when we consider that much of the literature on affect contains certain pre-theoretical assumptions that are very problematic, and I would like to focus on just three. The first is that these theories locate affect both in relations between things (human, non-human, post-human), at what we might term the 'trans-individual' level, and in a moment or place before intentional consciousness, the 'sub-individual' level (see Venn, 2010). The assumption is that affect, however it is defined – sensation, energy, intensity, pulse – is the same kind of thing/propensity/effect at both levels. A second and related assumption is that since affect comes before thought and is the product of a relation to an environment broadly understood, it is a form of practical attunement to a lived world that is autonomous of propositional intentionality (Barnett, 2008: 188–9). This explains why many contemporary approaches to affect are extremely hostile to poststructuralist approaches to power, to theories of social construction and, in particular, to discursive and psychoanalytic theories of the subject and subjectification (see Hemmings, 2005). The third assumption concerns what may be called the 'tyranny of the present'. This arises from the relentless flow of generativity that is at the core of theories of affect, the ongoing nature of life as it is, the inherent potentiality of encounters and relations between bodies (human, non-human, post-human) and their environments. In much of the writing on affect, this is accompanied by a triumphalist claim to newness, a paean to an anti-foundationalism rooted in germinal life, a consolidation – or is it confusion? – of the vitality of affect with freedom itself. Generativity is not, however, the same thing as social transformation.

Cyprus

A rather good example of all three of these difficulties and how they are connected to the problem of forced choice between paradigms is provided by Yael Navaro-Yashin's brilliant analysis (2009) of how Turkish-Cypriots have managed to live with the houses, land and objects they appropriated from the Greek-Cypriots during the war of 1974. The situation described by Navaro-Yashin involves thousands of displaced people losing their land, animals, houses and personal belongings, and leaving behind their neighbours and friends to move to the north of Cyprus, where they were allocated land, houses and belongings to use and own that had just been abandoned by members of the other community who had been forced to flee in the opposite direction. The Turkish-Cypriot refugees were left with the memory of social relations with their former Greek-Cypriot neighbours, as well as the specific forms of fantasized sociality invoked in the imagination through inhabiting their abandoned houses and belongings (Navaro-Yashin, 2009: 2–3).

Navaro-Yashin's analysis focuses on the affect generated in a community that is forced to recreate its life and livelihood on the basis of spaces and objects belonging to another community designated as the 'enemy'. What is it like to live on someone else's land, to equip your house with furniture acquired on looting expeditions? What kinds of affect do these spaces, places and objects discharge, and what happens to the subjectivity of Turkish-Cypriots living in these expropriated spaces? Navaro-Yashin frames these questions within two broad lines of enquiry: what is the role of environment in engendering subjective feeling? and what is the intersection between subjectivity and affect (2009: 4)? Navaro-Yashin makes good use of theories of affect and ANT in her analysis, but she explicitly critiques the way scholarly practice associates innovation with refuting or outright discarding previous theoretical approaches and concepts. Instead, she asserts the right to dwell – as her Turkish-Cypriot informants do – with ruination and abjection, in the sense that she wants to retain certain theories of human agency, sit amidst 'the piles of debris of knowledge production', and discover what can be learned from retaining the apparently ruined and disavowed within the framework of analysis (2009: 7–8).

The point being made by Navaro-Yashin is that Latour's 'network' theory, and indeed affect theories in general, envisage subject–object relations, encounters and/or the movement of affect as being located in or rolling out across abstract terrains of space and time, when what is really required is an analysis of such processes in terms of the specifics of historical contingency and political affect. Contingency and affect have specific histories in given contexts, in part because of the human character of human agency. In any given context, not all potentialities have the same degree of potentiality – a point of which epigenetics is fully cognizant. For example, the 'assemblage' of subjects and objects that Navaro-Yashin has studied in Cyprus has been created through acts of violence, the erection of a border and the exclusion of specific persons and things, Therefore, it is not possible to theorize the resulting 'network/assemblage' or the movement and intensity of affect across it, as if it simply pertains to some all-inclusive, constantly differentiating, transcendental phenomena (2009: 9). Navaro-Yashin discusses how ANT seeks to return to 'things' as a way of unseating the primacy of language, representation and the anthropocentrism of social constructionism. But, while she acknowledges the validity of certain critiques of anthropocentrism, she makes the perfectly sound anthropological point that objects are not involved with human beings in ways that exclude language, and therefore it is not possible to cleave exclusively to a theoretical framework which, as a consequence of its direct attack on social constructionism and the 'linguistic turn', just casts this inconvenient problem aside. She argues perfectly reasonably that there is no reason why a turn to things should involve a turn away from language, nor indeed any particular rationale as to why a focus on the agency of non-human actants should force analysis to exclude human agency (2009: 9–10). I would go further and suggest that while affect clearly cannot be completely captured by language, or indeed be figured within the frame of the 'linguistic', nor can it be fully dissociated from language or signification. The materiality of signs and their non-arbitrary character (e.g. Moore, 1997; Keane, 2007) means that language cannot be so readily divided from the world, and it is worth recalling that as speaking/writing it is an everyday embodied practice, and one that is generative of affect.

Navaro-Yashin's critique begins with ANT, but she extends it to affect theory more generally. She discusses Deleuze's and Guattari's notion of the rhizome, with its intentional images of multiplicity and generation as a vehicle for figuring the movement of affect and its potential for creating relationality, and their metaphor of the 'plateau' as a boundless space across which potentialities unfold. She tellingly contrasts their imagined abstractions with the landscape of Northern Cyprus, which is far from infinite, and full of borders, fences, bullet holes and scrap. These ruins of human agency can be 'kept, lamented, cherished', and they leave marks on the memory and on the unconscious. Ruins extrude affect, but affects are projected onto them by human subjects (Navaro-Yashin, 2009: 14). Affect is not just a series of intensities and differentiating impulses that coalesce at certain moments into singularities – people, objects, landscape – because the experiences, feelings, sensation and emotions generated by relations and encounters in this specific environment are taken up and spun out in discourse – symbolized, politicized and projected forward as well as back in time, impacting on the processes and experiences of subjectification. Navaro-Yashin takes away a lesson from her own encounter with the rusty environment of Northern Cyprus, and it is one that inclines her to keep a range of theories on board, in order to mesh theories of affect with those of subjectivity, language and materiality (Navaro-Yashin, 2009: 14–15).

We can understand quite clearly in this context how analysis would be impoverished by having to choose between paradigms. However, we can also see that, while affect can be said to operate at the sub-individual and the

trans-individual levels, it is not the same kind of intensity/
energy/potentiality – however we might define it – at both
levels. Once affects enter into human relations – whether
between humans or between humans and heterogeneous
others – they are qualified, redirected and re-energized by
human agency and human subjectivity. The ruination of
Cyprus is experienced as melancholy, not as an autonomous energy. Human subjects recognize affect, register it
in their bodies and in their psyches, have views about it
and turn it to their own purposes. If we have an ethical
requirement to rethink our bodily materialism, then this
must extend to other human subjects' views of and
responses to affect. In a similar vein, we can see that it is
not enough to talk about affect and relationality as a kind
of 'practical attunement to a lived world' and certainly not
one that is independent of signification. Human agency
does not always 'go with the flow' or act in ways that are
adaptive. As the case of Cyprus shows, humans very often
act in ways that set out to cut themselves off from their
environments, to distance themselves from established
ways of being and doing, to work against the grain, to
redirect the movement of affect, to engender in others new
hopes, desires and satisfactions. Political oratory, affective
marketing and behavioural economics are all perfectly
good examples. There are many ways in which humans
interfere in the generativity of life – biology being only
one of them – but they also have the capacity to imagine
relations and forms of life that do not exist in nature, and
yet become crucial for human functioning and well-being.
What affect theories sometimes seem in danger of forget-
ting is that it is not possible simply to reject theories of
epistemology in favour of 'new' ontologies because many
of the theories of knowledge we need to take account of
in the social sciences and humanities concern theories of
being, and being in the world, held by people other than
academics. These theories are about the kinds of beings/
selves/persons people hold themselves to be, and they are
subject to considerable degrees of variation and change

across space and time (see Chapter 3). Any theory of the relation of being to the world therefore has to take account of historical ontologies and the way they refigure the relation of human beings to the worlds they inhabit (Hacking, 2002). It seems likely that not all aspects of human agency are exclusive to humans, but it is equally the case that some aspects of human agency are specifically human. There comes a moment in which, while recognizing the value of theories of affect and the welcome significance they give to embodied experience in the world and the agency of non-human actants, we might want to retain some aspects of those theories which specifically pertain to human agency, to human experiences of subjectification, and to human aspirations for social transformation.

Egypt

By way of example, I would like to turn to another empirical case based on material from Egypt, where the analyst explicitly explores the limitations of the feminist poststructuralist subject for analysing forms of self-making that depend on attention to the transformative potential of somatic affect. What makes this case material particularly relevant – and worth citing at some length – is the way it simultaneously reveals the inadequacies both of feminist accounts of a subject constructed in language and of theories of relationality that depend on a radical decentring of the human subject. Saba Mahmood (2005) has studied an urban women's mosque movement that is part of a larger Islamic revival in Egypt. In this movement, women from a variety of socioeconomic backgrounds provide each other with instruction on Islamic scriptures, and on the social practices and bodily comportment required for the cultivation of piety and the ideal of the virtuous self. Although Egyptian women have always had a measure of training in piety, the movement represents the first time in Egyptian history that such a large number of women have gathered publicly in mosques to teach one another Islamic doctrine, and it has had an substantial impact on the male-centred character of mosques, Islamic teaching and theological reasoning (Mahmood, 2005: 2). This development has been facilitated by women's enhanced mobility and sense of entitlement brought about by greater access to education and employment in postcolonial Egypt in the past 40 years. According to participants, the movement emerged in response to a perception that religious knowledge, as a set of principles and as a form of conduct, had become marginalized in the context of secularization and westernization, reduced to an abstract system of beliefs with no direct bearing on daily living. Consequently, the aim of the mosque movement is to educate ordinary women in the virtues, ethical capacities and forms of religious reasoning conducive and foundational not only to religious duties and acts of worship, but also to styles of dress and speech, the consumption of entertainment, financial and household management, the care of the poor and the character of public debate (Mahmood, 2005: 4). What kind of theories of social transformation and the subject are required to understand these processes of self-making?

As Mahmood points out:

> The Pious subjects of the mosque movement occupy an uncomfortable place in feminist scholarship because they pursue practices and ideals embedded within a tradition that has historically accorded women a subordinate status. Movements such as these have come to be associated with terms such as fundamentalism, the subjugation of women, social conservatism, reactionary atavism, cultural back-wardness . . . associations that, in the aftermath of September 11th, are often treated as 'facts' that do not require further analysis. (2005: 4–5)

One of the difficulties in analysing the mosque movement is that women are seen to assert themselves in domains previously thought of as male-dominated, but the mechanisms and idioms they use to gain access, particularly the emphasis on feminine virtues such as shyness, modesty and humility, are grounded in discourses that are normally associated with subordination to male authority.

Historically, feminist theories have explained such conundrums with reference to a variety of premises and theories, including false consciousness on the part of the women concerned and/or their internalization of patriarchal norms. Alternatively, they have seen women's activities as part of a larger strategy, involving the reworking of structures and discourses in line with their own interests, needs and agendas – that is, as a form of covert resistance. Explanations based on women's strategy have the advantage at least of providing a space for women's agency, as well as a mechanism for explaining why women appear to connive with their own subordination, while simultaneously resisting it (Mahmood, 2005: 6–10). However, explanations of this sort also locate women's agency within a binary logic of submission or subversion, constraint and freedom, and Mahmood enquires as to whether feminist theories of agency are of any value in trying to make sense of the agency of the women in the mosque movement and their practical ethics of piety – and if not, where can we turn? She suggests that we cannot just claim that the women are reinforcing patriarchal norms, because the movement itself is a challenge to the male-dominated space of the mosque and of Islamic pedagogy. Also many of these women have changed their lifestyles and their values to conform to a notion of the virtuous Islamic self against the wishes of their families, husbands and other kin. Equally, we cannot refer unproblematically to tradition and culture. The mosque movement is not a return to tradition in any straightforward sense, but a complex and sophisticated response to the challenges of modernity, because one of the consequences of secularism has been the politicization of religion. One of Mahmood's informants makes the point eloquently:

It is the project of the government and the secularists to transform religion into conventions or customs. . . . [W]hat they do . . . is to turn religion into no more than a folkloric custom! An example of this is the use of the veil as a custom rather than as a religious duty. When you . . . look at Egyptian society right now and see all these women wearing the hijab you must remember that a lot of them wear it as a custom, rather than a religious duty that also entails other responsibilities. These people are in fact no different than those who argue against the hijab and who say that the hijab is [an expression of] culture [and therefore a matter of personal choice], rather than a religious command. So what we have to do is to educate Muslim women that it is not enough to wear the veil, but that the veil must also lead us to behave in a truly modest manner in our daily lives, a challenge that far exceeds the simple act of donning the veil. (2005: 50–1)

What this respondent stresses, as Mahmood points out, is the distinction between a practice that is Islamic in outward appearance, a matter of custom and culture, a marker of ethnic identity, and a religious practice that is part of a larger project of realizing Islamic virtues, and which contributes to an ethical disposition or set of practices that transforms one's everyday living and one's relation to God. Individual responsibility and choice – a particular relation to the self – are key parts of the movement. The practices of the movement 'presuppose the existence of a divine plan for human life – embodied in the Quran, the exegetical literature, and moral codes'. Members of the movement are called upon to recognize their moral obligations through readings of the divine texts and other literature. This form of morality, while recognizing the authority of God, relies on no other authorities to enforce moral codes, but rather is based on a strongly individualizing orientation that requires each person to adopt a set of embodied and affective practices for shaping moral conduct and realizing aspects of self. 'Each individual must interpret the moral codes, in accord with traditional guidelines, in order to discover how she, as an individual, may best realize the divine plan for her life' (Mahmood, 2005: 30–1).

As Mahmood makes clear, women's agency cannot be simply glossed as internalizing patriarchal values or following tradition, but nor, in its adherence to an elaborate code of moral ethics and embodied practices connected to the realization of a virtuous self through an acceptance of God's will can it be viewed as liberatory in any of the senses of that term that we understand from Marxism or feminism. It is not, in short, intending to raise consciousness to overthrow a system. Unlike some of the more militant and state-centred Islamist activists, the mosque movement does not argue for the promulgation of the shari'a. They therefore do not confront the project of secularization from the perspective of the separation of religion from the affairs of state; rather, their goal is to introduce ethical practices by which individuals can judge their conduct in diverse realms of ordinary life, such as employment, domestic duties and leisure. They refuse secularism's confinement of religion to its own sphere, one circumscribed by private devotion and morality. They seek a space in which the ethics of self are realized through the practical embodiment of a living faith.

What Mahmood draws attention to is that it is not only that feminist theories of agency are insufficient to explain the agency of these women, but that their ethics of self pose a fundamental challenge to feminist theories of the poststructuralist subject. The poststructuralist subject differentiated by race, class and ethnicity evolved in response to the presumed autonomy of the transcendental liberal subject, and as an antidote to the universal pretensions of feminism. Its purpose was to move away from a notion of the self-authored subject and to take account, through the notion of difference, of different constructions of subjectivity across space and time. What Mahmood demonstrates is that if we actually enquire into the creation of historically specific forms of subjectivity and how they require and make possible particular forms of self-reflection and embodied practices, we see quite clearly that the forms of subjectification relevant to the women in the mosque movement are not captured by a notion of the subject constructed in and through difference whose agency is modelled on aspirations to liberation and freedom from authority.

The micro-practices which are the concern of the women's mosque movement have not emerged as a result of the redirection of critical knowledge alone; they are not just the conceptual result of new modes of reasoning, but have been provoked by the specific challenge posed by trying to reorient the body and the senses, in order that women can reorganize their daily living in accordance with Islamic standards of virtue in a world increasingly characterized by values perceived as inimical to their maintenance and flourishing (Mahmood, 2005: 55–6).[1] The participants' engagement with classical commentaries on the Quran and the Hadith are not geared to an abstract understanding of these texts or of religious injunctions, but at changes in practical conduct and affective responses that will transform day-to-day living. As Mahmood makes clear, this practical ethics reverses the usual analytic move from an interior self to outward behaviour, so instead of seeing bodily comportment as an expression of ideas, values or norms, the women concerned see affective bodily engagement as a means to build up or body forth the architecture of the virtuous self. From this perspective, it is the physical and material character of ethical practice that requires attention and analysis, as well as the power and potentiality of the affects produced though such practices. The gestures, styles and physical practices that materially embody one's relation to a moral code are not a contingent, but an absolutely necessary means of understanding the relation that is established between the self and structures of authority, between what one is, what one desires and the kind of work one performs on oneself in order to realize or embody a particular mode of being, a specific form of self as agent (Mahmood, 2005: 120). For example, the women in the mosque movement discuss how they hone and nurture the desire to pray through the performance of ordinary activities during the day, such as cooking, cleaning, running an errand, until that desire becomes a way of being, second nature. They do not assume that the desire to pray is the simple following of a moral precept or that it is natural, but that it must be created through a set of embodied disciplinary acts. Thus, desire is not the cause of moral action, but its product. The techniques through which pious desires are created involve a reorientation of the body and the senses, avoiding seeing, hearing or speaking about things that may weaken faith and engaging in forms of orientation and practice that strengthen the ability to enact obedience to God's will. This is a cumulative process, and its purpose is to make desires emerge spontaneously in accord with pious Islamic conventions, to make required behaviour natural to one's disposition in a manner that makes that behaviour inseparable in any a priori way from one's feelings (Mahmood, 2005: 124–31).

A tradition of moral cultivation – the development of habitus through assiduous practice of acts until they take root in one's character and cannot be expunged – is not exclusive to Islam. As Mahmood discusses, the term habitus is familiar in the social sciences from the work of Pierre Bourdieu, who uses it to describe how the objective conditions of society are learned through practice and unconsciously inscribed in the bodies and dispositions of social actors. However, the practice of ethical formation that the women in the mosque movement are engaged in is rather different, as Mahmood illustrates, because it is not just a question of acting virtuously through the enactment of the logic of social structures; it is also a matter of how one practises virtue, and with what degree of intention, commitment and emotion. Constant vigilance and monitoring of one's practices is a critical element in this tradition. Mahmood's point is that we need to attend to how a person acquires a habitus or we will lose sight of how specific kinds of bodily practice 'come to articulate different conceptions of the ethical subject, and how bodily form does not simply express social structures but also endows the self with particular capacities through which the subject comes to act in the world' (Mahmood, 2005: 138–9). For the women in the mosque movement, what is at stake is a particular conceptualization of the role the body plays in the making of the self, one in which the outward behaviour and practices of the body constitute both the affective potential and the means through which the interior self is realized (Mahmood, 2005: 159).

It is possible to explore more easily what Mahmood means by this by turning to another ethnographic study. Charles Hirschkind's discussion of cassette sermons in Egypt demonstrates how Islamic ethical traditions give explicit recognition to forms of bodily or somatic learning and cultivation (2006: 79). He argues that cassette sermons are now an omnipresent part of urban life in many Middle Eastern cities, and as part of what is termed the Islamic revival, they punctuate people's daily lives, forming part of their work and leisure, reformulating the experiences of pleasure and boredom, and structuring Islamic argumentation and debate. As a form of portable technology, they have extended the reach of theological reasoning into everyday life and political discussion, but contrary to the standard view that they are simply part of processes of militant indoctrination, Hirschkind argues that they act as vehicles for honing the sensibilities and affects of pious living. The focus of ethical attention is not on hearing the tape, but on listening carefully, that is, 'to incline one's ear towards the preacher's words' (2006: 70). This is part of what Hirschkind terms the physiology of the Quran, the affective-kinesthetic experience of a body opening towards God and permeated by faith. One writer describes the effect of hearing Quranic verses:

> [W]hen the true people of faith, the people of the eternal and deeply rooted doctrine hear the verses of warning their

flesh trembles in fear, their hearts are filled with despair, a violent angst shakes their backs, and their hearts become intoxicated with fear and dread. But if they hear the verses of mercy and forgiveness, their chests are opened and relaxed, and their hearts are left tranquil. (Badawi, 1996: 11–12; cited in Hirschkind, 2006: 75)

This moral physiology is immensely enhanced by the mimetic and repetitive gestures and forms of bodily comportment that attend listening, where each sermon requires a vocal or sub-vocal response from the listener, who may also follow the words by moving the lips and the tongue, inclining the body towards the sound of God's voice through the preacher's words, catching the breath to follow the passional movement of the argument, gesturing and moving in affective kinesthetic response. The listener ideally seeks not only to understand God's message, but to make himself or herself an adequate 'host' for the word of God, bodying forth the attitudes and expressions corresponding to the verses heard or recited (Hirschkind, 2006: 79–81).

What are acquired through listening are not only forms of moral reasoning and argumentation which operate at the level of language, interpretation and ostensible reference, but also somatic and affective potentialities which form the vital substrate of the techniques and practices of the self (Hirschkind, 2006: 81–3). 'Sermons impart not simply moral lessons, but affective energies of ethical potential' connected to practices and modes of sociability, inhabiting the world in a way appropriate to the faith and among a community of believers (Hirschkind, 2006: 98). Here we see that feminist and poststructuralist theories of agency based on performativity, where the potential for transformation is tethered to the iterability of the sign and shifts in referential meaning, would only capture a small part of the form, content and intent of these forms of agency. However, what the work of both Mahmood and Hirschkind also demonstrates is how affective and somatic responses and potentialities are involved in new forms and processes of subjectification. But these new experiences and mechanisms of subjectification cannot simply be understood as forms of attunement to a lived world that is autonomous of language and propositional intentionality. The ethical disciplines of Islam connect their practitioners to debates about virtue and the common good, to the duties of Muslims as Egyptian citizens, to the challenges faced by diverse Muslim communities around the world, and ultimately to God.

The Return of the Subject?

Historically, specific forms of subjectivity require and make possible specific forms of self-reflection: they operationalize particular forms of desire, anticipation, expectation, pleasure and satisfaction. They engage with specific forms of the ethical imagination. They create not just new forms of knowledge, but new ontologies. Affect as intensity, as relentless germinal creativity, connecting and reconnecting relations between humans, the non-human and the inhuman, does not just traverse these ontologies – which are also epistemologies (Moore, 2007; 2009b) – creating forms of expression and unique singularities, but encounters them as part of an 'environment' in the broadest sense, and one which has been touched by specific forms of human agency (Venn, 2010), including the virtual world-making powers of language, cognition and imagination. In much writing on affect theory, the problems of human ideas, dispositions, politics and forms are treated as if they are all versions of 'past states' or 'memories' that somehow alter intensities and create new possibilities for differentiation. But the situation is surely more complex when we observe that bodily and affective practices articulate different conceptions of the ethical subject, and when we are forced to recognize that the historical ontologies we are confronting incorporate other people's theories of affect. In such contexts, we surely cannot work with a theory of affect that is disembedded, just a life force, moving relentlessly across space and time, making connections between bodies, objects and matter.

The life that 'may not have "me" or any "human" at the centre' (Braidotti, 2006: 40) does have one aspect of its complex philosophical history (see Braidotti, 2010) that bears reflection here, and that is the analytic shift from difference to differentiation. One way to characterize this is to use the example of feminism. Insofar as the twentieth-century feminist project begins with the differences between women and men, then analyses the differences within the category of 'woman' to arrive at a reformulation of the differences within the female subject, it has drawn variously and unevenly on poststructuralist theories of difference and the non-unitary subject, as well as on deconstructionist theory and its notions of différance and deferral as constitutive of the postponement of meaning in language and signification. In this movement, we have a genealogy – more explicitly developed elsewhere, notably in the thought of Derrida, and inflected in much of twentieth-century philosophy – that emphasizes differing and deferral as constitutive of life, of the worlds we live in, and of the kinds of people we have become. At the most general level, instability and indeterminacy are not exactly new either in life or in theory, and they have always provided – in various measures and subject to certain qualifications – spaces and opportunities for change. What is significant about affect theory is that notions of difference and deferral have morphed into ideas about differentiation, processes of becoming that are not just based on biological metaphors but are intrinsic to the movement of affect and to the generative, unfolding character of 'life itself'. In this sense, theories of affect foreclose other philosophical positions and theories because they are not just proffered as a comprehensive theory of life, but actually encompass 'life itself'. The vitality of affect exceeds all the forms of its manifestation – preceding and transcending them – enduring across space and time, acting as a surplus, the remainder in which nothing can remain.

This shift from difference to differentiation is significant because in analytic terms it displaces the effects of agency and power – as affect theorists intend – but in so doing it raises the question of how and to what degree we need to engage with these issues at all. From a biological point of view, life is nothing without the forms it takes, and logically this would suggest that we cannot be satisfied with a theory that focuses only on the generative capacities of 'life itself', without a consideration of the resulting forms and their subsequent impact on their 'environment'. In the human and social sciences, this problem is more acute, since we also need an account of the meanings and values particular life forms attribute to themselves and to their existence as a 'form of life' at specific moments in time. Affects may attach to many things and, clearly, they may do so in unexpected and unforeseen ways. It is one thing, however, to suggest – quite reasonably – that affect is not necessarily under human control – much of it is not human in any event – but it is quite another to insist on the absolute autonomy of affect. Affects move through the body and the psyche in ways that are registered, but also interpreted. Such interpretation does not necessarily involve the bringing of sensation or experience into language; it may be only a matter of a somatic reorientation. However, human agents create associations – affective and otherwise – between feelings and contexts. These associations may be outside language, but given the historical nature of our ontogeny, they are rarely outside signification. The psyche forms itself through its relations to a world that both precede and exceed it, but the subject comes into being by distinguishing itself from that world, while simultaneously identifying with objects (human, non-human, inhuman) within it. Processes of differentiation involve ascribing meaning and significance to objects in the world, becoming part of a world of social meaning. Affects are introjected into the psyche and reprojected onto the world, and the self is formed by making relationships. Affective responses have deeply sedimented personal and social histories, and while they can surprise us, they are rarely random. Affective and somatic responses to the recognition of socially inscribed differences are good examples. In 2010, France banned the wearing of the burqa, a contentious move that generated heated debate, but at the crux of the matter was a view, viscerally held by many, that women should not cover their faces. Many complex theological and social arguments were advanced on both sides, but what the burqa debate reveals very clearly is that affect attaches differentially to bodies in social contexts: some bodies pass unremarked and others do not.

Our bodies have formative histories, but none that are wholly independent of the psyche even though they may be recalcitrant to self-reflection and linguistic articulation. We come into being in a world of relations that are not of our making, and our ongoing affective responses to them tie our personal histories to social and political horizons. This means, I suggest, that any encompassing theory of affect requires a theory of the subject and of subjectivity. As it turns out, a number of theorists are committed to some form of subjectivity, but its formulation is increasingly opaque to critique, and unsurprisingly the provocations hinge on the difficulties of power and agency, and how we might imagine new forms and practices of the political. For example, Nigel Thrift suggests that a theory of affect requires a theory of subjectivity because all sorts of corporate and state institutions are now trying to formulate bodies of knowledge relating to affect – and to life itself – and that these will inevitably require or be constitutive of new political practices. He does not provide details of what these new political practices are or might be, but simply states that for those who view these developments as worrying or inclining towards 'a new kind of velvet dictatorship', the response should be to produce 'relevant analyses and political agendas' (Thrift, 2008: 188).

In answering the question, 'What then is the agenda?', Thrift suggests that perhaps it is a form of 'emotional liberty', but acknowledges that this must surely go beyond a naive expression or maximization of individual emotions. Given the propensity for emotive politics to be harnessed to political identities and populist causes, this must surely be right (e.g. Berlant, 1997; Marcus, 2002). Thrift proposes a 'navigation of feeling' comprising three 'moments'. The first entails choosing 'the richness of the possible processuality, irreversibility and resingularization'. The second involves a 'politics of hope'. The third is more concrete and resolute, and requires the kind of disciplinary exercises and ethical reflexivity encompassed by Foucault's 'the care of the self'. Thrift's interest in Foucault's critique connects to a set of propositions about embodied practices. He points to 'skillful comportment' (2008: 189), a way of being open to receiving new affects, where the political project is to make receptivity into the 'top ontological good' (2008: 190). Learning to be open is associated here with a version of the Foucauldian project that would take up 'reparative positions' against negative affects, allowing the release of positive energies. This process is part of a broader project of expanding the 'potential number of interactions a living thing can enter into' (2008: 191). Thrift sets these ideas of embodied practice within the context of a 'microbiopolitics' that operates between action and cognition, a recognition of the way gestures, movements, stutters, laughter and the like 'move the world of concepts and belief' (Connolly, 2002: 43–4; cited in Thrift, 2008: 192).

Rosi Braidotti, like Thrift, wants to engage in an affirmative politics that entails the production of social horizons of hope (2010: 42), and, like him, she wants to maintain a residual connection to 'practices of the self' or self-styling, in large part because of the demands that politics makes on agency. Braidotti's nomadic subject is certainly based on an understanding of life/zoe as relentlessly generative, and actualizes a Spinozist-Deleuzean ethics based on a non-unitary and post-individualistic vision of the subject (Braidotti, 2006: 117). However, within this project, and contrary to what she terms the Kantians, the ethical instance is not 'located within the confines of a self-regulating subject of moral agency, but rather in a set of interrelations with both human and inhuman forces . . . The notion of the non-human, the inhuman, or post-human emerges . . . as the defining trait of this new kind of ethical subjectivity' (Braidotti, 2010: 44). Braidotti, like Thrift, seeks to open up subjectivity to sets of new relations that transcend the human, and she associates this move with a 'qualitative leap' in ethical liberty, where the anthropocentric other is no longer the privileged site or horizon of otherness (2010: 48): 'The fundamental political desire is for an individual and collective reappropriation of the production of subjectivity, along the lines of "ontological heterogenesis". . . . We need actively to desire to reinvent subjectivity as a set of mutant values and to draw our pleasure from that' (Braidotti, 2006: 123). The ethical ideal is to privilege co-dependence rather than recognition, and it is a laudable one.

Braidotti's allegiance is to a Deleuzean concept of rhizomes as a way of overcoming the negativity of Hegelian dialectics, with its own roots in the traditional equation of political subjectivity with critical oppositional consciousness (Braidotti, 2010: 44; 2006: 178). The core of Braidotti's argument is that oppositional thinking does not need to be tied to the present by negation, but should emerge out of 'different premises, affects and conditions'. These differences are the consequence of the potentialities created through forms of radical relationality with others. The result is an affirmative politics that imagines sustainable futures through mobilizing, actualizing and deploying 'cognitive, affective and collective forces' which have so far not been activated (2010: 45).

Braidotti explicitly states that her position is an anti-rationalist one, and that a subject's ethical core is not her 'moral intentionality', but the effects of the power her

actions have upon the world. The ethical good is thus
equated with 'radical relationality', the ability to 'increase
one's ability to enter into modes of relation with multiple
others', including non-human, post-human and inhuman
forces' (2010: 45). In this project, the 'other-than', the
'minoritarian' – all that had been excluded from the rational, humanist subject – women, gays, ethnic and racialized
others, the natural, animal and environmental others –
constitute the 'threshold of transformative encounters'
(2010: 46–7). Colebrook makes a similar argument:
'Minoritarian politics moves in the opposite direction from
recognition and aims to maximize the circumstances for
the proliferation and pulverization of differences'; one
should not see politics in terms of representation (women's
issues, gay rights, minority values), but 'as mobilization'
(Colebrook, 2010: 86). Colebrook, like Braidotti, views
those who figure as 'other-than' or the 'minoritarian', as
the site or locale of transformation. Her focus is on bodies,
not individuals. 'No body fully knows its own powers, and
can only become joyful (or live) not by attaining the ideal
it has of itself – being who I really am – but by maximizing
that in ourselves which exceeds the majoritarian, or which
is not yet actualized' (Colebrook, 2010: 88). Both Braidotti and Colebrook are committed to a politics of inclusion, one in which enhanced or expanded relations with
others – but specifically those previously designated as
minoritarian, and including the non-human – operate
according to a logic of reciprocity and co-dependence,
based on 'the compassionate acknowledgement of our
common need' (Braidotti, 2006: 270).

There is a new passion for difference in the writings of
these theorists, but is their commitment to radical relationality enough? If the point of reference in this political
project is the relation not the subject (Braidotti, 2010: 49),
how useful are their theories in recognizing alternative
theories of subjectivity, especially those which are simultaneously historical accounts of being, of affect, of ontology (Moore, 2009b)? The ethical intent here is recuperative,

but this privileging of a new theory of the ontological, of becoming as opposed to knowing, seems to position those who occupy the site of differences, those who figure as 'other-than', as those with whom the subject has expanded forms of relationality, rather than as those who might initiate forms of relation. As I have argued throughout this book, the ethical imagination is about the forms and means through which individuals imagine relationships to themselves and to others. It is the way we problematize the vexed question of what we share, of how we set our personal and political horizons, how we figure contemporary forms of belonging and the complex relations they entail. A truly radical relationality would have to acknowledge that the ethical imagination, with all that it implies about self–other relations, and our fantasized relations with them, is historically specific and coexists with other historically specific forms. Arguing for the decentring of the rational, humanist subject and the reinstatement of somatic engagement with the world are important moves, but they are not historically or culturally neutral. Does it not make a difference where we begin? What would it look like to begin from elsewhere?

Theorists of affect very often seem to argue that the autonomy of affect is all about what escapes the frameworks of social meaning, and yet surely we have an ethical requirement to take other people's theories of affect and ontology into account. For human subjects, affect (somatic engagement) is constitutive, but it is registered in social fields and encounters as something which is already within economies of signification, and not just as pulse, energy and intensity (Venn, 2010: 159). Life itself, and indeed affect, may be relentlessly vital, working towards differentiation, but neither has any interest in political transformation, nor even in the joy of being connected to others. Human subjects on the other hand are interested in both. They have a sense of themselves as agents, as beings who make themselves under conditions they may then choose to transform. All 'human' subjects – even if they are not individuals – must in some sense be self-styled, because for social transformation to occur they must have a sense of self in order to recognize the disparity between the hopes, desires and anticipations of that self, and the milieu, matrix or environment of which it is a part (Venn, 2010: 147). The affective subject is thus a being that requires the intelligibility of the world, and cannot encounter it outside of culture. In this sense, signification inheres in the human form of being, in its life form, and is not exterior to or subtractable from its being or from affect. One of the aspects of human subjectivity is the way it uses affectivity – somatic engagement with the world – not just for self-reflection, but for reflection also on all that is more-than-being.

Hope and desire are created by shifts in subjectification. The academic theoreticians themselves experience hopes and desires through their engagement with an alternative view of the human and the non-human subject, and they use the affect and energy thus created to drive forward a project of critique and social transformation. Shifts in subjectification create new political ontologies, as well as new forms of the political; we want to connect to others and to the world, in all its forms: human, non-human and inhuman. We want to capture something of life's relentless life force, to create an affirmative politics in the face of massive, almost super-human challenges. We recognize that we need to change ourselves in order to change our world, but this view of the co-dependence and co-constitution of all life is founded in a particular vision of responsibility for the world and for others – human, animal, non-human. It is in this sense more than a theory or a set of political aspirations; it is a form of the ethical imagination, a fantasy of self–other relations, and one that is historically contingent.

So perhaps it is too early yet to abandon a notion of the human subject marked by what is specifically human, most especially our desires, hopes and satisfactions. We need to remain critically alert. We need to explore the limits, as well as the potentialities, of these new theories of the affective (nomadic) subject. But should experience not alert us to the limitations of its moment of historical production? If earlier theories of subjectivity were about division and difference, those currently in vogue draw on images of inclusion, connection and relation. The oppositional consciousness of earlier feminist, postcolonial and Marxist subjects which animated theories of social transformation has been replaced by theories of affect that apparently do not take the human subject as their reference point, but somehow end up requiring a subject fashioned through heterogeneous, differentiating forms and sites of subjectification and engaged in a continuous process of relation with others. This affective/nomadic subject is at one with the matrix of its production. It is no longer bounded within the human body, but a hybrid involving aspects of the natural and non-human worlds, as well as informatics. A composite figure for composite times. Its grounding metaphors are life itself, ecology and sustainability. All the hope of the future, a time beyond capitalism, when the arts of the possible are realized, encompassing and encompassed by the image of the planet, wherein, like a craft with the fair wind of hope, we sail together.

Notes

Chapter 1 Thinking Again

1. I am deliberately using the Derridean term here with its intentional 'misspelling' (Derrida, 1982).
2. A similar argument about the limitations of a focus on identity has been made in linguistics (see Hastings and Manning, 2004 and Cameron and Kulick, 2002).
3. My discussion of the ethical imagination is provoked by Foucault's work on ethics, specifically Foucault (1985; 1990; 1998). I have also been particularly influenced in my thinking by two important essays: Faubion (2001) and Bernauer and Mahon (2005). However, I am not concerned here with delineating either a Foucauldian or an anti-Foucauldian theory of ethics; rather, I am interested in developing a theory of the ethical imagination as a way of taking us beyond the limitations of current theories of globalization, culture and agency.
4. Faubion (2001: 101) argues that the era of globalization is one of 'increasing intensity of problematization' because of increased information flow. My emphasis is rather different, and moves away from problematization primarily defined as a difficulty about thought or information.
5. The government of Bhutan has measured the happiness of its population since 1972, known as Gross National Happiness (GNH): http://www.grossnationalhappiness.com/. See also the report on economic performance, well-being and social progress commissioned by the President of France (Stiglitz et al., 2009). The government of the UK started asking citizens in April 2011 to rate well-being; the first happiness index will be produced in 2012.

Chapter 2 Still Life

1. United Nations Educational, Scientific and Cultural Organization (UNESCO), International Labour Organization (ILO), World Intellectual Property Organization (WIPO), non-governmental organization (NGO).
2. ILO, Convention 169, Concerning Indigenous and Tribal Peoples in Independent Countries, 27 June 1989, art. 13(1).
3. Terminology is very contentious here (see Hernlund and Shell-Duncan, 2007). FGM (female genital mutilation) is the commonest phrase used in Kenya. Female genital cutting and female circumcision are also used.
4. Ashoka is the global association of the world's leading social entrepreneurs. It promotes sustainable social change and supports social entrepreneurs.
5. Kenya ratified the UN Convention on the Rights of the Child on 31 July 1990. The enactment of the Children's Act of 2001 gave effect to the obligations of Kenya under the Convention on the Rights of the Child (CRC) and the African Children's Charter. The Children's Act is an Act of Parliament to make provision for parental responsibility, fostering, adoption, custody, maintenance, guardianship, care and protection of children and to give effect to the principles of the Convention on the Rights of the Child and the African Charter on the Rights and Welfare of the Child.

   Under this Act, a child is entitled to protection from physical and psychological abuse, neglect and any other form of exploitation; Section 127 makes it an offence for any person who has parental responsibility, custody, charge or care of any child to wilfully assault, ill-treat, abandon or expose, in any manner likely to cause unnecessary suffering or injury to health (including injury or loss of sight, hearing, limb or organ of the body, and any mental derangement).
6. After that date, World Vision withdrew from the Sibou area and the ARP went into decline, largely because the community business organizations that had devolved responsibility for its continuation lacked resources and support.
7. They also occur in other African countries (see Hernlund and Shell-Duncan, 2007).

8. The German development aid agency, Deutsche Gesellschaft für Technische Zusammenarbeit (GTZ) and The Netherlands Fund for Performing Arts (NFPK).
9. The Marakwet are one of the groups that make up the Kalenjin (see Moore, 1986).
10. For a discussion of these issues and an analysis of this song and the one that follows, see Moore, 2009b.

Chapter 3 Slips of the Tongue

1. Recent historical and postcolonial scholarship has emphasized the mutuality in constructions of the other in colonial contexts, and the fact that colonialism as a generic term occludes a vast array of historical conditions and processes. See, for example, Bayart, 2000; Dirlik, 2002; Cooper, 2005. My larger point, which I take up below, is that insofar as processes of othering are a necessary and essential condition for subjectification and self-fashioning, it is important not to assume that specific hierarchical binaries, or particular forms of alienation and abjection, always structure self–other relations. Othering, alienation and abjection all have histories.
2. For contemporary analyses of the intersections between revelation and concealment, the visible and the invisible, see Meyer and Pels, 2003.
3. Charles Taylor defines a social imaginary as 'something much broader and deeper than the intellectual schemes people may entertain when they think about social reality in a disengaged mode. I am thinking, rather, of the ways people imagine their social existence, how they fit with others, how things go on between them and their fellows, the expectations that are normally met, and the deeper normative notions and images that underlie these expectations. . . . the social imaginary is that common understanding that makes possible common practices and a widely shared sense of legitimacy' (Taylor, 2004: 23). I am in broad agreement with Taylor's definition, but my understanding specifically includes a key role for the imaginary processes of psychic life (fantasy and identification) and their foundational location in the constitution of social imaginaries. One

of the major assumptions here is that individuals consistently misrecognize themselves as coherent and self-produced, failing to recognize the otherness that is the core of identification and self–other relations. Consequently, while it is important to underline the conscious, purposive and tacit identifications with specific meanings, values and practices, it is also necessary to have regard for the dynamic processes of the unconscious. The social imaginary engages with the fantasies of the subject to structure desire and enjoyment, thus fantasies are never simply internal to the subject, but connect to relations with others and thereby engage in the construction of the social (Moore, 2007: ch. 3).

4. Mamadou Diouf (2000) makes the same point in his discussion of the Murid brotherhood in Senegal and their strategies of engaging with globalization, arguing that the antinomy of appropriation versus resistance, with its implied fulcrum of western modernity, does not capture the complexities of contemporary circumstances.

5. Here, we need to be clear that this applies to 'hybridity' understood as social science/cultural studies/postcolonial analytic category, and to its deployment in contexts where its imbrication with modernity effectively assumes specific sets of hierarchical relations and spatializations. This does not, of course, refer to those social and national contexts were the concept of hybridity has been part of lived experience and woven into nationalist discourses of identity and citizenship. As, for example, is the case in Latin America with the concepts of 'creolization' and 'mestizaje' (e.g. Anzaldúa, 1987; Garcia Canclini, 1995; Yúdice, 2003). In such contexts, the concept of hybridity, associated with cultural and racial mixing, does have a particular genealogy and a 'regional' value that also circulates through academic, arts, media and cultural milieu as a global good (Jiménez López, 2011). The recognition and analysis of regional specificities are essential, because in the European context, for example, hybridity as a sign and as a marker of cultural identity has become embedded in popular culture and celebrated through various mediations, and cultural and institutional forms. Thus it has become part of a series of identifications and possibilities for self-fashioning, and a

constitutive element of what is discussed in Chapters 2 and 7 as 'the anthropologization of everyday life', which also includes the use of cultural difference as a form of governmentality, as in policies of multiculturalism (Yúdice, 2003; Ewing, 2008: ch. 2).

6. A number of well-known studies have focused on the imitation of Europeans, national governments, and elites in dances, dress and performances across sub-Saharan Africa (e.g. Ranger, 1975; Kramer, 1993[1987]; Stoller, 1995; Geary, 1996). Mimicry is certainly a key element in such practices, but it only captures a small part of the relations of the performers to colonial and postcolonial power and its overdeterminations. It also as a concept sheds very little light on how power is perceived, experienced and negotiated by those who are subject to it, nor does it provide sure grounds for the mutuality of the constructions of power between 'rulers' and 'subjects'.

7. A number of scholars have noted that contemporary popular culture in Africa, and elsewhere is never simply about westernization or the appropriation of western fashions, because 'external' influences include such things as wahabi teachings from Saudi Arabia (Kresse, 2009), Indian films (Larkin, 1997), Nigerian films, Brazilian and South African soap operas, West Indian football and Chinese-language programmes, alongside American rap and hip-hop style. Nigeria, the Congo and South Africa are three locations for the production of images, sounds and cultural forms that have a major influence across sub-Saharan Africa and beyond.

8. I do not intend these as Kantian categories

9. In 2009, under-sea cables provided massively increased band width in East Africa, which has made participation in online communities, especially social networking sites like Facebook, and the downloading of music and films a much more accessible and a much more regular feature of people's lives.

10. See Ferguson's (1999) discussion of the perplexities of life on the Zambian Copperbelt, and Durham's (2002) helpful exploration of uncertainty and moral puzzlement in Botswana.

11. The use of 'we/our' here is fictive (see Moore, 1994).

12. Tsing's insights are powerful, but even her project is held back by a residual language of encounter: 'the cultural work of encounter emerges as formative' (2005: 12). The notion of encounter reinstates distinctions between the inside and the outside, the local and the global, quite against the intentions of the author, and so the question becomes, how can we reframe accounts of social change?

13. Just as contemporary capitalisms cannot be fruitfully analysed by reducing the analytic framework to sets of binaries, we cannot make much progress with power, inequality and hegemony by treating them as monoliths operating within binary codes. Dipesh Chakrabarty's discussion of the problem of 'history' shows how deep the roots of binary modelling are. He argues that 'history is precisely the site where the struggle goes on to appropriate, on behalf of the modern [the] hyperreal Europe . . . other collocations of memory' (2000: 37). Thus, in telling/writing non-European histories, for example Indian history, one can never get rid of a lag and an incompleteness that is written into the pre-theoretical commitments to evolutionism (and perhaps even imperialism). Chakrabarty points out that since history is the teleological narrative of the nation-state, and its true subject Europe, Indian history cannot be anything but a mimetic one (2000: 40). He argues that the way out of this conundrum lies not in rejecting modernism and its narrative forms, but in configuring alternative histories 'that aim to displace a hyperreal Europe from the centre toward which all historical imagination currently gravitates' (2000: 45). Frederick Cooper has criticized Chakrabarty for reinstituting the very binary he seeks to displace by focusing on a 'hyperreal' Europe instead of a more historical, more provincial Europe, that changes its contours and is more than a self-evident monolithic hegemonic force (Cooper, 2005: 31).

14. For example, for cultural studies, see Jameson, 1991; for psychoanalysis, see Dufour, 2007; for sociology, see Bauman, 2007.

15. Werbner argues that in analytic terms 'subjectivities may be defined as *political*, a matter of subjugation to state authority; *moral*, reflected in the conscience and agency of subjects who bear rights, duties and obligations; and *realised*

existentially, in the subject's consciousness of their personal or intimate relations' (2002: 2). He recognizes that these terms are not exhaustive. While this typology is helpful for the purposes of clarification on modes of subjectivity and forms of subjectification, it takes us no further in understanding how these modes intersect either personally or across long-run processes of social, economic and political transformation. The analytic problem is akin to the feminist desire to differentiate the feminist subject across race, class, gender, sexuality and other axes of difference, and then realizing that this impedes our ability to theorize the intersections between forms of difference.

16. Kleinman and Fitz-Henry begin by affirming the 'variability, heterogeneity, and contingency' of subjectivities, pointing out that they are forever in flux, 'fluid, contingent and open to transformation (2007: 53–5). They ground this capacity for variability and transformation in experience.

17. For a discussion of the intersections between anthropology and psychoanalysis, and the variations in the manner of addressing theories of person, self, psyche and the unconscious in feminism, anthropology and psychoanalysis, see Moore, 2007.

18. For a critique of this position, see Moore, 2007: ch. 2.

Chapter 4 Other Modes of Transport

1. With the exception, of course, of feminist and poststructuralist accounts of the non-unitary subject (for example, Braidotti, 2002; 2006). For an exception from anthropology, see Rofel, 2007.

2. For a critique of this, see Moore, 2007. For exceptions, see Ewing, 1998 and Boellstorff, 2005.

3. As Ewing argues, a theory of the creative, interactive self requires a theory of the subject if it is to avoid voluntarism on the one hand and over-determination on the other (1998: 18–19).

4. Some *gay* men and *lesbi* women do try to delay marriage, and may have anxieties about heterosexual sex, and some cases of individuals being forced into marriage or finding the marriage of a long-term partner traumatic

certainly exist (Boellstorff, 2005: 110–12). Of Boellstorff's own informants, 10 per cent stated that they had chosen not to marry, and for some this choice is correlated with class (2005: 120–1).

Chapter 5 Second Nature

1. Economic theories of rationality, utility and satisfaction are, I suggest, distinct from theories and ideas about intellectual, affective and somatic satisfactions, and their links to personal histories and social imaginaries. As described in Chapter 1, new work on behavioural economics and emotional prosperity does depend on reformulated understandings of well-being that draw on older theories of satisfaction, but seek to develop new models for social action and economic performance.
2. 'Nutter' and 'fruitcake' are both English slang terms used to refer to individuals with mental health problems and/or those whose behaviour is thought to be eccentric.
3. Internet movie data base blog, 20 December 2007: http://www.imdb.com/title/tt0410387/usercomments.
4. See Moore, 2011 for an earlier discussion of this material.
5. According to Susan Napier, when asked what impression they had gained of the country through anime, a number of respondents clearly recognized that this was not a guileless question and responded along the lines of: '[Japan is] an interesting place. Every girl under nineteen wears a sailor suit, except when she transforms into a princess, and giant robots are lurking around every corner to save/destroy the world' (2007: 185–7).

Chapter 6 Arts of the Possible

1. Keynote Address to the 2004 Democratic Convention, 27 July 2004, Fleet Centre, Boston.
2. http://nobelprize.org/nobel_prizes/peace/laureates/2009/press.html.
3. http://www.whitehouse.gov/the-press-office/remarks-president-acceptance-nobel-peace-prize.

4. *Saturday Night Live* is a live television and sketch comedy show running in the US since 1975. *Bird and Fortune* is a satirical British comedy television show focusing on current events.

5. 'Candle in the wind' is an Elton John song originally written in 1973 in honour of Marilyn Monroe, and remade as a tribute to Diana, Princess of Wales in 1997: 'Goodbye England's Rose'.

6. Bradford and Bingley is a British bank which was formed in 2000 by the demutualization of the Bradford and Bingley Building Society. Partly as a result of the financial crisis, it was nationalized in 2008.

7. http://www.youtube.com/watch?v=kQdNLFVdwfQ.

8. http://www.youtube.com/watch?v=s_iMS31mqmU& feature=related. The 10 o'clock evening news in the UK is the flagship news broadcast for the BBC.

9. http://www.youtube.com/watch?v=gACEVoqT7cY.

10. http://www.facebook.com/allianceforyouthmovements.

11. http://www.kintera.org/TR.asp?a=mwK2JhMUIlJ0JmL&s= agJLLUOwGiJRKUPuHkE&m=8rIKL1MIKjJRJaJ.

12. Lady Gaga is an American recording and glam rock artist.

Chapter 7 New Passions for Difference

1. Clearly, education, literacy and the media have a major impact both on processes of subjectification and on modes of self-reflection. These are, after all, the grounds that made possible the women's mosque movement, but they also provide new spaces, as Mahmood demonstrates, in which questions of doctrine, piety and modesty have to be negotiated with issues such as public transport, workplaces and entertainment media.

References

Abu–Lughod, L. 1997 'The interpretations of culture(s) after television', *Representations* 59: 109–134.

Adam, B., J. W. Duyvendak and A. Krouwel 1999. *The Global Emergence of Gay and Lesbian Politics: National Imprints of a Worldwide Movement*. Philadelphia: Temple University Press.

Agamben, G. 1998. *Homo Sacer: Sovereign Power and Bare Life*. Stanford: Stanford University Press.

Agamben, G. 2005. *The Time that Remains: A Commentary on the Letter to the Romans*. Stanford: Stanford University Press.

Ahmed, S. 2007. 'The happiness turn', *New Formations* 63: 7–14.

Ahmed, S. 2010. *The Promise of Happiness*. Durham, NC: Duke University Press.

Ali, T. 2010. *The Obama Syndrome: Surrender at Home, War Abroad*. London: Verso.

Allison, A. 2006. *Millennial Monsters: Japanese Toys and the Global Imagination*. Berkeley: University of California Press.

Altman, D. 2001. *Global Sex*. Chicago: Chicago University Press.

Amin, A. 2010. 'The remainders of race', *Theory, Culture And Society* 27(1): 1–3.

Amselle, J.-L. 2002. 'Globalization and the future of anthropology', *African Affairs* 101: 213–229.

Anderson, B. 2006. 'Becoming and being hopeful: Toward a theory of affect', *Environment and Planning D: Society And Space* 24: 733–752.

Anderson, B. 2007. 'Hope for nanotechnology: Anticipatory knowledge and the governance of affect', *Area* 39(2): 156–165.

Anderson, B. and P. Harrison (eds) 2010. *Taking Place: Non-Representational Theories and Geography*. Farnham: Ashgate.

Anheier, H. and Y. R. Isar 2011. *Heritage, Memory, and Identity*. The Cultures and Globalization Series, 4. London: Sage Publications.

Ansell Pearson, K. 1999. *Germinal Life: The Difference and Repetition of Deleuze*. London: Routledge.

Anzaldúa, G. 1987. *Borderlands/La Frontera: The New Mestiza*. San Francisco: Aunt Lute.

Appadurai, A. 1996. *Modernity at Large: Cultural Dimensions of Globalization*. Minneapolis: University of Minnesota Press.

Appadurai, A. 2004. 'The capacity to aspire: Culture and the terms of recognition', in V. Rao and M. Walton (eds), *Culture and Public Action*. Stanford: Stanford University Press.

Appadurai, A. 2007. 'Hope and democracy', *Public Culture* 19(1): 29–34.

Argenti, N. 2007. *The Intestines of the State: Youth, Violence, and Belated Histories in the Cameroon Grassfields*. Chicago: Chicago University Press.

Ariely, D. 2009. *Predictably Irrational: The Hidden Forces that Shape Our Lives*. London: HarperCollins.

Badiou, A. 2003. *Saint Paul: The Foundation of Universalism*. Stanford: Stanford University Press.

Barber, K. (ed.) 1997. *Readings in African Popular Culture*. Bloomington: Indiana University Press.

Barnett, C. 2008. 'Political affects in public space: Normative blind-spots in non-representational ontologies', *Transactions of the Institute of British Geographers* 33: 186–200.

Barth, F. 1975. *Ritual and Knowledge Among the Baktaman of New Guinea*. Oslo and New Haven, CT: Universitetsforlaget and Yale University Press.

Barth, F. 1989. 'The guru and the conjurer: Transactions in knowledge and the shaping of culture in Southeast Asia and Melanesia', *Man* 25(4): 640–653.

Bauman, Z. 2007. *Liquid Times: Living in an Age of Uncertainty*. Cambridge: Polity.

Bayart, J.-F. 2000. 'Africa in the world: A history of extraversion', *African Affairs* 99: 217–267.

Bayart, J.-F. 2001. 'The paradoxical invention of economic modernity', in A. Appadurai (ed.), *Globalization*. Durham, NC: Duke University Press.

Bayart, J.-F. 2007. *Global Subjects: A Political Critique of Globalization*. Cambridge: Polity.

Behrend, H. 2002. ' "I am like a movie star in my street": Photographic self-creation in postcolonial Kenya', in R. Werbner (ed.), *Postcolonial Subjectivities in Africa*. London: Zed books.

Beidelman, T. O. 1997. *The Cool Knife: Imagery of Gender, Sexuality and Moral Education in Kaguru Initiation Ritual*. Washington, DC: Smithsonian Institution Press.

Benjamin, W. 1992. *Illuminations*. London: Fontana Press.

Berlant, L. 1997. *The Queen of America Goes to Washington City: Essays on Sex and Citizenship*. Durham, NC: Duke University Press.

Berlant, L. 2007. 'Cruel optimism: On Marx, loss and the senses', *New Formations* 63: 33–51.

Bernauer, J. and M. Mahon 2005. 'Michel Foucault's ethical imagination', in G. Gutting (ed.), *The Cambridge Companion to Foucault*. Cambridge: Cambridge University Press.

Biehl, J. 2005. *Vita: Life in a Zone of Social Abandonment*. Berkeley: University of California Press.

Biehl, J., B. Good and A. Kleinman 2007. *Subjectivity: Ethnographic Investigations*. Berkeley: University of California Press.

Bisley, N. 2007. *Rethinking Globalization*. London: Routledge.

Blackman, L. 2007. 'Is happiness contagious?', *New Formations* 63: 15–32.

Blackman, L. and C. Venn 2010. 'Affect', *Body and Society* 16(1): 7–28.

Boellstorff, T. 2005. *The Gay Archipelago: Sexuality and Nation in Indonesia*. Princeton: Princeton University Press.

Boellstorff, T. 2007. *A Coincidence of Desires: Anthropology, Queer Studies, Indonesia*. Durham, NC: Duke University Press.

Boellstorff, T. 2008. *Coming of Age in Second Life*. Princeton: Princeton University Press.

Bolter, J. and R. Grusin 1999. *Remediation: Understanding New Media*. Cambridge, MA: MIT Press.

Bourriaud, N. 2002. *Relational Aesthetics*. Dijon: Les Presses du Réel.

Boyce, P. 2005. ' "Conceiving kothis": Men who have sex with men in India and the cultural subject of HIV prevention', *Medical Anthropology* 26: 175–203.

Boyd, D. 2006. 'Friends, friendsters, and MySpace top 8: Writing community into being on social network sites', *First Monday* 11(12); http://www.firstmonday.org/issues/issue11_12/boyd/index.html.

Brader, T. 2006. *Campaigning for Hearts and Minds: How Emotional Appeals in Political Ads Work*. Chicago: University of Chicago Press.

Braidotti, R. 2002. *Metamorphoses: Towards a Materialist Theory of Becoming*. Cambridge: Polity.

Braidotti, R. 2006. *Transpositions*. Cambridge: Polity.

Braidotti, R. 2008. 'In spite of the times: The postsecular turn in feminism', *Theory, Culture and Society* 25(6): 1–24.

Braidotti, R. 2010. 'On putting the active back into activism', *New Formations* 68: 42–57.

Bronk, R. 2009. *The Romantic Economist: Imagination in Economics*. Cambridge: Cambridge University Press.

Brown, M. 2003. *Who Owns Native Culture?* Cambridge, MA: Harvard University Press.

Brown, M. 2005. 'Heritage trouble: Recent work on the protection of intangible cultural property', *International Journal of Cultural Property* 12: 47–49.

Burgess, J. and J. Green 2009. *YouTube: Online Video and Participatory Culture*. Cambridge: Polity.

Butler, J. 1997. 'Merely cultural', *Social Text* 52/53: 265–277.

Butler, J. 2004a. *Undoing Gender*. London: Routledge.

Butler, J. 2004b. *Precarious Life*. London: Verso.

Butler, J. 2005. *Giving an Account of Oneself*. New York: Fordham University Press.

Cameron, D. and D. Kulick 2002. 'Introduction: Language and desire in theory and practice', *Language and Communication* 23: 93–105.

Candea, M. (ed.) 2010. *The Social After Gabriel Tarde*. London: Routledge.

Carrier, J. and D. Miller (eds) 1998. *Virtualism: A New Political Economy*. Oxford: Berg.

Castells, M. 1996. *The Rise of the Network Society*. Oxford: Blackwell.

Chakrabarty, D. 2000. *Provincializing Europe: Postcolonial Thoughts and Historical Difference*. Princeton: Princeton University Press.

Ching, L. 2000. 'Globalizing the regional, regionalizing the global: Mass culture and Asianisms in the age of late capital', *Public Culture* 12(1): 233–257.

Clark, A. 2008. *Supersizing the Mind: Embodiment, Action and Cognitive Extension*. Oxford: Oxford University Press.

Clough, P. 2007. *The Affective Turn*. Durham, NC: Duke University Press.

Clough, P. 2008. 'The affective turn: Political economy, biomedia and bodies', *Theory, Culture and Society* 25(1): 1–23.

Cohen, L. 2005. 'The kothi wars: AIDS cosmopolitanism and the morality of classification', in S. Pigg and V. Adams (eds), *Sex in Development: Science, Sexuality, and Morality in Global Perspective*. Durham, NC: Duke University Press.

Colebrook, C. 2010. 'Queer vitalism', *New Formations* 68: 77–92.

Comaroff, J. and J. Comaroff 1991. *Of Revelation and Revolution: Christianity, Colonialism and Consciousness in South Africa*, vol. 1. Chicago: University of Chicago Press.

Comaroff, J. and J. Comaroff 1999. 'Occult economies and the violence of abstraction: Notes from the South African postcolony', *American Ethnologist* 26: 279–301.

Comaroff, J. and J. Comaroff 2000a. *Millennial Capitalism and the Culture of Neoliberalism*. Durham, NC: Duke University Press.

Comaroff, J. and J. Comaroff 2000b. 'Millennial capitalism: First thoughts on the second coming', *Public Culture* 12(2): 291–343.

Connolly, W. 2002. *Neuropolitics: Thinking, Culture, Speed*. Minneapolis: University of Minnesota Press.

Coombe, R. 1998. *The Cultural Life of Intellectual Properties: Authorship, Appropriation, and the Law*. Durham, NC: Duke University Press.

220 References

Cooper, F. 2005. *Colonialism in Question: Theory, Knowledge, History*. Berkeley: University of California Press.

Cooper, M. 2008. *Life as Surplus: Biotechnology and Capitalism in the Neoliberal Era*. Washington, DC: Washington University Press.

Corner, J. and D. Pels (eds) 2003. *Media and the Re-styling of Politics*. London: Sage.

Cornwall, A. and S. Jolly 2006. 'Introduction: Sexuality matters', *IDS Bulletin* 37(5): 1–11.

Cornwall, A. and S. Jolly 2009. 'Sexuality and the development industry', *Development* 52(1): 5–12.

Correa, S. and R. Parker 2004. 'Sexuality, human rights and demographic thinking: Connections and disjunctions in a changing world', *Sexuality Research and Social Policy: NSRC Journal* 1(1): 15–38.

Couldry, N. and T. Markham 2007. 'Celebrity culture and public connection: Bridge or chasm?', *International Journal of Cultural Studies* 10: 403–421.

Crapanzano, V. 2003. 'Reflections on hope as a category of social and psychological analysis', *Cultural Anthropology* 18(1): 3–32.

Cryle, P. 2009. 'Les choses et les mots: Missing words and blurry things in the history of sexuality', *Sexualities* 12: 437–450.

Davis, M. 2009. 'Obama at Manassas', *New Left Review 56*.

Deleuze, G. 1994. *Difference and Repetition*. London: Athlone.

Deleuze, G. 2005[1983]. *Cinema I: The Movement Image*. London: Continuum.

Deleuze, G. and F. Guattari 1987. *A Thousand Plateaus: Capitalism and Schizophrenia*. London: Athlone.

Deleuze, G. and F. Guattari 1994. *What is Philosophy?* London: Verso.

Deleuze, G. and F. Guattari 2004[1977]. *Anti-Oedipus*. London: Continuum.

Derrida, J. 1974. *Of Grammatology*. Baltimore, MD: Johns Hopkins University Press.

Derrida, J. 1982. 'Différance', in *Margins of Philosophy*. Chicago: Chicago University Press.

Diouf, M. 2000. 'The Senegalese Mouride trade diaspora and the making of a vernacular cosmopolitanism', *Public Culture* 12(3): 679–702.

Dirlik, A. 2002. 'Historical colonialism in contemporary perspective', *Public Culture* 14(3): 611–615.

Dufour, D.-R. 2007. *The Art of Shrinking Heads: The New Servitude of the Liberated in the Era of Total Capitalism*. Cambridge: Polity.

Durham, D. 2002. 'Uncertain citizens: Herero and the new intercalary subject in postcolonial Botswana', in R. Werbner (ed.), *Postcolonial Subjectivities in Africa*. London: Zed Books.

Echchaibi, N. 2011. 'Al Jazeera and the promise of the Arab revolution', *Huffington Post*; http://www.huffingtonpost.com/nabil–echchaibi/al–jazeera–and–the–promis_b_821105.html.

Etling, B., J. Kelly, R. Faris and J. Palfrey 2009. 'Mapping the Arabic blogosphere: Politics, culture, and dissent', Internet & Democracy Project, Berkman Center for Internet & Society, Harvard University; http://cyber.law.harvard.edu/sites/cyber.law.harvard.edu/files/Mapping_the_Arabic_Blogosphere_0.pdf.

Ewing, K. 1998. *Arguing Sainthood*. Durham, NC: Duke University Press.

Ewing, K. 2008. *Stolen Honor: Stigmatizing Muslim Men in Berlin*. Stanford: Stanford University Press.

Fahmi, S. 2009. 'Blogger's street movement and the right to the City. (Re)claiming Cairo's real and virtual "spaces of freedom"', *Environment and Urbanization* 21(1): 89–107.

Fahmy, N. 2010. 'Revealing the "agenda-cutting" through Egyptian blogs: An empirical study'; http://online.journalism.utexas.edu/2010/papers/Fahmy10.pdf.

Fanon, F. 1986[1970]. *Black Skin, White Masks*. London: Pluto.

Fardon, R. 1988. *Raiders and Refugees: Trends in Chamba Political Development, 1750–1950*. Washington, DC: Smithsonian Institution Press.

Fardon, R. 2000. ' "Metissage" or curate's egg?', *Africa* 70(1): 144–151.

Faubion, J. 2001. 'Toward an anthropology of ethics: Foucault and the pedagogies of autopoiesis', *Representations* 74: 83–104.

Feierman, S. 2001. 'The Comaroffs and the practice of historical ethnography', *Interventions* 3(1): 24–30.

Ferguson, J. 1999. *Expectations of Modernity: Myths and Meanings of Urban Life on the Zambian Copperbelt.* Berkeley: University of California Press.

Ferme, M. 2001. *The Underneath of Things: Violence, History, and the Everyday in Sierra Leone.* Berkeley: University of California Press.

Fernandez, J. 1982. *Bwiti: An Ethnography of the Religious Imagination in Africa.* Princeton: Princeton University Press.

Foster, R. 2002. *Materializing the Nation: Commodity Consumption and Commercial Media in Papua New Guinea.* Bloomington: Indiana University Press.

Foster, R. 2008a. *Coca-Globalization: Following Soft Drinks from New York to New Guinea.* New York: Palgrave Macmillan.

Foster, R. 2008b. 'Commodities, brands, love and kula: Comparative notes on value creation in honor of Nancy Munn', *Anthropological Theory* 8(1): 9–25.

Foucault, M. 1976. *The History of Sexuality.* Vol. I: *The Will to Knowledge.* Harmondsworth: Penguin.

Foucault, M. 1977. *Discipline and Punish: the Birth of the Prison.* New York: Pantheon.

Foucault, M. 1985. *The History of Sexuality.* Vol. II: *The Use of Pleasure.* New York: Pantheon.

Foucault, M. 1990. *The History of Sexuality.* Vol. III: *The Care of the Self.* Harmondsworth: Penguin.

Foucault, M. 1998. *Ethics: Subjectivity and Truth (Essential Works of Michel Foucault, 1954–1984).* New York: New Press.

Foucault, M. 2007. *Security, Territory, Population: Lectures at the Collège de France, 1977–1978,* trans. G. Burchell. New York: Palgrave Macmillan.

Foucault, M. 2008. *The Birth of Biopolitics: Lectures at the Collège de France, 1978–1979,* trans. G. Burchell. New York: Palgrave Macmillan.

Franklin, S. 2006. 'The cyborg embryo: Our path to transbiology', *Theory, Culture and Society* 23(7–8): 167–187.

Franklin, S. and M. Locke (eds) 2003. *Remaking Life and Death: Toward an Anthropology of the Biosciences.* Santa Fe, NM: School of American Research Press.

Franklin, S., C. Lury and J. Stacey (eds) 2000. *Global Nature, Global Culture.* London: Sage.

Fraser, N. 1997. *Justice Interruptus: Critical Reflections on the 'Postsocialist' Condition*. London: Routledge.

Fraser, N. 1998. 'Heterosexism, misrecognition, and capitalism: A response to Judith Butler', *New Left Review* I/228: 140–149.

Fraser, N. 2000. 'Rethinking recognition', *New Left Review* 3: 107–120.

Fraser, N. 2009. 'Feminism, capitalism and the cunning of history', *New Left Review* 56: 97–117.

Fraser, N. and L. Nicholson 1988. 'Social criticism without philosophy: An encounter between feminism and postmodernism', in A. Ross (ed.), *Universal Abandon? The Politics of Postmodernism*. Edinburgh: Edinburgh University Press.

Friedman, J. 2000. 'Globalization, class and culture in global systems', *Journal of World Systems Research* 6(3): 636–656.

Garcia Canclini, N. 1995. *Hybrid Cultures: Strategies for Entering and Leaving Modernity*. Minneapolis: University of Minnesota press.

Geary, C. 1996. 'Political dress: German-style military attire and colonial politics in Bamum', in I. Fowler and D. Zeitlyn (eds), *African Crossroads: Intersections between History and Anthropology in Cameroon*. Oxford: Berghahn Books.

Gell, A. 1998. *Art and Agency*. Oxford: Blackwell.

Gell, A. 1999. 'Strathernograms, or, the semiotics of mixed metaphors', in *The Art of Anthropology: Essays and Diagrams*. London: Athlone.

Geschiere, P. 1997. *The Modernity of Witchcraft: Politics and the Occult in Postcolonial Africa*. Charlottesville: University of Virginia Press.

Geschiere, P. 2009. *The Perils of Belonging: Autochthony, Citizenship, and Exclusion in Africa and Europe*. Chicago: Chicago University Press.

Geschiere, P. and F. Nyamnjoh 2000. 'Capitalism and autochthony: The seesaw of mobility and belonging', *Public Culture* 12(2): 423–452.

Gilroy, P. 2004. *After Empire: Melancholia or Convivial Culture?* London: Routledge.

Gosine, A. 2009a. 'Speaking sexually: The heteronationalism of MSM', in C. Barrow, M. de Bruin and R. Carr (eds), *Sexualities, Social Exclusion and Rights*. Kingston, Jamaica: Ian Randle Press.

Gosine, A. 2009b. 'Monster, womb, MSM: The work of sex in international development', *Development* 52(1): 25–33.

Guyer, J. 2007. 'Prophecy and the near future: Thoughts on macroeconomic, evangelical and punctuated time', *American Ethnologist* 34(3): 409–421.

Hacking, I. 2002. *Historical Ontology*. Cambridge, MA: Harvard University Press.

Harris, M. 2008. 'Barack to the future', *Engineering & Technology* 3(20): 25–25.

Harrison, S. 2003. 'Cultural difference as denied resemblance: Reconsidering nationalism and ethnicity', *Comparative Studies in Society and History*, 45(2): 343–361.

Harvey, D. 1990. *The Condition of Postmodernity: An Enquiry into the Origins of Cultural Change*. Oxford; Blackwell.

Harvey, D. 2000. *Spaces of Hope*. Berkeley: University of California Press.

Harvey, D. 2002. 'The art of rent: Globalization, monopoly and the commodification of culture', *Socialist Register* 38: 93–110.

Harvey, D. 2005. *Neoliberalism*. Oxford: Oxford University Press.

Hastings, A. and P. Manning 2004. 'Introduction: Acts of alterity', *Language and Communication* 24: 291–311.

Held, D. and A. McGrew (eds) 2007. *Globalization Theory: Approaches and Controversies*. Cambridge: Polity.

Hemmings, C. 2005. 'Invoking affect: Cultural theory and the ontological turn', *Cultural Studies* 19(5): 548–567.

Henare, A., M. Holbraad and S. Wastell (eds) 2007. *Thinking Through Things: Theorising Artefacts Ethnographically*. London: Routledge.

Hernlund, Y. and B. Shell-Duncan (eds) 2007. *Transcultural Bodies: Female Genital Cutting in Global Context*. New Brunswick, NJ: Rutgers University Press.

Hirschkind, C. 2006. *The Ethical Soundscape: Cassette Sermons and Islamic Counterpublics*. New York: Columbia University Press.

Hoofd, I. 2010. 'Between Baudrillard, Braidotti and Butler: Rethinking left-wing feminist theory in light of neoliberal acceleration', *International Journal of Baudrillard Studies* 7(2): 1–24; http://www.ubishops.ca/baudrillardstudies/vol-7_2/v7-2-hoofd.html.

Iwabuchi, K. 2002. *Recentering Globalization: Popular Culture and Japanese Transnationalism*. Durham, NC: Duke University Press.

Jackson, P. 2001. 'Pre-gay, post-queer: Thai perspectives on proliferating gender/sex diversity in Asia', *Journal of Homosexuality* 40(3–4): 1–25.

Jackson, P. 2004. 'Gay adaptation, tom-dee resistance, and kathoey indifference: Thailand's gender/sex minorities and the episodic allure of queer English', in W. Leap and T. Boellstorff (eds), *Speaking in Queer Tongues: Globalization and Gay Language*. Urbana: University of Illinois Press.

Jameson, F. 1991. *Postmodernism or the Cultural Logic of Late Capitalism*. Durham, NC: Duke University Press.

Jenkins, H. 2006. *Convergence Culture: Where Old and New Media Collide*. New York: New York University Press.

Jiménez López, L. 2011. 'Contemporary creativity and heritage', in H. K. Anheier and Y. R. Isar (eds), *Heritage, Memory and Identity*. Cultures and Globalization Series, 4. London: Sage Publications.

Johnson, M. 1997. *Beauty and Power: Transgendering and Cultural Transformation in the Southern Philippines*. New York: Berg.

Jones, D. 2007. 'Queered virtuality: The claiming and making of queer spaces and bodies in the user-constructed world of second life', MA thesis, Georgetown University.

Judt, T. 2010. *Ill Fares the Land*. London: Allen Lane.

Karlström, M. 2004. 'Modernity and its aspirants: Moral community and developmental eutopianism in Buganda', *Current Anthropology* 45(5): 595–618.

Keane, W. 1998. 'Calvin in the tropics: Objects and subjects at the religious frontier', in P. Spyer (ed.), *Border Fetishisms: Material Objects in Unstable Spaces*. London: Routledge.

Keane, W. 2003. 'Self-interpretation, agency, and the objects of anthropology: Reflections on a genealogy', *Comparative Studies in Society and History* 45(2): 222–248.

Keane, W. 2007. *Christian Moderns: Freedom and Fetish in the Mission Encounter*. Berkeley: University of California Press.

Khanna, A. 2009a. 'Taming of the shrewd Meyeli Chhele: A political economy of development's sexual subject', *Development* 52(1): 43–51.

Khanna, A. 2009b. 'Meyeli Chhele becomes MSM: Transformation of idioms of sexualness into epidemiological forms in India', in A. Cornwall, J. Edstrom and A. Grieg (eds), *Politicising Masculinity*. London: Zed Press.

Kleinman, A. and E. Fitz-Henry 2007. 'The experiential basis of subjectivity: How individuals change in the context of societal transformation', in J. Biehl, B. Good and A. Kleinman (eds), *Subjectivity: Ethnographic Investigations*. Berkeley: University of California Press.

Knorr Cetina, K. and U. Bruegger 2002. 'Traders' engagement with markets: A postsocial relationship', *Theory, Culture and Society* 19(5/6): 161–185.

Kramer, F. 1993[1987]. *The Red Fez: Art and Spirit Possession in Africa*. London: Verso.

Kramer, L. 2002. *Musical Meaning: Towards a Critical History*. Berkeley: University of California Press.

Kresse, K. 2007. *Philosophising in Mombasa: Knowledge, Islam and Intellectual Practice on the Swahili Coast*. Edinburgh: Edinburgh University Press.

Kresse, K. 2009. 'Muslim politics in postcolonial Kenya: Negotiating knowledge on the double-periphery', *Journal of the Royal Anthropological Institute* 15(1): 76–94.

Laidlaw, J. 2002. 'For an anthropology of ethics and freedom', *Journal of the Royal Anthropological Institute* 8(2): 311–332.

Lambek, M. 2000. 'The anthropology of religion and the quarrel between poetry and philosophy', *Current Anthropology* 41(3): 309–320.

Laqueur, T. 1990. *Making Sex: Body and Gender from the Greeks to Freud*. Cambridge, MA: Harvard University Press.

Laqueur, T. 2009. 'Sexuality and the transformation of culture: The longue durée', *Sexualities* 12: 418–436.

Larkin, B. 1997. 'Indian films and Nigerian lovers: Media and the creation of parallel modernities', *Africa* 67(3): 406–440.

Larvie, S. 1999. 'Queerness and the specter of Brazilian national ruin', *Gay and Lesbian Quarterly* 5(4): 527–558.

Latour, B. 1993. *We Have Never Been Modern*. Hemel Hempstead: Harvester Wheatsheaf.

Latour, B. 1996. *Aramis: Or the Love of Technology*. Cambridge, MA: Harvard University Press.

Latour, B. 1999. *Pandora's Hope: An Essay on the Reality of Science Studies*. Cambridge, MA: Harvard University Press.

Latour, B. 2005. *Reassembling the Social: An Introduction to Actor-Network Theory*. Oxford: Oxford University Press.

Layard, R. 2006. *Happiness: Lessons from a New Science*. Harmondsworth: Penguin.

Leadbeater, C. 2005. 'Design your own revolution', *Observer*, 19 June; http://www.guardian.co.uk/life/science/story/0, 1509833,00.html.

Little, W. 2000. 'Home as a place of exhibition and performance: Mayan household transformations in Guatemala', *Ethnology* 39(2): 163–181.

Lovibond, S. 1989. 'Feminism and postmodernism', *New Left Review* 178: 5–28.

Luhrman, T. 2006. 'Subjectivity', *Anthropological Theory* 6(3): 345–361.

Lunn, P. 2008 *Basic Instincts: Human Nature and the New Economics*. London: Marshall Cavendish.

Luvaas, B. 2010. 'Designer vandalism: Indonesian indie fashion and the cultural practice of cut 'n' paste', *Visual Anthropology Review* 26(1): 1–16.

Magubane, B. 1971. 'A critical look at indices used in the study of social change in Africa', *Current Anthropology* 12: 419–431.

Mahmood, S. 2005. *The Politics of Piety: The Islamic Revival and the Feminist Subject*. Princeton: Princeton University Press.

Marcus, G. 2002. *The Sentimental Citizen: Emotion in Democratic Politics*. Philadelphia: University of Pennsylvania Press.

Massumi, B. 2002. *Parables for the Virtual: Movement, Affect, Sensation*. Durham, NC: Duke University Press.

Mbembe, A. 2001. *On the Postcolony*. Berkeley: University of California Press.

Mbembe, A. 2002. 'African modes of self–writing', *Public Culture* 14(2): 239–273.

Mbembe, A. 2003. 'Necropolitics', *Public Culture* 15(1): 11–40.

Meldrum, A. 2006. 'Stealing beauty', *Guardian*, 15 March; http://www.guardian.co.uk/artanddesign/2006/mar/15/art.

Meyer, B. and P. Pels (eds) 2003. *Magic and Modernity: Interfaces of Revelation and Concealment*. Stanford: Stanford University Press.

Miller, D. (ed.) 2005. *Materiality*. Durham, NC: Duke University Press.

Mitchell, J. C. 1956. *The Kalela Dance: Aspects of Social Relationships among Urban Africans in Northern Rhodesia.* Manchester: Manchester University Press.

Miyazaki, H. 2005. 'From sugar cane to "swords": Hope and the extensibility of the gift in Fiji', *Journal of the Royal Anthropological Institute* 11: 277–295.

Miyazaki, H. 2006. 'Economy of dreams: Hope in global capitalism and its critiques', *Cultural Anthropology* 21(2): 147–172.

Miyazaki, H. 2007. *The Method of Hope: Anthropology, Philosophy, and Fijian Knowledge.* Stanford: Stanford University Press.

Mohamud, A., S. Radeny and K. Ringheim 2006. 'Community-based efforts to end female genital mutilation in Kenya: raising awareness and organizing alternative rites of passage', in R. Abusharaf (ed.), *Female Circumcision.* Philadelphia: University of Pennsylvania Press.

Mohanty, C., A. Russo and L. Torres (eds) 1991. *Third World Women and the Politics of Feminism.* Bloomington: Indiana University Press.

Moore, H. L. 1986. *Space, Text and Gender: an Anthropological Study of the Marakwet of Kenya.* Cambridge: Cambridge University Press.

Moore, H. L. 1988. *Feminism and Anthropology.* Cambridge: Polity.

Moore, H. L. 1994. *A Passion for Difference: Essays in Anthropology and Gender.* Cambridge: Polity.

Moore, H. L. 1997. 'Sex, symbolism and psychoanalysis', *Differences* 9(1): 68–94.

Moore, H. L. 2004. 'Global anxieties: Concept-metaphors and pre-theoretical commitments in anthropology', *Anthropological Theory* 4(1): 71–88.

Moore, H. L. 2006. 'The future of gender or the end of a brilliant career?', in P. Geller and M. Stockett (eds), *Feminist Anthropology: Past, Present and Future.* Philadelphia: University of Pennsylvania Press.

Moore, H. L. 2007. *The Subject of Anthropology: Gender, Symbolism and Psychoanalysis.* Cambridge: Polity.

Moore, H. L. 2008. 'The problem of culture', in D. Held and H. L. Moore (eds), *Cultural Politics in a Global Age.* Oxford: One World.

Moore, H. L. 2009a. 'Forms of knowing and un-knowing: Secrets about society, gender and sexuality in Northern Kenya', in R. Ryan-Flood and R. Gill (eds), *Secrecy and Silence in the Research Process: Feminist Perspectives*. New York: Routledge.

Moore, H. L. 2009b. 'Epistemology and ethics: Perspectives from Africa', in C. Toren and J. Pina-Cabral (eds), 'Epistemology and Anthropology'. Special Issue, *Social Analysis* 53(2): 207–218.

Moore, H. L. 2010. 'Feminist anthropology', in A. Barnard and J. Spencer (eds), *The Routledge Encyclopedia of Social and Cultural Anthropology*, 2nd edn. London: Routledge.

Moore, H. L. 2011. 'Intangibles: Culture, heritage and identity', in H. K. Anheier and Y. R. Isar (eds), *Heritage, Memory, and Identity*. The Cultures and Globalization Series, 4. London: Sage Publications.

Moore, H. L. and T. Sanders (eds) 2001. *Magical Interpretations, Material Realities: Modernity, Witchcraft and the Occult in Postcolonial Africa*. London: Routledge.

Mudimbe, V. Y. 1988. *The Invention of Africa*. Bloomington: Indiana University Press.

Napier, S. 2007. *From Impressionism to Anime: Japan as Fantasy and Fan Cult in the Mind of the West*. New York: Palgrave Macmillan.

Navaro-Yashin, Y. 2009. 'Affective spaces, melancholic objects: Ruination and the production of anthropological knowledge', *Journal of the Royal Anthropological Institute* 15: 1–18.

Norris, P. 2002. *Democratic Phoenix: Reinventing Political Activism*. Cambridge: Cambridge University Press.

Nunley, J. 1987. *Moving with the Face of the Devil: Art and Politics in Urban West Africa*. Urbana: University of Illinois Press.

Nyamnjoh, F. 2002. ' "A child is one person's only in the womb": Domestication, agency and subjectivity in the Cameroonian Grassfields', in R. Werbner (ed.), *Postcolonial Subjectivities in Africa*. London: Zed Books.

Olds, K. and N. Thrift 2005. 'Cultures on the brink: Reengineering the soul of capitalism – on a global scale', in A. Ong and S. Collier (eds), *Global Assemblages: Technology, Politics, and Ethics as Anthropological Problems*. Oxford: Blackwell.

Ondrejka, C. 2004. 'Escaping the gilded cage: User-created content and building the metaverse', *New York Law School Law Review* 49(1): 81–101.

Ong, A. and S. Collier (eds) 2005. *Global Assemblages: Technology, Politics and Ethics as Anthropological Problems*. Oxford: Blackwell.

Ortner, S. 2005. 'Subjectivity and cultural critique', *Anthropological Theory* 5(1): 31–52.

Oswald, A. 2010. 'Emotional prosperity and the Stiglitz commission', *British Journal of Industrial Relations* 48(4): 651–669.

Parisi, L. 2004. *Abstract Sex, Philosophy, Bio-Technology and the Mutations of Desire*. London: Continuum.

Parry, B. 2004. 'Bodily transactions: Regulating a new space of flows in "bio-information"', in K. Verdery and C. Humphrey (eds), *Property in Question: Value Transformation in the Global Economy*. Oxford: Berg.

Perry, R. and B. Maurer 2003. 'Globalization and governmentality', in R. Perry and B. Maurer (eds), *Globalization Under Construction: Governmentality, Law, and Identity*. Minneapolis: University of Minnesota Press.

Phillips, A. 1997. 'From inequality to difference: A severe case of displacement', *New Left Review* I/224: 143–153.

Phillips, A. 1999. *Which Equalities Matter?* Cambridge: Polity.

Phillips, A. 2007. *Multiculturalism Without Culture*. Princeton: Princeton University Press.

Pigg, S. and V. Adams (eds) 2005. *Sex in Development: Science, Sexuality, and Morality in Global Perspective*. Durham, NC: Duke University Press.

Povinelli, E. 2001. 'Radical worlds: The anthropology of incommensurability and inconceivability', *The Annual Review of Anthropology* 30: 319–334.

Povinelli, E. 2006. *The Empire of Love: Toward a Theory of Intimacy, Genealogy, and Carnality*. Durham, NC: Duke University Press.

Rabinow, P. 2003. *Anthropos Today: Reflections on Modern Equipment*. Princeton: Princeton University Press.

Radsch, C. 2008. 'Core to commonplace: The evolution of Egypt's blogosphere'; http://www.arabmediasociety.com/UserFiles/AMS6%20Courtney%20Radsch.pdf.

Radsch, C. 2011. 'Repertoires of repression and the Egypt street: This is not a Facebook, Twitter or Wiki revolution!', *Huffing-*

ton Post, 1 February; http://www.huffingtonpost.com/court-ney–c–radsch/repertoires–of–repression_b_815714.html.

Ranger, T. 1975. *Dance and Society in Eastern Africa, 1890– 1970: The Beni Ngoma*. London: Heinemann.

Rieff, D. 1993. 'Multiculturalism's silent partner: It's the new globalized consumer economy, stupid', *Harper's* 287 (August): 62–72.

Robbins, J. 2003. 'On the paradoxes of global pentecostalism and the perils of continuity thinking', *Religion* 33(3): 221–231.

Robbins, J. 2007a. 'Between reproduction and freedom: Morality, value and radical cultural change', *Ethnos* 72(3): 293–314.

Robbins, J. 2007b. 'Causality, ethics and the near future', *American Ethnologist* 34(3): 433–436.

Roberts, K. 2006. *Lovemarks: The Future Beyond Brands*. New York: Power House Books.

Rofel, L. 2007. *Desiring China: Experiments in Neoliberalism, Sexuality, and Public Culture*. Durham, NC: Duke University Press.

Roitman, J. 2005. *Fiscal Disobedience: An Anthropology of Economic Regulation in Central Africa*. Princeton: Princeton University Press.

Rose, N. 2007. *The Politics of Life Itself: Biomedicine, Power, and Subjectivity in the Twenty-First Century*. Princeton: Princeton University Press.

Sassen, S. 2001. 'Spatialities and temporalities of the global: Elements for a theorization', in A. Appadurai (ed.), *Globalization*. Durham, NC: Duke University Press.

Shapiro, S. 2009. 'Revolution, Facebook-style', *New York Times*, 22 January.

Simmel, G. 1950. *The Sociology of Georg Simmel*. New York: Free Press.

Simpson, A. 2003. *'Half-London', in Zambia: Contested Identities in a Catholic Mission School*. Edinburgh: Edinburgh University Press.

Sinnott, M. 2004. *Toms and Dees: Transgender Identity and Female Same-Sex Relationships in Thailand*. Honolulu: University of Hawaii Press.

Spivak, G. 1988. 'Can the subaltern speak?', in C. Nelson and L. Grossberg (eds), *Marxism and the Interpretation of Culture*. Basingstoke: Macmillan.

Stephens, C. 2008. 'Animal', in M. Gale and C. Stephens (eds), *Francis Bacon*. London: Tate Publishing.

Sterling, B. 2003. 'Every other movie is the blue pill', in K. Haber (ed.), *Exploring the Matrix: Visions of the Cyber Present*. New York: St Martin's Press.

Stiglitz, J., A. Sen and J.-P. Fitoussi 2009. 'Report by the Commission on the Measurement of Economic Performance and Social Progress'; http://www.stiglitz-sen-fitoussi.fr/en/index.htm.

Stoler, A. 2002. *Carnal Knowledge and Imperial Power: Race and the Intimate in Colonial Rule*. Berkeley: University of California Press.

Stoller, P. 1995. *Embodying Colonial Memories: Spirit Possession, Power and the Hauka in West Africa*. London: Routledge.

Strathern, M. 1988. *The Gender of the Gift*. Berkeley: University of California Press.

Strathern, M. 2001. 'The patent and the Malanggan', *Theory, Culture and Society* 18(4): 1–26.

Surin, K. 2001. 'The sovereign individual and Michael Taussig's politics of defacement', *Nepantla: Views from South* 2(1): 205–220.

Sylvester, D. 1975. *Interviews with Francis Bacon*. London: Thames and Hudson.

Taylor, C. 2004. *Modern Social Imaginaries*. Durham, NC: Duke University Press.

Taylor, T. 2006. 'Beyond management: Considering participatory design and governance in player culture', *First Monday*, special issue 7; http://firstmonday.org/issues/special11_9/taylor.

Terdiman, D. 2006. ' "Second Life" dreams of electric sheep', http://news.cnet.com/Second-Life-dreams-of-Electric-Sheep/2100-1043_3-6056759.html.

Thacker, E. 2004. *Biomedia*. Minneapolis: University of Minnesota Press.

Thacker, E. 2006. *The Global Genome, Biotechnology, Politics and Culture*. Cambridge, MA: MIT Press.

Thaler, R. and C. Sunstein 2008. *Nudge: Improving Decisions about Heath, Wealth and Happiness*. New Haven, CT: Yale University Press.

Thompson, J. 2005. 'The new visibility', *Theory Culture and Society* 22(6): 31–51.

Thornton, R. 2007. 'Marginal utilities, time, and zombies: Comment on Jane Guyer's "Prophecy and the near future: Thoughts on macroeconomic, evangelical, and punctuated time', *American Ethnologist* 34(3): 437–439.

Thrift, N. 2008. *Non-Representational Theory: Space, Politics, Affect*. London: Routledge.

Tobin, J. (ed.) 2004. *Pikachu's Global Adventure: The Rise and Fall of Pokemon*. Durham, NC: Duke University Press.

Tsing, A. 2005. *Friction: An Ethnography of Global Connection*. Princeton: Princeton University Press.

Turkle, S. 1995. *Life on the Screen Identity in the Age of the Internet*. New York: Simon and Schuster.

Turkle, S. 2009. *Simulation and its Discontents*. Cambridge, MA: MIT Press.

Van Gennep, A. 1961. *Rites of Passage*. Chicago: Chicago University Press.

Van Zoonen, L. 2005. *Entertaining the Citizen: When Politics and Popular Culture Converge*. Lanham, MD: Rowman and Littlefield.

Venn, C. 2009. 'Identity, diasporas and subjective change: The role of affect, the relation to the other, and the aesthetic', *Subjectivity* 26: 3–28.

Venn, C. 2010. 'Individuation, relationality, affect: Rethinking the human in relation to the living', *Body and Society* 16(1): 129–161.

Von Hippel, E. 2005. *Democratizing Innovation*. Cambridge, MA: MIT Press.

Wagner, R. 1986. *Symbols that Stand for Themselves*. Chicago: Chicago University Press.

Walsh, V. 2008. 'Real imagination is technical imagination', in M. Gale and C. Stephens (eds), *Francis Bacon*. London: Tate Publishing.

Weber, M. 1948. *Essays in Sociology*. London: Routledge.

Webmoor, T. 2008. 'From Silicon Valley to the Valley of Teotihuacan: The "Yahoo!s" of new media and digital heritage', *Visual Anthropology Review* 24(2): 183–200.

Weinberger, D. 2007. *Everything is Miscellaneous: The Power of the New Digital Disorder*. New York: Holt.

Weiss, B. 2009. *Street Dreams and Hip Hop Barber Shops: Global Fantasy in Urban Tanzania*. Bloomington: Indiana University Press.

Werbner, P. 1997 'Introduction: The dialectics of cultural hybridity'. In P. Werbner and T. Modood (eds), *Debating Cultural Hybridity: Multi-Cultural Identities and the Politics of Anti-Racism*. London: Zed Books.

Werbner, R. 2002. 'Introduction – postcolonial subjectivities: The personal, the political and the moral', in R. Werbner (ed.), *Postcolonial Subjectivities in Africa*. London: Zed Books.

Whitehead, N. 2004. 'Rethinking anthropology of violence', *Anthropology Today* 20(5): 1–2.

Wilson, G. and M. Wilson 1945. *The Analysis of Social Change*. Cambridge: Cambridge University Press.

Yanagisako, S. 2002. *Producing Culture and Capital: Family Firms in Italy*. Princeton: Princeton University Press.

Yang, M. 2000. 'Putting global capitalism in its place: Economic hybridity, Bataille, and ritual expenditure', *Current Anthropology* 41(4): 477–509.

Young, I. 2000. *Inclusion and Democracy*. Oxford: Oxford University Press.

Yúdice, G. 2003. *The Expediency of Culture: Uses of Culture in the Global Era*. Durham, NC: Duke University Press.

Zaloom, C. 2005. 'The discipline of speculator', in A. Ong and S. Collier (eds), *Global Assemblages: Technology, Politics, and Ethics as Anthropological Problems*. Oxford: Blackwell.

Zaloom, C. 2009. 'How to read the future: The yield curve, affect, and financial prediction', *Public Culture* 21(2): 245–268.

Zigon, J. 2007. 'Moral breakdown and the ethical demand: A theoretical framework for an anthropology of moralities', *Anthropological Theory* 7(2): 131–150.

Žižek, S. 1999. *The Ticklish Subject: The Absent Centre of Political Ontology*. London: Verso.

Žižek, S. 2003. *The Puppet and the Dwarf: The Perverse Core of Christianity*. Cambridge, MA: MIT Press.

Žižek, S. 2004. *Organs Without Bodies: On Deleuze and Consequences*. London: Routledge.

Zournazi, M. 2003. *Hope: New Philosophies for Change*. London: Routledge.

Index

abjection and alienation 58, 64, 68–9, 71
actor network theory (ANT) 178–9, 183–4
advertising and marketing 107–15
aesthetics
  art and 34–5, 120–5
  of the self 56, 57, 61, 62, 64–5
affect theories
  art, aesthetics and 120–5
  assumptions 181–2
  body and biology 171–81, 198–9
  Cyprus 182–7
  and economics 156–9
  Egypt 187–96
  and language 115–20, 184–5
  and politics 159–60, 171–2, 199–202
  and power 168
  subject and subjectivity 196–205
Africa
  connected worlds 66–71, 74–5
  real of fantasy 60–6
  see also female genital mutilation (FGM), Kenya; 'Half-London'
African art 121–2
Agamben, G. 140, 171–2
agency
  actor network theory (ANT) 178–9, 183–4
  biological model 177
  Cyprus 185–7
  and knowledge 145–9
  and subjectivity 13–15, 17–18
  women's 189, 191–2
Agha-Soltan, N. 165–6
AIDS/HIV 49–50, 97, 98, 100–1

Al Jazeera 167
Allison, A. 128–9, 130
alternative rites of passage
(ARP) 44–7, 48–52
Anderson, B. 175, 176
anime and manga 127–30
Ansell Pearson, K. 177
Appadurai, A. 139, 144–5
Argenti, N. 67
art and aesthetics 34–5,
120–5
Asia
India 101
South East 81–8
Australian Aboriginal
sexuality 102–5
avatars 131–4

Bacon, F. 122–3, 125
Barth, F. 52
Benjamin, W. 34, 53
Berlant, L. 29
Biehl, J. 172
et al. 71, 72
biopolitics 172
biotechnologies 172, 173–5,
180–1
Blackman, L. 26, 27
and Venn, C. 175
body
and biology 171–81,
198–9
Malanggan funerary
sculptures 125–7
Boellstorff, T. 81–3, 85–7,
94, 113, 132, 133,
134
Bolter, J. and Grusin, R.
107
Bourdieu, P. 193
Bourne, M. 115–16

Braidotti, R. 14, 81, 158,
177, 180–1, 197,
200–1
Bronk, R. 157
Butler, J. 79, 101, 171

capitalism 5, 24–5, 142–3
global 3, 6, 113–14, 141
and identity movements
160
marketing and advertising
107–15
see also market economics
Centre for Human Rights and
Democracy (CHRD)
39, 40–2
Christianity 35, 36, 39, 62
anti-female genital
mutilation (FGM)
campaign 42–7
Catholic mission school,
Africa 56–61
citizenship
cultural elements 33–4
global 7–8, 9
Clough, P. 172, 173
Colebrook, C. 176, 177, 202
colonial/postcolonial issues
see Africa;
'Half-London'
commodification 113–15
connected worlds 66–76,
81–8
Crapanzano, V. 137–9, 144
'The credit crunch anthem'
161–2
crisis
financial (2008) 156–7,
161–3
of subject 71–2
Cryle, P. 92

cultural diversity   32–4, 141
cultural meanings and
        interpretation   6–8,
        17–18
cultural property rights   32–3
cultural specificities and
        sexuality   97–9
culture
    perspectives on   30–5
    and subjectivity   10–15
Cyprus   182–7

The Day I Will Never Forget
        (Longinotto)   41
Deleuze, G.   119, 120,
        178–9, 201
    and Guattari, F.   89, 185
Les Demoiselles d'Avignon
        (Picasso)   121–2
democracy
    Centre for Human Rights
        and Democracy
        (CHRD)   39, 40–2
    hopes of   156–69
Derrida, J.   55, 59
desire
    hope and satisfaction
        21–9, 204–5
    for other   58–9
digital technology *see* film;
        information/digital
        technologies; media
Dirlik, A.   63

Echchaibi, N.   167
economics *see* market
        economics
education
    'Half-London', Zambia
        (Catholic mission
        school)   56–61

see also female genital
        mutilation (FGM),
        Kenya
Edwards, J.   168
Egypt   163, 166–7, 187–96
Equality Now   41
ethics   59, 193–4, 200–3
    and ethical imagination
        15–21, 22–3, 57,
        64–5

Facebook   163–4, 165, 169
fandom   108–11, 129–30
fantasy   16–17, 18
    fandom   129
    futurism and enforced
        presentism   153, 154
    history of   76
    real of   60–6
Fardon, R.   63
Feierman, S.   70
female genital mutilation
        (FGM), Kenya
        35–9
    alternative rites of passage
        (ARP)   44–7, 48–52
    campaign against   39–47
    education as knowledge
        47–54
femininity *see* gender
        identities, Asia
feminist theory   141, 197
    women's mosque
        movement, Egypt
        187, 188–9, 191
film   119–20
    Japanese animation
        127–30
    The Matrix   109–11
financial crisis (2008)
        156–7, 161–3

238   Index

Foucault, M.   2, 15–16,
    19–20, 21, 56, 84,
    90–1, 92, 94–6, 105,
    172, 200
Franklin, S.   173–4
    et al.   172
    and Locke, M.   172

Gell, A.   125–7
gender identities, Asia   81–8
ghazals   118
global capitalism   3, 6,
    113–14, 141
globalization   71, 142–3
    connected worlds   66–76,
        81–8
    as metaphor and process
        3–4, 8–9
    theoretical approaches   2–9
Guyer, J.   149, 153, 154

habitus   193–4
'Half-London'   63–4, 69
    Catholic mission school,
        Zambia   56–61
    Kenya   55–6
happiness   25–6
Harvey, D.   31, 140, 158
Hayek, F. von   149
'Heidenröslein' (Schubert/
    Goethe)   117–18
hip-hop and rap music, Africa
    65–6
Hirschkind, C.   194–6
HIV/AIDS   49–50, 97, 98,
    100–1
hope   137–40, 144–5
    of democracy   156–69
    desire and satisfaction
        21–9, 204–5
    faith and reason   148–56

hybridity   63–4, 70, 75, 80,
    114

identity   12–13
    and identification   16–17,
        64, 80–1
    movements   160
    see also sexuality
India   101
Indonesia   81–3, 85–8
inequalities   9
information/digital
    technologies   5–6, 8,
        26–8
    financial markets   145–8,
        151–2, 155–6
    political action   163–9
    Second Life   112–13,
        130–5
    YouTube   161–3, 165–6,
        167
    see also film; media
initiation rituals   124–5
international development
    theory and sexuality
        97
International Labour
    Organization (ILO)
        33
Iran   165–6
Islam   61–2
    cassette sermons, Egypt
        194–6
    women's mosque
        movement, Egypt
        187–94

Japan
    animation   127–30
    financial traders   145–8,
        151–2

Jenkins, H.   108, 109,
    110–11, 127–8, 160–1,
    168
Johnson, M.   83, 84
Jones, D.   132, 133

Karlström, M.   70, 137
Keane, W.   62, 143
Kennedy, J. F.   (US President)
    138
Kenya   55–6
    see also female genital
    mutilation (FGM)
Khanna, A.   100–1
Kierkegaard, S.   137
Kleinman, A. and Fitz-Henry,
    E.   72–4
Knorr Cetina, K. and
    Bruegger, U.   156
knowledge
    and agency   145–9
Kenya
    anti-female genital
    mutilation (FGM)
    campaign   47–54
    Marakwet culture   36–9
    and power   19–20, 57,
    94–5
Koran see Islam
Kramer, L.   117–18

language
    and affect theory   115–20,
    184–5
    of analysis   4–6
    of sexuality   92–4, 100–1
Laqueur, T.   91, 92, 93–4
Latour, B.   178–9, 181, 184
'Lehman bros and financial
    crisis revisited song'
    162–3

'life itself', resurgence of
    171–80
Lincoln, A. (US President)
    138
Longinotto, K.   41
Luhrman, T.   71, 72
Luvaas, B.   6–8

Mahmood, S.   187–96
Malanggan funerary
    sculptures, New
    Ireland   125–7
manga and anime   127–30
Marakwet culture see female
    genital mutilation
    (FGM), Kenya
market economics
    and affect theories   156–9
    faith and reason   148–56
    financial crisis (2008)
    156–7, 161–3
    Japanese traders   145–8
    see also capitalism
marketing and advertising
    107–15
masculinity see gender
    identities, Asia
Massumi, B.   176, 177–8,
    179–80, 181
The Matrix   109–11
Mbembe, A.   74, 172
media   5–6, 66–7, 68, 82–3,
    160–1
    Al Jazeera   167
    see also film; information/
    digital technologies
melancholia of the Left   4,
    140, 141–2, 147–8
men who have sex with men
    (MSM)   100–1
mimicry   6, 63, 64

minoritarian politics 202
Miyazaki, H. 23, 144,
146–8, 149, 150
Moi, D. (President of Kenya)
40
Moore, H. L. 10, 18, 31,
32, 33, 37, 39, 52,
58–9, 69, 72, 74, 77,
79, 87, 111, 114, 120,
121, 124, 129, 140–1,
142, 196
multi-constituted subject
79–80
MySpace 169

nanotechnology 175
Napier, S. 128, 129–30
Navaro-Yashin, Y. 181,
182–5
New Ireland: Malanggan
funerary sculptures
125–7
Norris, P. 159
The Nutcracker (ballet)
114–16
Nyamnjoh, F. 74

Obama, B. (US President)
136–9, 159, 162–3,
167, 169
Olds, K. and Thrift, N. 155
Ortner, S. 71, 72, 73–4
otherness 58–9

Philippines 83
Picasso, P. 121–2
Pigg, S. and Adams, V. 96,
98, 99
politics
and affect theories
159–60, 171–2,
199–202

biopolitics 172
and culture 31–5
and hopes of democracy
156–69
identity movements 160
and information
technologies 163–9
minoritarian 202
representation 142–4
popular music 65–6, 106–7,
161–3
Povinelli, E. 10, 102–4
power
and affect 168
and knowledge 19–20,
57, 94–5
problematization of self
19–20, 21, 84–5

Quran see Islam

Rabinow, P. 171
rap and hip-hop music, Africa
65–6
relational subjects 78–81
gender identities 81–8
see also self–other
relationships
religion
faith and reason 148–56
and popular music, Africa
65–6
see also Christianity; Islam
representation
language and affect
115–20
political 142–4
resistance 7–8, 64
rhizome concept 185, 201
Rieff, D. 141
Robbins, J. 67–8, 154
Rofel, L. 67, 70–1

The Romantic Economist
(Bronk) 157

satisfaction 106-7
hope, desire and 21-9,
204-5
Saudi Arabia 164
Second Life 112-13,
130-5
self
aesthetics 56, 57, 61, 62,
64-5
problematization 19-20,
21, 84-5
techniques 26, 80, 195
see also subject/subjectivity
self-other relationships
15-16, 18, 21
Catholic mission school,
Zambia 57, 59
financial trading 156
intersubjectivity, Africa
73-5
Second Life 130-5
see also relational subjects
self-stylization 2, 28, 29,
39, 154-5
sexuality
gender identities, Asia
81-8
and sexual practices
88-105
Shapiro, S. 163, 164
Simmel, G. 57, 59
Simpson, T. 56-60
Sinnott, M. 84
Strathern, M. 125-6
subject-object distinctions
25-6, 125
subject/subjectivity
and affect theories
196-205

Africa 56-7, 59, 61, 66,
68-73
and intersubjectivity
73-5
and agency 13-15, 17-18
and politics 199-200, 201
subjectification process
79-81
Surin, K. 116
Sylvester, D. 122-3

Tanzanian Muslims 61-2
techniques of the self 26,
80, 195
technology
biotechnologies 172,
173-5, 180-1
and commodification
113-15
nanotechnology 175
see also film; information/
digital technologies;
media
*Three Studies at the Base of a
Crucifixion* (Bacon)
122-3
Thrift, N. 168, 181,
199-200
Olds, K. and 155
Tunisia 166

UNESCO 33
Universal Declaration of
Human Rights 32-3,
40
user communities and
user-created worlds
111-13

Venn, C. 196, 203-4
Blackman, L. and 175
virtuality 125, 130-5

Index

Wagner, R.   117
Weber, M.   4
Weiss, B.   61–2, 65–6, 68, 78
Werbner, P.   74–5
World Vision: anti-female
    genital mutilation
    (FGM) campaign
    42–7

YouTube   161–3, 165–6,
    167
Yúdice, G.   32, 33

Zaloom, C.   152, 155–6
Zambia: Catholic mission
    school   56–61
Žižek, S.   141